GUNNERS ON THE TARGET

Gunners on the Target

Written for

THE ARSENAL FOOTBALL SUPPORTERS' CLUB

by

GEOFFREY MOWBRAY

Foreword by

HARRY HOMER

STANLEY PAUL
London

STANLEY PAUL & CO. LTD

178–202 Great Portland Street, London, W.1

AN IMPRINT OF THE  HUTCHINSON GROUP

London Melbourne Sydney
Auckland Bombay Toronto
Johannesburg New York

First published 1961

*This book has been set in Times New Roman type
face. It has been printed in Great Britain by The
Anchor Press, Ltd., in Tiptree, Essex, on Antique
Wove paper and bound by Taylor Garnett Evans
& Co., Ltd., in Watford, Herts*

Contents

INTRODUCTION

Arsenal Football Club: some outstanding dates;
Arsenal's early history.

page 11

PART ONE

A season-by-season review of Arsenal Football
Club's League history, including F.A. Cup results,
players' appearances, goal-scorers and honours.

page 23

PART TWO

Career records of some of the leading Arsenal
players.

page 147

Illustrations

Tom Whittaker, M.B.E., Manager 1947–56   *frontispiece*

Woolwich Arsenal F.C. Players and Officials,
1906–7   *facing page* 16

Herbert Chapman, Manager 1925–34   17

Arsenal Football Club 1953–4   17

The Arsenal teams of 1930–1   32

Mr. George Allison with the six members of the Arsenal
team who played for England against Wales in 1936   32

Arsenal Football Club 1956–7   33

A. Baker, W. Barnes, C. S. Bastin and W. Blyth   48

E. R. Bowden, J. Bloomfield, D. Bowen and C. Buchan   49

M. Charles, D. Clapton, D. Compton and L. Compton   64

W. Copping, J. Crayston, R. Daniel and T. Docherty   65

E. Drake, G. Eastham, A. Forbes and V. Groves   80

E. Hapgood, J. Henderson, D. Herd and J. Hulme   81

D. B. N. Jack, A. James, R. John and C. Jones   96

B. Joy, R. Lewis, D. Lishman and J. Logie   97

J. Kelsey, A. Macaulay, A. Mackie and G. Male   112

I. McPherson, J. Mercer, F. Moss and T. Parker   113

H. Roberts, R. Rooke, D. Roper and L. Scott   128

J. Shaw, L. Smith, D. Tapscott and G. Swindin   129

Foreword

'The fans will love it!' said one who ought to know, when he had been through a proof copy of this book. Who was he? Let us first look at football statistics.

The official *Arsenal F.C. Handbook* was written for years by the late W. N. Johnston as 'Recorder' during the great Arsenal years of the 1920's and 1930's. For seasons I was very close to him and lost a good friend when he died in the early days of the war. He was the finest football statistician that I have ever known and taught me much that was beyond value when I took over his mantle as 'Marksman'.

After me came W. R. Wall, a man of figures if ever there was one —one-time Comptroller and now Secretary of Arsenal F.C.—a fine statistician. It was he who made the remark concerning this book with which I have opened my Foreword.

Now Geoffrey Mowbray has entered the field with this really splendid record of the famous Gunners, season by season over the years. This is indeed a rich book and one that with all my heart I wish every success.

It will surely fire the imagination of those who were too young to have been at the earlier matches, and for those who were lucky enough to have been there it will conjure up great memories. And to all football fans who argue about Arsenal—and is there one from Southend to Sunderland who does not?—it will form a most valuable and interesting book of reference. It should, then, be more than a good buy to every type of customer.

Good luck to you, Geoffrey, and thanks for your most excellent production!

HARRY HOMER

Heathfield
Sussex

Introduction

In compiling this work of reference I have had in mind the vast army of soccer enthusiasts of the Arsenal Football Supporters' Club who like to have the facts and figures of their favourite team readily to hand. It caters most especially for those who delight in collecting, year by year, the *Arsenal F.C. Handbook* and whose collections are not as extensive as they would wish. For instance, a big proportion possess post-war editions only and, as back numbers are rarely available, this volume becomes invaluable in filling in the gaps.

Naturally, a volume of this size cannot include everything, and I have tended to omit the history and policies of the boardroom in favour of the results and personalities of the playing field.

To the many players and officials who have helped put the Club in the exalted position it holds in the footballing world today and who have not received a mention I tender my humble apologies.

I am deeply grateful to my friend Harry Headington of Barkingside, an avid collector of soccer statistics, who helped with some of the pre-1930 figures and also to Mr. L. W. Neves, Managing Editor of the *Kentish Independent*, for permission to investigate their files of the years 1886 to 1893.

GEOFFREY MOWBRAY

April 1961

Arsenal F.C.: some outstanding dates

1893–4   Entered Football League Division II

1903–4   Runners-up Football League Division II
          P.34 W.21 D.7 L.6 Goals 91—22 Pts.49 2nd

1912–13   Relegated from Division I
          P.38 W.3 D.12 L.23 Goals 26—74 Pts.18 20th

1919–20   Elected to Football League Division I

1925–6   Runners-up Football League Division I
          P.42 W.22 D.8 L.12 Goals 87—63 Pts.52 2nd

1926–7   Finalists F.A. Cup   Arsenal 0 *v.* Cardiff City 1
          Team: Lewis; Parker, Kennedy; Baker, Butler, John;
          Hulme, Buchan, Brain, Blyth, Hoar.

1929–30   WINNERS F.A. Cup   Arsenal 2 *v.* Huddersfield Town 0
                              (James, Lambert).
          Team: Preedy; Parker, Hapgood; Baker, Seddon, John;
          Hulme, Jack, Lambert, James, Bastin.

1930–1   CHAMPIONS Football League Division I
          P.42 W.28 D.10 L.4 Goals 127—59 Pts.66 1st

          Appearances: Baker 1, Bastin 42, Brain 16, Cope 1, Hapgood
          38, Harper 19, Haynes 2, Hulme 32, Jack 35, James 40,
          John 40, Johnstone 2, Jones (C.) 24, Keyser 12, Lambert
          34, Male 3, Parker 41, Preedy 11, Roberts 40, Seddon 18,
          Thompson 2, Williams 9.

Goal-scorers: Lambert 38, Jack 31, Bastin 28, Hulme 14, James 5, Brain 4, John 2, Williams 2, Johnstone 1, Jones (C.) 1, Roberts 1. Total 127.

1931–2 Runners-up Football League Division I

P.42 W.22 D.10 L.10 Goals 90—48 Pts.54 2nd

Finalists F.A. Cup.   Arsenal 1 *v.* Newcastle United 2 (John).

Team: Moss; Parker, Hapgood; Jones (C.), Roberts, Male; Hulme, Jack, Lambert, Bastin, John.

1932–3 CHAMPIONS Football League Division I

P.42 W.25 D.8 L.9 Goals 118—61 Pts.58 1st

Appearances: Bastin 42, Bowden 7, Coleman 27, Compton (L.) 4, Cope 4, Hapgood 38, Haynes 6, Hill 26, Hulme 40, Jack 34, James 40, John 37, Jones (C.) 16, Lambert 12, Male 35, Moss 41, Parker 5, Parkin 5, Preedy 1, Roberts 36, Sidey 2, Stockhill 4.
Goal-scorers: Bastin 33, Coleman 24, Hulme 20, Jack 18, Lambert 14, James 3, Stockhill 3, Bowden 2, Hill 1. Total 118

1933–4 CHAMPIONS Football League Division I

P.42 W.25 D.9 L.8 Goals 75—47 Pts.59 1st

Appearances: Bastin 38, Beasley 23, Birkett 15, Bowden 32, Coleman 12, Cox 2, Dougall 5, Drake 10, Dunne 21, Hapgood 40, Haynes 1, Hill 25, Hulme 8, Jack 14, James 22, John 31, Jones (C.) 29, Lambert 3, Male 42, Moss 37, Parkin 5, Roberts 30, Sidey 12, Wilson 5.
Goal-scorers: Bastin 13, Bowden 13, Beasley 10, Dunne 9, Drake 7, Birkett 5, Hulme 5, Jack 5, James 3, John 1, Lambert 1, Coleman 1, Roberts 1, o.g. 1. Total 75.

1934–5 CHAMPIONS Football League Division I

P.42 W.23 D.12 L.7 Goals 115—46 Pts.58 1st

Appearances: Bastin 36, Beasley 20, Birkett 4, Bowden 24, Compton (L.) 5, Copping 31, Crayston 37, Davidson 11, Dougall 8, Drake 41, Dunne 1, Hapgood 34, Hill 15, Hulme 16, James 30, John 9, Kirchen 7, Male 39, Marshall 4, Moss 33, Roberts 36, Rogers 5, Sidey 6, Trim 1, Wilson 9,

14

Goal-scorers: Drake 42, Bastin 20, Bowden 14, Hulme 8, Beasley 6, James 4, Crayston 3, Hill 3, Birkett 2, Davidson 2, Kirchen 2, Rogers 2, Compton (L.) 1, Dougall 1, Hapgood 1, Moss 1, o.g. 3. Total 115.

1935-6   WINNERS F.A. Cup   Arsenal 1 *v.* Sheffield United 0
                                       (Drake).

        Team: Wilson; Male, Hapgood; Crayston, Roberts, Copping; Hulme, Bowden, Drake, James, Bastin.

1937-8   CHAMPIONS Football League Division I

        P.42 W.21 D.10 L.11 Goals 77—44 Pts.52 1st

        Appearances: Bastin 38, Biggs 2, Boulton 15, Bowden 10, Bremner 2, Carr 11, Cartwright 6, Collett 5, Compton (D.) 7, Compton (L.) 9, Copping 38, Crayston 31, Davidson 5, Drake 27, Drury 11, Griffiths 9, Hapgood 41, Hulme 7, Hunt 18, Jones (L.) 28, Joy 26, Kirchen 19, Lewis 4, Male 34, Milne 16, Roberts 13, Sidey 3, Swindin 17, Wilson 10.

        Goal-scorers: Drake 17, Bastin 15, Carr 7, Kirchen 6, Griffiths 5, Crayston 4, Milne 4, Hunt 3, Jones 3, Cartwright 2, Davidson 2, Hulme 2, Lewis 2, Bowden 1, Bremner 1, Compton (D.) 1, Compton (L.) 1, o.g. 1. Total 77.

1947-8   CHAMPIONS Football League Division I

        P.42 W.23 D.13 L.6 Goals 81—32 Pts.59 1st

        Appearances: Barnes 35, Compton (D.) 14, Compton (L.) 35, Fields 6, Forbes 11, Jones (B.) 7, Lewis 28, Logie 39, Macaulay 40, McPherson 29, Male 8, Mercer 40, Rooke 42, Roper 40, Scott 39, Sloan 3, Smith (L.) 1, Swindin 42, Wade 3.

        Goal-scorers: Rooke 33, Lewis 14, Roper 10, Logie 8, Compton (D.) 6, McPherson 5, Forbes 2, Jones (B.) 1, Moss (Aston Villa), Robinson (Middlesbro'). Total 81.

1949-50   WINNERS F.A. Cup   Arsenal 2 *v.* Liverpool 0
                                         (Lewis 2).

        Team: Swindin; Scott, Barnes; Forbes, Compton (L.), Mercer; Cox, Logie, Goring, Lewis, Compton (D.).

1951-2   Finalists F.A. Cup   Arsenal 0 *v.* Newcastle United 1

        Team: Swindin; Barnes, Smith (L.); Forbes, Daniel, Mercer; Cox, Logie, Holton, Lishman, Roper.

15

1952–3   CHAMPIONS Football League Division I
P.42 W.21 D.12 L.9 Goals 97—64 Pts.54 1st

Appearances: Bowen 2, Chenhall 13, Cox 9, Daniel 41,
Dodgin 1, Forbes 33, Goring 29, Holton 21, Kelsey 25,
Lishman 39, Logie 32, Marden 8, Mercer 28, Milton 25,
Oakes 2, Platt 3, Roper 41, Shaw 25, Smith (L.) 31,
Swindin 14, Wade 40.

Goal-scorers: Lishman 22, Holton 19, Roper 14, Goring 10,
Logie 10, Milton 7, Daniel 5, Marden 4, Mercer 2, Cox 1,
Forbes 1, Oakes 1, o.g. 1.   Total 97.

16

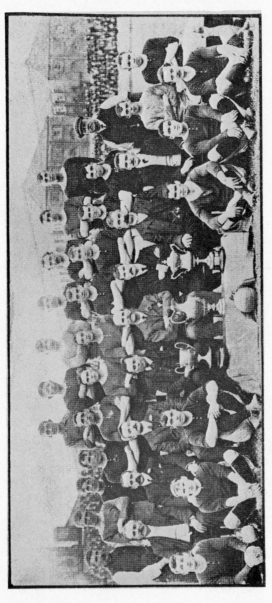

WOOLWICH ARSENAL F.C. PLAYERS AND OFFICIALS, 1906–7

G. H. Lee, Sharp, Bateup, Bigden, McEachrane, Ferguson, Sutherland,
A. Smith, Low, P. Sands (capt.), Kyle, Scollard, Blair, Minter, Cross, Ashcroft, Coleman, Bellamy, R. Dunmore (*Trainer*).
Mr. Beardsley, Mr. Titlow, Mr. Weeks, Mr. E. Mercer, Mr. A. E. Kennedy, Mr. P. Kelso, Mr. Craib, Mr. Radford, T. Lee, Gray,
Garbutt, Neave, Satterthwaite, THE STAR CUP, SOUTHERN CHARITY CUP, S.E. LEAGUE CUP, Dick, Freeman, Theobald

HERBERT CHAPMAN
Manager 1925–34

ARSENAL FOOTBALL CLUB 1953–4
Winners Football League Div. I 1952–3, F.A. Charity Shield 1953

Back row: W. J. Crayston (Assistant Manager), A. Shaw, D. J. Oakes, C. Holton, C. A. Milton, A. J. Kelsey, W. Dodgin, H. Goring, L. Wills, R. Marden, J. E. Shaw, W. Milne (*Trainer*). *Front row:* S. J. Wade, D. G. Roper, L. Smith, A. R. Forbes, T. J. Whittaker, M.B.E. (*Secretary and Manager*), J. T. Logie, D. J. Lishman, W. Barnes, D. L. Bowen

Arsenal's early history

IN THE 1880's a group of men left their homes in Nottingham to find work at Woolwich Arsenal and brought with them a lively enthusiasm for the game of soccer which was then flourishing in the Midlands town. These ammunition workers, employed in the Dial Square section, decided to form a football club of their own. This historic meeting took place at the Royal Oak, Woolwich, in 1886, and the title chosen was Royal Arsenal F.C.

The close ties with Nottingham were further cemented when the Forest agreed to give a set of red jerseys for the first matches, which, incidentally, were played on Plumstead Common. The results of the first season, when seven matches were won, one drawn and two lost, with a goal aggregate of 36—8, were so encouraging that a private enclosure called Manor Field was obtained. There was, of course, nothing pretentious about the Club's headquarters of those days. The 'grandstand', for instance, was merely a few military wagons placed end to end.

1889–90

7th September 1889: Opening match *v.* London Caledonians, 2—2.
  Team: F. W. Beardsley; P. Connolly, J. McBean; D. Howatt, J. M. Bates (capt.), J. W. Julian; R. T. Horsington, R. J. Grandison, H. Barbour, H. S. Robertson, W. Scott.

By the middle of November, Royal Arsenal had the excellent record of P.10 W.8 D.2 L.0 Goals 61—9, and the following victories were among those to their credit: *v.* Casuals 6—1; *v.* Tottenham Hotspur 10—1; *v.* Unity 8—0; *v.* Lyndhurst (in F.A. Cup) 11—0; *v.* Northumberland Fusiliers 6—1; *v.* Unity (in London Cup) 4—1 and *v.* West Kent (in Kent County Cup) 10—1.

In the meantime the reserves were also going great guns, having P.8 W.6 D.1 L.1 Goals 52—11. Bates and Connolly were selected to represent Kent in a match against Middlesex and J. W. Meggs represented London against Sheffield.

Arsenal won three trophies during the season—the London Charity Cup, the Kent Senior Cup and the Kent Junior Cup—and were locally acclaimed 'Football Champions of the South'. The three silver trophies were on view to the public for several weeks in the window of Messrs. Hosegood, outfitters, Powis Street, Woolwich; the Kent Senior Cup was rather larger than the Kent Junior, while the London Charity Cup was enormous. In addition, an illustrated sporting paper published the portraits of the Arsenal football men and sold a prodigious number of copies. Such was Arsenal's success that a 2—0 defeat at Clapton was considered the worst beating of the season.

LONDON CHARITY CUP

Final: Arsenal beat Old Westminsters 3—1 before 10,000 spectators. Arsenal's team:

F. W. Beardsley (goal). Nottingham-born and had kept goal for the Forest. Was numbered amongst the hardest workers in the cause of football progress at Woolwich.

J. McBean (right-back). From Kircaldy Wanderers.

P. Connolly (left-back). From Kircaldy Wanderers. Came as centre-forward. Represented Kent in county matches several times.

D. Howatt (right-half). Born Preston and had played for the North End reserves.

J. M. Bates (centre-half). Captain and an ex-Forest player.

J. W. Julian (left-half). Born Boston, Lincolnshire.

H. Offer. Born Devizes. Utility man, had played full-back for Swindon Town.

A. Christmas. Born Wolverhampton and had played for Kidderminster.

H. S. Robertson. Born Glasgow, ex-Westburn player.

H. Barbour. Born Glasgow and had experience with Third Lanark and Airdrieonians.

W. F. Fry. Borrowed from London Caledonians in the absence of

18

Meggs who was unfit. Was described as 'C. Edwards', sometimes called 'A. N. Other'.

KENT SENIOR CUP

Semi-final: Arsenal beat Chatham, winners of the Kent Senior Cup for the previous three years, 5—0 on their own ground.
Final: Arsenal beat Thanet Wanderers 3—0 at Chatham.

LONDON SENIOR CUP

Semi-final: Royal Arsenal 3 *v.* London Caledonians 1 at Essex County Ground, Leyton. Robertson 2 and Horsington were Arsenal's scorers. *Team:* F. W. Beardsley; P. Connolly, J. McBean; D. Howatt, J. M. Bates (capt.), H. Offer; R. T. Horsington, J. W. Meggs, H. Barbour, J. W. Julian, H. S. Robertson. On the way to the semi-final Arsenal had beaten Unity 4—1, Foxes 4—1 and St. Martin's Athletic 6—0; while the Caledonians disposed of Old Harrovians 10—1, West End 7—0 and South West Ham 4—0.
Final: Royal Arsenal 0 *v.* Old Westminsters 1.

Arsenal lost one of their best men early in the game through injury and played ten against the best eleven in London, including Moon, one of the most renowned of goalkeepers. The gate receipts for this match amounted to £200—the highest on record for a cup match up to that time.

1890-1

The successes of the previous season led to Arsenal obtaining the use of the Invicta Ground which boasted a stand, terraces and dressing-rooms. It was on this ground that the supporters of the Club had a feast of football on the Easter Monday and Tuesday of this season. Heart of Midlothian—the Scottish champions—and Notts Forest were the visitors and Arsenal beat both, before 12,000 spectators on the Monday and before 7,000 on the following day.

Arsenal were knocked out of the London Charity Cup at the third attempt by Old Carthusians in the semi-final round. After draws of 1—1 and 2—2, Old Carthusians qualified for the final with a 2—1 victory. Arsenal, however, did win the London Senior Cup.

LONDON SENIOR CUP

Quarter-final: Royal Arsenal 3 *v.* Casuals 2 (H.T. 1—2).

Semi-final: Royal Arsenal 3 *v.* Clapton 2 at Kennington Oval. Clapton scored a goal in each half and were leading 2—0 twenty-five minutes from the end. Julian then moved up Connolly from the defence, Offer dropping back in his place. Connolly infused such life into the forward line that Arsenal scored three times in quick succession to pull the match out of the fire.

Final: Royal Arsenal 6 *v.* St. Bartholomew's Hospital Club 0.

The *Kentish Independent* newspaper described the scenes of Arsenal's victorious return thus: 'Excitement is a mild description of the scene in Woolwich and Plumstead on the return of the football champions on Saturday night. A host of admirers met them at the Dockyard Station and drove them in open carriages, shouting and singing and followed by many more enthusiasts on foot. There was shouting and singing everywhere all evening and, we fear, a good deal of drinking was mingled with the rejoicing and exultation. The refrain most in vogue was that of the modern legend "It's Another Colour Now".'

1891–2

In reaching the first round proper of the F.A. Cup for the first time, in 1891, Arsenal entertained Derby County at the Invicta Ground, losing narrowly by two goals to one. Goodall, an English international and formerly centre-forward with Preston North End, was the County's captain and wing-half. This experienced player was very impressed by the displays of Connolly and Buist and offered them professional terms with Derby.

Arsenal had built up a very successful side and here was practical evidence that amateur clubs could not retain their best players in face of the competition of attractive professional offers.

Mr. Jack Humble, one of the committee members, therefore proposed at the Annual General Meeting held at the Windsor

Castle Hotel in the summer of 1891 that 'Royal Arsenal F.C. do embrace professionalism'. The proposal was carried, but this bold step was almost suicide. Arsenal were expelled from the London F.A. and boycotted by the majority of the Southern clubs, with the result that the Club was obliged to arrange friendly fixtures with Midland and Northern clubs in order to struggle along.

Among these early fixtures of 1891–2 were:

Royal Arsenal F.C.	..	.. 0	v. Sheffield United..	..	.. 2
Royal Arsenal F.C.	..	.. 1	v. West Bromwich Albion		.. 1
Bootle (Midland Alliance)		.. 2	v. Royal Arsenal ..	..	.. 2
Royal Arsenal F.C.	..	.. 1	v. Sheffield Wednesday		
			(Midland Alliance) ..		.. 8

(Arsenal's worst defeat on record up to that time!)

Royal Arsenal F.C.	..	.. 3	v. Long Eaton Rangers ..		.. 1

At the end of the season Arsenal attempted to interest some leading London clubs in the formation of a Southern League to stimulate a competitive attraction but the idea fell through.

1892–3

Friendly games against Midland and Northern clubs continued to be played this season, but, with an unreliable fixture list and without the boost of competitive spirit, support was poor. At the end of the season a dispute arose between the owners of the Invicta Ground and Arsenal F.C. in the matter of rent. The owners demanded £350 a year plus taxes, whereas Arsenal refused to pay more than £300 a year inclusive of taxes.

The result was that a limited liability company, with a capital of £4,000, was formed and the Club purchased the Manor Ground, which was its home until the move to Highbury in 1913. Furthermore, another important step was made when admission to the Football League—Division II—was obtained during the close season.

When funds were low, in 1902–3, an archery tournament was held to raise money. The sum of £1,200 was obtained and was spent on strengthening the team. The following season promotion to the First Division was gained, but the Club still found it difficult to pay its way. In an effort to overcome the lack of support at Plumstead, the Directors decided to move to North London in 1913 to seek a new following at Highbury.

Following his great work for Huddersfield, Herbert Chapman was engaged as manager in 1925 and, thereafter, Arsenal Football Club was set on the road to greatness.

PART ONE

A season-by-season review

Season 1893-4

Football League—Division II

P.28 W.12 D.4 L.12 Goals 52—55 Pts.28 9th

The Second Division of the Football League was formed in 1892 and a year later it was decided to increase its membership by three, to fifteen. Accrington, relegated from Division I, dropped out of the League, so Arsenal, Middlesbrough Ironopolis, Newcastle United and Rotherham Town were elected to fill the four vacancies.

Arsenal, captained by right-back Powell, drew their first Football League match 2—2, a home game against Newcastle, but ended the season on a bleak note, losing the last three encounters: *v.* Notts County, Small Heath and Burton Swifts—all at home too!

FOOTBALL LEAGUE RESULTS

Home	Opponents	Away	Home	Opponents	Away
1—0	Ardwick ..	.. 1—0	1—0	Middlesbro' Iron.	.. 6—3
4—1	Burslem Port Vale	1—2	2—2	Newcastle United	.. 0—6
0—2	Burton Swifts	.. 2—6	6—0	Northwich Victoria	.. 2—2
3—2	Crewe Alex.	.. 0—0	1—2	Notts County..	.. 2—3
3—1	Grimsby Town	.. 1—3	3—0	Rotherham Town	.. 1—1
4—0	Lincoln City..	.. 0—3	1—4	Small Heath ..	.. 1—4
0—5	Liverpool ..	.. 0—2	4—0	Walsall T. Swifts	.. 2—1

F.A. CUP COMPETITION

1st Qual. Rd. *v.* Ashford United	..	(h)	12—0
2nd Qual. Rd. *v.* Clapton	..	(h)	6—2
3rd Qual. Rd. *v.* Millwall	..	(h)	2—0
4th Qual. Rd. *v.* 2nd Scots Guards	..	(a)	2—1
1st Rd. *v.* Sheffield Wednesday	..	(h)	1—2

Season 1894-5

Football League—Division II

P.30 W.14 D.6 L.10 Goals 75—58 Pts.34 8th

Arsenal opened the season at Lincoln with a 5—2 defeat, which was followed by Grimsby's 3—1 victory at Plumstead and yet a third successive defeat at Burton where the Swifts won 3—0. Thereafter, however, Arsenal won the next seven home games, dropping only three further points, and in fact that initial home defeat turned out to be the only one of the season. Away points, on the other hand, were scarce, and the Club managed to gain two only from each of Burslem, Newcastle and Rotherham.

Home record: P.15 W.11 D.3 L.1 Goals 54—20 Pts.25

FOOTBALL LEAGUE RESULTS

Home	Opponents	Away	Home	Opponents	Away
7—0	Burslem Port Vale	1—0	3—3	Leicester Fosse	1—3
3—0	Burton Swifts	0—3	5—2	Lincoln City ..	2—5
1—1	Burton Wanderers ..	1—2	4—2	Manchester City	1—4
4—2	Bury ..	0—2	3—2	Newcastle United	4—2
7—0	Crewe Alex. ..	0—0	3—2	Newton Heath	3—3
4—0	Darwen ..	1—3	2—1	Notts County..	2—2
1—3	Grimsby Town ..	2—4	1—1	Rotherham Town	2—1
			6—1	Walsall Town Swifts .. 1—4	

F.A. CUP COMPETITION

1st Rd. v. Bolton Wanderers .. (a) 0—1

HONOURS

Storer, H.: Football League v. Scottish League.

Season 1895-6

Football League—Division II

P.30 W.14 D.4 L.12 Goals 59—42 Pts.32 7th

Arsenal finished in seventh place behind Liverpool, Manchester City, Grimsby Town, Burton Wanderers, Newcastle and Newton Heath. Liverpool, relegated after the test matches of the previous season, scored 106 goals in the thirty games and had the biggest home and away wins of the season: 10—1 v. Rotherham and 7—0 at Burton Swifts and at Crewe Alexandra.

Arsenal's best victories were against Crewe Alexandra (7—0), who finished at the foot of the table and dropped out of the Football League until the Third Division (North) was formed in 1921, and against Loughborough Town (6—0), champions of the Midland League 1894-5, who were elected to the Football League at the expense of Walsall Town Swifts.

FOOTBALL LEAGUE RESULTS

Home	Opponents	Away	Home	Opponents	Away
2—1	Burslem Port Vale	2—0	4—0	Lincoln City ..	.. 1—1
5—0	Burton Swifts	.. 2—3	0—2	Liverpool ..	.. 0—3
3—0	Burton Wanderers	1—4	6—0	Loughboro' Town	.. 1—2
7—0	Crewe Alexandra	.. 1—0	0—1	Manchester City	.. 0—1
1—3	Darwen ..	.. 1—1	2—1	Newcastle United	.. 1—3
3—1	Grimsby Town	.. 1—1	2—1	Newton Heath	.. 1—5
1—1	Leicester Fosse	.. 0—1	2—0	Notts County..	.. 4—3
	5—0 Rotherham Town		.. 0—3		

F.A. CUP COMPETITION

1st Rd. v. Burnley .. .. (a) 1—6

Season 1896–7

Football League—Division II

P.30 W.13 D.4 L.13 Goals 68—70 Pts.30 10th

Season 1896–7 remains a notable one in Arsenal's history in the League for two reasons. Firstly, the tenth position in Division II is the lowest that Arsenal have ever been placed, and, secondly, the 8—0 defeat at Loughborough still remains the worst defeat in the whole of Arsenal's record in the Football League. In addition, the team was knocked out of the Cup by Millwall—a Southern League club!

Arsenal competed against new opponents in the League in Blackpool, Gainsborough Trinity and Walsall, who had replaced Burslem Port Vale, Crewe Alexandra and Rotherham Town. Arsenal, in the meantime, were still the only representative of the South in the Football League.

FOOTBALL LEAGUE RESULTS

Home	Opponents	Away	Home	Opponents	Away
4—2	Blackpool	1—1	6—2	Lincoln City	3—2
3—0	Burton Swifts ..	2—1	2—0	Loughborough Town	0—8
3—0	Burton Wanderers	3—0	1—2	Manchester City ..	1—1
1—0	Darwen	1—4	5—1	Newcastle United ..	0—2
6—1	Gainsborough Trinity	1—4	0—2	Newton Heath ..	1—1
4—2	Grimsby Town ..	1—3	2—3	Notts County.. ..	4—7
2—1	Leicester Fosse ..	3—6	2—3	Small Heath	2—5
1—1	Walsall	3—5			

F.A. CUP COMPETITION

4th Qual. Rd. *v.* Leyton	(h)	5—2
5th Qual. Rd. *v.* Chatham	(h)	4—0
Final Suppl'y Rd. *v.* Millwall	(a)	2—4

Reserves: Champions Kent County League.

Season 1897-8

Football League—Division II

P.30 W.16 D.5 L.9 Goals 69—49 Pts.37 5th

Now known as Woolwich Arsenal (the title 'Royal' was dropped at the beginning of the previous season), the Club appointed T. B. Mitchell, from Blackburn Rovers, as manager. Also, for the first time, it broke new ground in supplying a player for a current international: Caesar Llewellyn Jenkins, captain of Arsenal, being chosen to represent Wales v. England.

Only one club—Leicester Fosse—managed to win a League game at Manor Field during the season, where the record was W.10 D.4 L.1. On away midden, Arsenal had a particularly good spell in December, January and February, when victories were registered at Loughborough, Lincoln, Burton Swifts and Grimsby. Together with a drawn game at Blackpool, these made up nine points out of a possible ten in five successive away fixtures.

FOOTBALL LEAGUE RESULTS

Home	Opponents	Away	Home	Opponents	Away
2—1	Blackpool ..	.. 3—3	2—2	Lincoln City ..	.. 3—2
1—1	Burnley ..	.. 0—5	4—0	Loughborough Town	3—1
3—0	Burton Swifts	.. 2—1	3—0	Luton ..	.. 2—0
3—1	Darwen ..	.. 4—1	2—2	Manchester City	.. 1—4
4—0	Gainsborough Trinity	0—1	0—0	Newcastle United	.. 1—4
4—1	Grimsby Town	.. 4—1	5—1	Newton Heath	.. 1—5
0—3	Leicester Fosse	.. 1—2	4—2	Small Heath ..	.. 1—2
	4—0 Walsall		..	.. 2—3	

F.A. CUP COMPETITION

3rd Qual. Rd. v. St. Albans	..	.. (h) 9—0
4th Qual. Rd. v. Sheppey United	..	.. (h) 3—0
5th Qual. Rd. v. New Brompton	..	.. (h) 4—2
1st Rd. Proper v. Burnley	..	.. (a) 1—3

Season 1898–9

Football League—Division II

P.34   W.18   D.5   L.11   Goals 72—41   Pts.41   7th

Mr. T. B. Mitchell resigned at the end of 1897–8 and Mr. G. Elcoat, from Stockton, was appointed to succeed him as manager. For this season, each of the Divisions was increased to eighteen clubs and test matches were abolished; promotion and relegation being automatic as it is today. The vacancies in Division I were filled by Burnley and Newcastle, while the newcomers to Division II were Barnsley, Glossop, New Brighton Tower and Burslem Port Vale.

At the foot of Division II at the end of the season were Darwen, who were defeated 10—0 by Loughborough, Manchester City and Walsall. Their away record read: P.17   W.0   D.1   L.16   Goals 6—109.

In the Cup Arsenal were soundly defeated at Manor Ground by Derby County who, for the second season in succession, failed to win the trophy at the last hurdle. A year previously Notts Forest beat them 3—1; this time Sheffield United, after three replays *v.* Liverpool in the semi-final, won 4—1.

FOOTBALL LEAGUE RESULTS

Home	Opponents	Away	Home	Opponents	Away
3—0	Barnsley	1—2	4—0	Leicester Fosse	1—2
6—0	Blackpool	1—1	4—2	Lincoln City	0—2
1—0	Burslem Port Vale	0—3	3—1	Loughborough Town	0—0
2—1	Burton Swifts	2—1	6—2	Luton	1—0
6—0	Darwen	4—1	0—1	Manchester City	1—3
5—1	Gainsborough Trinity	1—0	4—0	New Brighton Tower	1—3
3—0	Glossop North End	0—2	5—1	Newton Heath	2—2
1—1	Grimsby Town	0—1	2—0	Small Heath	1—4
	0—0 Walsall	1—4			

F.A. CUP COMPETITION

1st Rd. *v.* Derby County   .. (h) 0—6

Football League—Division II

P.34 W.16 D.4 L.14 Goals 61—43 Pts.36 8th

For the third successive year there was a change of manager at Arsenal. This time the services of Mr. H. Bradshaw were obtained.

During the season Arsenal established the Club record score for a League game when they beat Loughborough 12—0. It is a coincidence that Arsenal's worst defeat in the League (8—0 at Loughborough three years previously) involved the same club. At the end of the season Loughborough, who could engineer but one solitary victory, dropped out of the Football League after a five-year membership.

Arsenal's marathon cup-tie against New Brompton, which the latter won in the fifth meeting after playing eight hours, was the longest tie on record until 1924 when Barrow and Leyton each took nine hours to beat Gillingham and Ilford respectively.

FOOTBALL LEAGUE RESULTS

Home	Opponents	Away	Home	Opponents	Away
5—1	Barnsley	2—3	2—1	Lincoln City	0—5
0—1	Bolton Wanderers	0—1	12—0	Loughborough Town	3—2
1—0	Burslem Port Vale	1—1	3—1	Luton	2—1
1—1	Burton Swifts	0—2	3—0	Middlesbrough	0—1
2—0	Chesterfield	1—3	5—0	New Brighton Tower	2—0
2—1	Gainsborough Trinity	1—1	2—1	Newton Heath	0—2
2—0	Grimsby Town	0—1	1—2	Sheffield Wednesday	1—3
0—2	Leicester Fosse	0—0	3—0	Small Heath	1—3
	3—1	Walsall			0—2

F.A. CUP COMPETITION

3rd Qual. Rd. *v.* New Brompton .. (h) 1—1 (a) 0—0
(at Millwall) 2—2; (at Tottenham) 1—1; (at Gravesend) 0—1

Football League—Division II

P.34 W.15 D.6 L.13 Goals 39—35 Pts.36 7th

In the League during the season there were thirteen occasions (more than a third of the total) in which games were won or lost by an orphan goal and more than half of the away fixtures were lost in such a manner.

Arsenal progressed beyond the first round proper in the F.A. Cup for the first time when they beat Blackburn Rovers 2—0 in that stage. It was also the first occasion that the London club had beaten a First Division side.

Among Mr. Bradshaw's efforts to strengthen the team, two notable players were signed during the previous season, goalkeeper Ashcroft from Sheppey and full-back Cross from Dartford. Both gave valuable service to the Club; Cross being a regular first-team player for ten years, while Ashcroft represented the Football League and England in 1905 and 1906.

FOOTBALL LEAGUE RESULTS

Home	Opponents	Away	Home	Opponents	Away
1—2	Barnsley	0—3	1—1	Grimsby Town	0—1
3—1	Blackpool	1—1	2—1	Leicester Fosse	0—1
3—1	Burnley	0—3	0—0	Lincoln City	3—3
3—0	Burslem Port Vale	0—1	1—0	Middlesbrough	1—1
3—1	Burton Swifts	0—1	2—1	New Brighton Tower	0—1
1—0	Chesterfield	1—0	2—1	Newton Heath	0—1
2—1	Gainsborough Trinity	0—1	1—0	Small Heath	1—2
2—0	Glossop North End	1—0	2—0	Stockport County	1—3
1—1	Walsall	0—1			

F.A. CUP COMPETITION

Final Suppl'y Qual. Rd. v. Darwen	..	(a)	2—0
1st Rd. v. Blackburn Rovers	..	(h)	2—0
2nd Rd. v. West Bromwich Albion	..	(h)	0—1

THE ARSENAL TEAMS OF 1930–1

(*Left to right*) *Back row:* Mr. J. E. Shaw (*Assistant Manager*), Cope, Robinson, Allison, Brain, Preedy, Haynes, Roberts, Harper, Seddon, Lewis, Male, Parkin, Mr. W. Milne (*Assistant Trainer*). *2nd row:* Williams, Thompson, Maycock, Baker, Diaper, Bastin, Hapgood, Lewis, John, Lambert, Mr. J. McEwan (*Coach*). *Front row:* Hulme, Parker, Mr. H. Chapman (*Secretary-Manager*), Mr. T. Whittaker (*Trainer*), Jack, Jones

Mr. George Allison with the six members of the Arsenal team who played for England against Wales in 1936. *Left to right:* Male, Drake, Bastin, Hapgood, Bowden and Crayston

ARSENAL FOOTBALL CLUB 1956–7

(*Left to right*) *Top row:* R. Swallow, A. Biggs, J. Smailes, H. Dove, R. Greenwood, V. Groves. *Second row:* L. Garrett, B. McGreevey, D. Barrett, E. Cox, D. McBennett, E. Doughty, L. Vernon, D. Bennett. *Third row:* S. Charlton, J. Fotheringham, P. Goy, C. Sullivan, A. J. Kelsey, W. Dodgin, D. Herd, D. Tapscott. *Front row (seated):* D. Clapton, L. Wills, D. Evans, C. Holton, H. Goring, D. Roper, J. Bloomfield, M. Tiddy, G. Nutt. *Seated on ground:* J. Haverty, J. Barnwell, T. Petts, B. Crouch

Season 1901-2

Football League—Division II

P.34 W.18 D.6 L.10 Goals 50—26 Pts.42 4th

In attaining fourth position, Arsenal experienced their most success-ful season so far in Division II and, in particular, the pleasing feature was the solidarity of the defence. Only twenty-six goals were conceded in the thirty-four matches and in almost half of them the opposition failed to find the net. At Manor Field no more than six teams managed to score and Arsenal's goal aggregate there was 35—9.

Although finishing in fourth place, Arsenal were not at any time during the season one of the challengers for promotion. West Bromwich Albion were always way out in front with Middlesbrough following in their wake. The Albion ended the season as champions of Division II, thirteen points ahead of Arsenal, while Middles-brough, who claimed the very fine goal aggregate of 90—24, were nine points superior to the Gunners.

FOOTBALL LEAGUE RESULTS

Home	Opponents	Away	Home	Opponents	Away
2—1	Barnsley	0—2	5—0	Gainsborough Trinity	2—2
0—0	Blackpool	3—1	4—0	Glossop	1—0
2—0	Bristol City	3—0	2—0	Leicester Fosse	1—2
4—0	Burnley	0—0	2—0	Lincoln City	0—0
3—1	Burslem Port Vale	0—1	0—3	Middlesbrough	0—1
0—1	Burton United	0—2	2—0	Newton Heath	1—0
3—2	Chesterfield	3—1	0—0	Preston North End	0—2
1—0	Doncaster Rovers	0—1	3—0	Stockport County	0—0
		2—1	West Bromwich Albion	1—2	

F.A. CUP COMPETITION

Final Suppl'y Rd. v. Luton	(h)	1—1
Replay v. Luton	(a)	2—0
1st Rd. v. Newcastle United	(h)	0—2

HONOURS

Jackson, J.: England trial.

Season 1902-3

Football League—Division II

P.34 W.20 D.8 L.6 Goals 66—30 Pts.48 3rd

Arsenal climbed one position nearer promotion, finishing third, six points behind the champions Manchester City and three behind Small Heath. Losing only six games during the season, the least successful period was in December when three successive away fixtures resulted in defeats, v. Small Heath, Manchester City and Burton United. Thereafter, Arsenal collected twenty-eight points out of a possible thirty-six, with a solitary defeat at Manchester United who had, earlier in the season, registered the only away victory at Plumstead.

Sheffield United provided the opposition in the attractive fixture in the first round proper of the F.A. Cup. The United during the previous five years had been champions, runners-up, cup-winners (twice) and finalists. Little wonder, then, that 25,000 spectators turned up to see this team in action.

FOOTBALL LEAGUE RESULTS

Home	Opponents	Away	Home	Opponents	Away
4—0	Barnsley	1—1	6—1	Gainsborough Trinity	1—0
2—1	Blackpool	0—0	0—0	Glossop	2—1
2—1	Bristol City	0—1	0—0	Leicester Fosse	2—0
5—1	Burnley	3—0	2—1	Lincoln City	2—2
3—0	Burslem Port Vale	1—1	1—0	Manchester City	1—4
3—0	Burton United	1—2	0—1	Manchester United	0—3
3—0	Chesterfield	2—2	3—1	Preston North End	2—2
3—0	Doncaster Rovers	1—0	6—1	Small Heath	0—2
	3—1 Stockport County	1—0			

F.A. CUP COMPETITION

Final Suppl'y Rd. v. Brentford	(a)	1—1
Replay v. Brentford	(h)	5—0
1st Rd. v. Sheffield United	(h)	1—3

HONOURS

Shanks, T.: Ireland v. Scotland.

34

Season 1903-4

Football League—Division II

P.34   W.21   D.7   L.6   Goals 91—22   Pts.49   2nd

Promotion! At the half-way stage Preston and Arsenal seemed to have the race on their own, but a late challenge from Manchester United put the issue in doubt until the final games were played. As both of their rivals had inferior goal averages, Arsenal had to obtain one point from their last fixture, *v.* Port Vale, to be sure of going up. This they did, while Preston, who beat Blackpool 1—0, went to the top.

Arsenal were unbeaten at home—winning all apart from the last two—and had a goal aggregate of 67—5. The promotion team generally consisted of Ashcroft; Cross, Jackson; Dick, Sands, McEachrane; Briercliffe, Coleman, Gooing, Shanks, Linward. Ashcroft and Gooing played in all thirty-four matches and Shanks, with twenty-five goals, was the leading scorer.

FOOTBALL LEAGUE RESULTS

Home	Opponents	Away	Home	Opponents	Away
3—0	Barnsley	1—2	6—0	Chesterfield	0—1
3—0	Blackpool	2—2	6—0	Gainsborough Trinity	2—0
3—0	Bolton Wanderers ..	1—2	2—1	Glossop	3—1
4—1	Bradford City ..	3—0	5—1	Grimsby Town ..	2—2
2—0	Bristol City	4—0	8—0	Leicester Fosse ..	0—0
4—0	Burnley	0—1	4—0	Lincoln City	2—0
0—0	Burslem Port Vale ..	3—2	4—0	Manchester United ..	0—1
8—0	Burton United ..	1—3	0—0	Preston North End ..	0—0
	5—2 Stockport County .. 0—0				

F.A. CUP COMPETITION

Final Suppl'y Rd. *v.* Bristol Rovers   .. (a) 1—1   (h) 1—1
                              (at Tottenham)   1—0
1st Rd. *v.* Fulham   ..   ..   .. (h) 1—0
2nd Rd. *v.* Manchester City   ..   .. (h) 0—2

HONOURS

Coleman, J., Linward, W. and *Sands, P.:* England trial
Shanks, T.: Ireland *v.* Wales.

Season 1904-5

Football League—Division I

P.34 W.12 D.9 L.13 Goals 36—40 Pts.33 10th

Mr. Bradshaw surprisingly left to take up the managerial chair at Fulham during the close season, and Mr. P. Kelso, a Scot from Hibernian, was appointed as his successor at Arsenal.

Still the only team in the Football League south of Birmingham (apart from Bristol City in the Western region), Arsenal made a fair start among the 'big names' of the First Division. They averaged just under a point per match and obtained two-thirds of them at home. The top and bottom clubs (Newcastle and Notts County) and Notts Forest (16th) were the only ones to win at Plumstead, while Arsenal turned the tables on both of the Nottingham teams on their own midden. One team only managed to complete the double over Arsenal—that was Newcastle, who were not only the champions but also narrowly beaten cup-finalists as well.

FOOTBALL LEAGUE RESULTS

Home	Opponents	Away	Home	Opponents	Away
1—0	Aston Villa ..	.. 1—3	1—2	Notts County ..	.. 5—1
2—0	Blackburn Rovers	.. 1—1	0—3	Notts Forest ..	.. 3—0
2—1	Bury ..	.. 1—1	0—0	Preston North End ..	0—3
0—0	Derby County ..	.. 0—0	1—0	Sheffield United ..	.. 0—4
2—1	Everton ..	.. 0—1	3—0	Sheffield Wednesday	3—0
1—0	Manchester City	.. 0—1	1—1	Small Heath ..	.. 1—2
1—1	Middlesbrough ..	.. 0—1	2—1	Stoke City ..	.. 0—2
0—2	Newcastle United	.. 0—3	0—0	Sunderland ..	.. 1—1

2—0 Wolverhampton Wanderers .. 1—4

F.A. CUP COMPETITION

1st Rd. *v.* Bristol City .. .. (h) 0—0
Replay *v.* Bristol City .. .. (a) 0—1

HONOURS

Ashcroft, J.: Football League *v.* Irish League.
Coleman, J., Sands, P. and *Satterthwaite, C.:* England trial.
Shanks, T.: Ireland *v.* England.

Football League—Division I

P.38 W.15 D.7 L.16 Goals 62—64 Pts.37 12th

The First Division was increased to twenty clubs this season. Bury and Notts County (17th and 18th in 1904-5) remained in the upper sphere and Liverpool and Bolton (champions and runners-up in Division II) joined them. Liverpool, incidentally, followed up their Division II success by carrying off the League title twelve months later.

Arsenal progressed beyond the second round of the Cup for the first time, and reached the semi-final stage, but in the League the results were not so encouraging. Particularly from October to February, when only three games were won and two drawn in sixteen—eight points out of thirty-two. The Club, however, pulled out of danger with nine victories in the next ten encounters and finished in twelfth position.

FOOTBALL LEAGUE RESULTS

Home	Opponents	Away	Home	Opponents	Away
2—1	Aston Villa ..	.. 1—2	2—2	Middlesbrough	.. 0—2
5—0	Birmingham ..	.. 1—2	4—3	Newcastle United	.. 1—1
3—2	Blackburn Rovers	.. 0—2	1—1	Notts County	.. 0—1
0—0	Bolton Wanderers	.. 1—6	3—1	Notts Forest	.. 1—3
4—0	Bury ..	.. 0—2	2—2	Preston North End ..	2—2
1—0	Derby County	.. 1—5	5—1	Sheffield United	.. 1—3
1—2	Everton ..	.. 1—0	0—2	Sheffield Wednesday	2—4
3—1	Liverpool ..	.. 0—3	1—2	Stoke City ..	.. 1—2
2—0	Manchester City	.. 2—1	2—0	Sunderland ..	.. 2—2
		2—1 Wolverhampton Wanderers .. 2—0			

F.A. CUP COMPETITION

1st Rd. v. West Ham United	.. (h)	1—1
Replay v. West Ham United	.. (a)	3—2
2nd Rd. v. Watford ..	.. (h)	3—0
3rd Rd. v. Sunderland ..	.. (h)	5—0
4th Rd. v. Manchester United	.. (a)	3—2
S.F. v. Newcastle United (at Stoke)	0—2

HONOURS

Ashcroft, J. : England *v.* Scotland, Ireland and Wales; Football League *v.* Scottish League; England trial (2).
Coleman, J : England trial.
Cross, A. G. : England trial.
Sands, P. R.: Football League *v.* Irish League.

38

Season 1906-7

Football League—Division I

P.38 W.20 D.4 L.14 Goals 66—59 Pts.44 7th

For a few weeks early in their third season in Division I Arsenal held the supreme position at the head of the Football League for the first time. In a very fine start, the Club dropped only three points out of eighteen and included away wins *v.* Manchester City, Preston and Bristol City. The top six positions in the table on 20th October and at the end of the season are given below:

Arsenal	W.7	D.1	L.1	Pts.15
Everton	W.6	D.2	L.2	Pts.14
Newcastle Utd. ..	W.6	D.1	L.2	Pts.13
Aston Villa ..	W.6	D.1	L.3	Pts.13
Bolton Wand. ..	W.5	D.2	L.2	Pts.12
Manchester Utd.	W.3	D.4	L.2	Pts.10

Newcastle Utd. ..	W.22	D.7	L.9	Pts.51
Bristol City ..	W.20	D.8	L.10	Pts.48
Everton	W.20	D.5	L.13	Pts.45
Sheffield Utd. ..	W.17	D.11	L.10	Pts.45
Aston Villa ..	W.19	D.6	L.13	Pts.44
Bolton Wand. ..	W.18	D.8	L.12	Pts.44

Although deposed by Everton at the end of October, Arsenal were still among the leaders at the half-way stage. A poor spell in February when four successive League games were lost (two of which were at home!) pulled them back, however, and seventh place was the final reward.

During the lean period in the League, Arsenal's effort in the knock-out competition was much more satisfactory. They reached the penultimate stage for the second successive season running, being beaten by the eventual winners Sheffield Wednesday at Birmingham.

FOOTBALL LEAGUE RESULTS

Home	Opponents	Away	Home	Opponents	Away
3—1	Aston Villa ..	.. 2—2	2—0	Blackburn Rovers ..	3—2
2—1	Birmingham ..	.. 1—5	2—2	Bolton Wanderers ..	0—3

Home	Opponents	Away	Home	Opponents	Away
1—2	Bristol City ..	.. 3—1	2—0	Middlesbrough	.. 3—5
3—1	Bury	.. 1—4	2—0	Newcastle United	.. 0—1
3—2	Derby County	.. 0—0	1—0	Notts County..	.. 1—4
3—1	Everton ..	.. 1—2	1—0	Preston North End	.. 3—0
2—1	Liverpool ..	.. 0—4	0—1	Sheffield United	.. 2—4
4—1	Manchester City	.. 4—1	1—0	Sheffield Wednesday	1—1
4—0	Manchester United	.. 0—1	2—1	Stoke City ..	.. 0—2
	0—1 Sunderland	.. .. 3—2			

LEAGUE APPEARANCES (24 PLAYERS)

Ashcroft, J. ..	.. 35	Dick, J.	.. 1	Low, A. B.	.. 2		
Batup, E. ..	.. 3	Ducat, A.	.. 4	McEachrane, R. J.	34		
Bellamy, J. T.	.. 12	Ferguson, J.	.. 1	Mordue, J.	.. 3		
Bigden, J. H.	.. 37	Freeman, B. C.	12	Neave, D.	.. 33		
Blair, J. ..	.. 1	Garbutt, W.	.. 24	Sands, P. R.	.. 24		
Coleman, J. ..	.. 34	Gray, A.	.. 23	Satterthwaite, C.	38		
Cross, A. J. ..	.. 16	Hynds, T.	.. 13	Sharp, J.	.. 36		
Crowe	.. 1	Kyle, P.	.. 29	Theobald, S. W. ..	2		

LEAGUE GOAL-SCORERS

Satterthwaite, C.	.. 18	Neave, D.	.. 4	Bigden, J. H.	.. 1
Coleman, J. ..	.. 14	Garbutt, W.	.. 3	Ducat, A.	.. 1
Kyle, P. ..	.. 13	Sands, P. R.	.. 3	Sharp, J.	.. 1
Freeman, B. C.	.. 7	Bellamy, J. T. ..	1		Total 66

F.A. CUP COMPETITION

1st Rd. *v.* Grimsby Town	..	(a)	1—1
Replay *v.* Grimsby Town	..	(h)	3—0
2nd Rd. *v.* Bristol City ..	..	(h)	2—1
3rd Rd. *v.* Bristol Rovers..	..	(h)	1—0
4th Rd. *v.* Barnsley	..	(a)	2—1
S.F. *v.* Sheffield Wednesday	..		1—3 (at Birmingham)

HONOURS

Ashcroft, J.: England trial.
Coleman, J.: England *v.* Ireland; Football League *v.* Scottish League,
    Irish League; England trial (2).
Cross, A. J.: England trial.
Sharp, J.: Scotland *v.* England, Wales.

Season 1907-8

Football League—Division I

P.38   W.12   D.12   L.14   Goals 51—63   Pts.36   14th (Equal)

Arsenal and Blackburn Rovers ended the season bracketed together in fourteenth place with identical records, including goals scored and conceded. This situation is absolutely unique, never having happened before or since in the long history of the Football League.

Arsenal, the pioneers of professional soccer in the South, who had been for so long the sole representatives of the southern half of England in the League, were joined this season in Division I by fellow Londoners Chelsea. With Clapton Orient and Fulham in the lower Division, London now had four clubs in the Football League. Arsenal were admitted in 1893, Chelsea and Clapton in 1905 and Fulham in 1907.

At the end of the season Arsenal made a concentrated tour of Scotland, with the following results:

21st April *v.* Hearts .. 1—3	27th April *v.* Motherwell .. 1—1
22nd April *v.* Raith R. .. 0—1	28th April *v.* Rangers .. 1—1
23rd April *v.* Aberdeen .. 1—4	29th April *v.* Morton .. 0—1
25th April *v.* Dundee .. 1—2	30th April *v.* Kilmarnock 2—1

P.8   W.1   D.2   L.5   Goals 7—14

FOOTBALL LEAGUE RESULTS

Home	Opponents	Away	Home	Opponents	Away
0—1	Aston Villa ..	.. 1—0	2—1	Manchester City	.. 0—4
1—1	Birmingham ..	.. 2—1	1—0	Manchester United ..	2—4
2—0	Blackburn Rovers	.. 1—1	4—1	Middlesbrough	.. 0—0
1—1	Bolton Wanderers	.. 1—3	2—2	Newcastle United	.. 1—2
0—4	Bristol City ..	.. 2—1	1—1	Notts County..	.. 0—2
0—0	Bury ..	.. 2—3	3—1	Notts Forest ..	.. 0—1
0—0	Chelsea	.. 1—2	1—1	Preston North End ..	0—3
2—1	Everton	.. 1—1	5—1	Sheffield United	.. 2—2
2—1	Liverpool	.. 1—4	1—1	Sheffield Wednesday	0—6
	4—0 Sunderland ..	.. 2—5			

41

LEAGUE APPEARANCES (24 PLAYERS)

Ashcroft, J.	.. 36	Garbutt, W.	.. 8	Neave, D.	.. 35
Batup, E. ..	.. 2	Gray, A.	.. 30	Rodger, J.	.. 1
Bigden, J. H.	.. 6	Hoare, G. R.	.. 1	Sands, P. R.	.. 34
Coleman, J. ..	.. 26	Kyle, P.	.. 23	Satterthwaite, C.	23
Cross, A. G.	.. 11	Lee, H. G.	.. 18	Satterthwaite, J.	3
Dick, J. ..	.. 17	Lewis, C.	.. 13	Sharp, J. ..	.. 32
Ducat, A. ..	.. 18	McEachrane, R.J.	38	Shaw, J. ..	.. 1
Freeman, B. C.	.. 15	Mordue, J.	.. 23	Theobald, S. W. ..	3

LEAGUE GOAL-SCORERS

Coleman, J. ..	.. 9	Freeman, B. C.	4	Mordue, J.	.. 1
Kyle, P. ..	.. 8	Satterthwaite, C.	3	Satterthwaite, J. ..	1
Lewis, C. ..	.. 8	Garbutt, W.	.. 2	Sharp, J. ..	.. 1
Neave, D. ..	.. 6	Sands, P. R.	2		Total 51
Lee, H. G. ..	.. 5	Ducat, A.	.. 1		

F.A. CUP COMPETITION

1st Rd. *v.* Hull City .. .. (h) 0—0
Replay *v.* Hull City .. .. (a) 1—4

HONOURS

Ducat, A.: England trial.
Sharp, J.: Scotland *v.* England.

Football League—Division I

P.38   W.14   D.10   L.14   Goals 52—49   Pts.38   6th

A season of contrasts—in particular for Arsenal, Notts Forest and Newcastle. It is often said that to draw away and win at home is championship form. Arsenal almost achieved the more difficult part of this target by claiming seventeen points in nineteen away fixtures. Form at home, on the other hand, was not equal to championship standards, because seven teams managed to take away full points from Plumstead and three others each gained a point there. Only Nottingham Forest suffered more home defeats than Arsenal. In contrast, the Forest had the satisfaction of equalling the Division I record home victory when they defeated Leicester Fosse by twelve goals to nil.

Arsenal failed to achieve the double over any club during the season, while they conceded four points to Aston Villa, Newcastle and Sunderland. Four successive defeats in November and December included Sunderland's visit on 21st November, when they returned the winners by 4—0. A fortnight later, on 5th December, Sunderland reached a new peak and created the present record for an away win: 9—1 at Newcastle. The United, nevertheless, went on undaunted to win the championship, with Sunderland nine points behind in third place.

Newcomers to the League in place of Stoke, Tottenham won the Division II title at the first attempt and so became the third London club in the First Division.

FOOTBALL LEAGUE RESULTS

Home	Opponents	Away	Home	Opponents	Away
0—1	Aston Villa ..	.. 1—2	3—0	Manchester City	.. 2—2
0—1	Blackburn Rovers	.. 3—1	0—1	Manchester United	.. 4—1
1—0	Bradford City	.. 1—4	1—1	Middlesbrough	.. 1—1
1—1	Bristol City ..	.. 1—2	1—2	Newcastle United	.. 1—3
4—0	Bury	.. 1—1	1—0	Notts County..	.. 1—2
0—0	Chelsea ..	.. 2—1	1—2	Notts Forest ..	.. 1—0
0—4	Everton ..	.. 3—0	1—0	Preston North End ..	.. 0—0
2—1	Leicester Fosse	.. 1—1	1—0	Sheffield United	.. 1—1
5—0	Liverpool ..	.. 2—2	2—0	Sheffield Wednesday	2—6
	0—4 Sunderland ..	.. 0—1			

LEAGUE APPEARANCES (23 PLAYERS)

Beney, B.	 8	Greenaway, D.	37	Neave, D.	.. 25
Chisholm, N. W.	.. 3	Hoare, G. R.	.. 11	Raybould, S.	.. 26
Cross, A. G.	.. 13	Lee, H. G.	.. 17	Sands, P. R.	.. 32
Curie, W.	 3	Lewis, C.	.. 23	Satterthwaite, J.	.. 18
Dick, J.	 5	McDonald, H.	.. 38	Shaw, J.	 28
Ducat, A.	 33	McEachrane, R.J.	36	Theobald, S. W.	.. 3
Fitchie, T. T.	.. 21	McKinnon, A.	.. 2	Thomson	 3
Gray, A.	 32	Maxwell, J. M.	1		

LEAGUE GOAL-SCORERS

Fitchie, T. T.	.. 8	Hoare, G. R.	.. 5	Greenaway, D.	.. 3
Lee, H. G.	 8	Neave, D.	.. 5	Ducat, A.	.. 1
Lewis, C.	 7	Satterthwaite, J.	4	Sands, P. R.	.. 1
Raybould, S.	.. 6	Beney, B.	.. 3	opponents	.. 1

Total 52

F.A. CUP COMPETITION

1st Rd. *v.* Croydon Common	..	1—1 (at Crystal Palace)
Replay *v.* Croydon Common	.. (h)	2—0
2nd Rd. *v.* Millwall	.. .. (h)	1—1
Replay *v.* Millwall	.. .. (a)	0—1

Football League—Division I

P.38 W.11 D.9 L.18 Goals 37—67 Pts.31 18th

Relegation loomed large in the affairs at Plumstead during 1909–10. This pattern was set at the start when only five points were mustered from the first dozen games. Arsenal did not pick up an away point until the second week in November, and the seven successive defeats produced an adverse goal aggregate of 6—32. Blackburn scored seven against them, Sunderland six and Aston Villa, Middlesbrough and Notts County each netted five.

The defence subsequently became less vulnerable because only Preston, Newcastle and Liverpool managed to score more than two goals against them afterwards. In failing to find the net in almost a third of the matches, the attack carried few guns, and not one individual totalled more than five goals during the season.

Arsenal escaped relegation by virtue of a run of five undefeated games in the last month (three wins and two draws with an aggregate of 4—1) and Chelsea's defeats by fellow relegation candidates Arsenal (0—1), Bristol City (0—1) and Tottenham (1—2).

THE FOOT OF DIVISION I

26th March 1910

Chelsea	.. P.32	W.9	D.7	L.16	Pts. 25
Bristol C.	.. P.31	W.9	D.7	L.15	Pts. 25
Middlesbro'	.. P.31	W.10	D.4	L.17	Pts. 24
Tottenham	.. P.31	W.8	D.7	L.16	Pts. 23
Arsenal	.. P.32	W.8	D.7	L.17	Pts. 23
Bolton W.	.. P.32	W.7	D.4	L.21	Pts. 18

30th April 1910

Tottenham	.. W.11	D.10	L.17	Pts. 32
Bristol C.	.. W.12	D.8	L.18	Pts. 32
Middlesbro'	.. W.11	D.9	L.18	Pts. 31
Arsenal	.. W.11	D.9	L.18	Pts. 31
Chelsea	.. W.11	D.7	L.20	Pts. 29
Bolton W.	.. W.9	D.6	L.23	Pts. 24

FOOTBALL LEAGUE RESULTS

Home	Opponents	Away	Home	Opponents	Away
1—0	Aston Villa ..	.. 1—5	0—0	Manchester United ..	.. 0—1
0—1	Blackburn Rovers ..	0—7	3—0	Middlesbrough	.. 2—5
2—0	Bolton Wanderers ..	0—3	0—3	Newcastle United ..	1—1
0—1	Bradford City ..	1—0	1—2	Notts County..	.. 1—5
2—2	Bristol City ..	.. 1—0	0—1	Notts Forest ..	.. 1—1
0—0	Bury	.. 2—1	1—3	Preston North End ..	4—3
3—2	Chelsea ..	.. 1—0	0—0	Sheffield United ..	0—2
1—0	Everton ..	.. 0—1	0—1	Sheffield Wednesday	1—1
1—1	Liverpool ..	.. 1—5	1—2	Sunderland ..	.. 2—6

1—0 Tottenham Hotspur .. 1—1

LEAGUE APPEARANCES (28 PLAYERS)

Bassett	..	.. 1	Heppinstall	.. 18	McKinnon, A.	..	.. 8
Beney, B.	..	.. 8	Hoare, G. R.	.. 1	Neave, D.		.. 21
Buckenham, W. E.		21	Lawrence	.. 25	Oliver	..	.. 1
Cross, A. G.		.. 9	Lee, H. G.	.. 6	Sands, P. R.		.. 12
Dick, J.	..	.. 7	Lewis, C.	.. 28	Shaw, J.	..	.. 29
Drain	..	.. 2	McDonald, D.	25	Steven	..	.. 7
Ducat, A.	..	.. 29	McDonald, H.	36	Satterthwaite, J.	..	4
Fisher	..	.. 2	McEachrane, R.J.	32	Thomson, M.		.. 30
Gray, A.	..	.. 13	McGibbon, C. E.	4			
Greenaway, D.		.. 36	McKellor	.. 3			

LEAGUE GOAL-SCORERS

Buckenham, W. E.	5	Beney, B.	.. 3	Lee, H. G.		.. 2
Greenaway, D.	.. 5	Ducat, A.	.. 3	McKellor ..		.. 1
Lawrence	.. 5	Lewis, C.	.. 3	Steven	..	.. 1
Neave, D. ..	.. 5	McGibbon, C. E.	3	Thomson, M.		.. 1

Total 37

F.A. CUP COMPETITION

1st Rd. v. Watford	..	.. (h)	3—0
2nd Rd. v. Everton	..	.. (a)	0—5

HONOURS

Ducat, A.: England v. Scotland, Wales, Ireland; England trial.

Season 1910–11

Football League—Division I

P.38 W.13 D.12 L.13 Goals 41—49 Pts.38 10th

As in a good many of the campaigns in Arsenal's history, the feature of 1910–11 was the poor start and the fine finish which enabled the Club to finish in a respectable mid-table position. The first victory came in the eighth match and, once again, the forwards found difficulty in planting the ball in the net. For, apart from a goal in each of the first two games, the following five produced no Arsenal goals.

After losing to Oldham, the newcomers to Division I, the Gunners played off their remaining eleven matches without a defeat. In this period seventeen points were gained and only three goals were conceded. The attack, still not very prolific, but with Common, who won fame as the first footballer to be transferred for £1,000, as the scheming inside-right, managed to penetrate the opposing defences just enough to gain the points, scoring fourteen goals in eleven games.

THE LAST ELEVEN MATCHES

11 March	*v.* Everton	..	(h) 1—0	14 April	*v* Liverpool	.. (h)	0—0
15 March	*v.* Aston V.	..	(h) 1—1	15 April	*v.* Middlesbro'	(a)	1—1
18 March	*v.* Sheff. Wed.		(a) 0—0	17 April	*v.* Liverpool	.. (a)	1—1
25 March	*v.* Bristol C.	..	(h) 3—0	22 April	*v.* Preston	.. (h)	2—0
1 April	*v.* Newcastle	..	(a) 1—0	29 April	*v.* Notts. Co.	(a)	2—0
8 April	*v.* Tottenham		(h) 2—0				

THE FIRST SEVEN MATCHES

1 Sept.	*v.* Man. Utd.		(h) 1—2	24 Sept.	*v.* Sunderland	.. (h)	0—0
3 Sept.	*v.* Bury	..	(a) 1—1	1 Oct.	*v.* Oldham	.. (h)	0—0
10 Sept.	*v.* Sheff. Utd.		(h) 0—0	8 Oct.	*v.* Bradford C.	(a)	0—3
17 Sept.	*v.* Aston V.	..	(a) 0—3				

FOOTBALL LEAGUE RESULTS

Home	Opponents	Away	Home	Opponents	Away
1—1	Aston Villa ..	.. 0—3	3—0	Bristol City ..	.. 1—0
4—1	Blackburn Rovers	.. 0—1	3—2	Bury	.. 1—1
0—0	Bradford City	.. 0—3	1—0	Everton ..	.. 0—2

47

Home	Opponents	Away	Home	Opponents	Away
0—0	Liverpool ..	.. 1—1	3—2	Notts Forest	.. 3—2
0—1	Manchester City	.. 1—1	0—0	Oldham Athletic	.. 0—3
1—2	Manchester United ..	0—5	2—0	Preston North End	.. 1—4
0—2	Middlesbrough	.. 1—1	0—0	Sheffield United	.. 2—3
1—2	Newcastle United	.. 1—0	1—0	Sheffield Wednesday	0—0
2—1	Notts County..	.. 2—0	0—0	Sunderland ..	.. 2—2
		2—0	Tottenham Hotspur ..	1—3	

LEAGUE APPEARANCES (26 PLAYERS)

Batup, E. ..	.. 28	Greenaway, D.	22	Peart, J. C.	.. 7
Burdett, G. ..	.. 10	Heppinstall ..	5	Quayle ..	.. 1
Calder, L. ..	.. 1	Hoare, G. R. ..	14	Rippon, W.	.. 9
Calvert, F. ..	.. 1	Lewis, C. ..	34	Sands, P. R.	.. 31
Chalmers, J.	.. 29	Logan ..	11	Shaw, J. ..	.. 35
Common, A. ..	.. 29	McDonald, D.	1	Short ..	.. 4
Ducat, A. ..	.. 33	McEachrane, R. J.	30	Thomson, M.	.. 17
Flannagan, J.	.. 9	McKinnon, A.	10	Winship, T.	.. 6
Gray, A. ..	.. 26	Neave, D. ..	15		

LEAGUE GOAL-SCORERS

Chalmers, J.	.. 15	Neave, D. ..	3	Flannagan, J. ..	1
Common, A.	.. 6	Greenaway, D.	2	opponents ..	1
Hoare, G. R.	.. 6	Lewis, C. ..	2		
Ducat, A. ..	.. 3	Rippon, W. ..	2	Total 41	

F.A. CUP COMPETITION

1st Rd. v. Clapton Orient .. (a) 1—0 (abandoned)
v. Clapton Orient .. (a) 2—1
2nd Rd. v. Swindon Town .. (a) 0—1

A. BAKER

W. BARNES

C. S. BASTIN

W. BLYTH

E. R. BOWDEN

J. BLOOMFIELD

D. BOWEN

C. BUCHAN

Football League—Division I

P.38 W.15 D.8 L.15 Goals 55—59 Pts.38 10th

In collecting thirty-eight points from an identical number of matches, Arsenal occupied tenth position at the final reckoning, all of which was a repetition of the previous season. It is interesting to note that the Club's away record was almost the exact reverse of that at home, even to goals for and against. At Manor Ground Arsenal averaged exactly two goals per match and conceded one per match (38—19), while on away midden the figures were 17—40.

Blackburn Rovers, who had already won the Cup on five occasions, won the League title for the very first time. In an unbeaten home record thirteen of the nineteen matches were won, and the brilliant defensive trio, Robinson, Crompton and Cowell, conceded in them only ten goals. Their best victory of the season was against Woolwich Arsenal at Ewood Park, when they won 4—0, but there was a sequel five months later at Manor Ground when the Rovers suffered the heaviest defeat of their championship year—Arsenal beat the prospective champions by five goals to one.

The forwards wearing the 'Blue and white' were Simpson, Shea, Chapman, Latheron and Hodkinson; with the exception of the centre-forward, all won England caps.

FOOTBALL LEAGUE RESULTS

Home	Opponents	Away	Home	Opponents	Away
2—2	Aston Villa ..	.. 1—4	3—1	Middlesbrough	.. 2—0
5—1	Blackburn Rovers	.. 0—4	2—0	Newcastle United	.. 2—1
3—0	Bolton Wanderers	.. 2—2	0—3	Notts County..	.. 1—3
2—0	Bradford City	.. 1—1	1—1	Oldham Athletic	.. 0—0
1—0	Bury	.. 1—3	4—1	Preston North End	.. 1—0
0—1	Everton ..	.. 0—1	3—1	Sheffield United	.. 1—2
2—2	Liverpool ..	.. 1—4	0—2	Sheffield Wednesday	0—3
2—0	Manchester City	.. 3—3	3—0	Sunderland ..	.. 0—1
2—1	Manchester United ..	0—2	3—1	Tottenham Hotspur ..	0—5
	0—2	West Bromwich Albion	.. 1—1		

LEAGUE APPEARANCES (24 PLAYERS)

Burdett, G. ..	.. 18	Grant, J. W. ..	4	Neave, D.	.. 4
Calvert, F. ..	.. 1	Gray, A. ..	5	Peart, J. C.	.. 34
Chalmers, J.	.. 19	Greenaway, D.	23	Randall, C. E.	.. 27
Common, A.	.. 36	Hoare, G. R. ..	3	Roose, L. R.	.. 13
Crawford, H. S.	.. 7	Lewis, C.	.. 29	Sands, P. R.	.. 34
Ducat, A. ..	.. 33	McEachrane,R.J.	18	Shaw, J. ..	.. 36
Flannagan, J.	.. 33	McKinnon, A.	22	Thomson, M.	.. 7
Grant, G. ..	.. 1	McLaughlin, J.	3	Winship, T.	.. 8

LEAGUE GOAL-SCORERS

Common, A.	.. 17	Ducat, A. ..	5	Winship, T.	.. 2
Randall, C. E.	.. 8	Grant, J. W. ..	3	Calvert, F.	.. 1
Flannagan, J.	.. 7	Lewis, C. ..	3	Hoare, G. R.	.. 1
Chalmers, J.	.. 6	Greenaway, D.	2	Total	55

F.A. CUP COMPETITION

1st Rd. *v.* Bolton Wanderers .. (a) 0—1

Season 1912-13

Football League—Division I

P.38 W.3 D.12 L.23 Goals 26–74 Pts.18 20th

In a vivid contrast to the feats of modern times comes the black season of 1912–13, when Arsenal registered only three victories and scored twenty-six goals. These figures are the worst on record in the history of the First Division. The first is also shared with Stoke. Thirteen players shared the twenty-six goals, and Randall topped the list with four, which is the smallest total by a club's leading scorer in the Football League.

Stoke's record was created in the second season of the League, 1889–90, when twenty-two matches were played, during which they scored twenty-seven goals (in one game they beat Accrington 7—1 too!). In comparison, then, the figures set up by Arsenal were infinitely worse, because the Londoners' programme included another sixteen matches beyond Stoke's total.

The very worst total in the history of the Football League was set up by Loughborough Town in 1899–1900, when the 2—1 victory over Burton Swifts was their solitary success of the season. Arsenal won at Bramall Lane 3—1, on 21st September 1912, but did not gain another victory until winning at Manchester City on 8th March 1913—a sequence of twenty-three matches without a victory.

This was the last season at the Manor Ground, Plumstead, which had been Arsenal's home since 1889 except for a break of two years (1891 and 1892) when the Invicta Ground was used.

FOOTBALL LEAGUE RESULTS

Home	Opponents	Away	Home	Opponents	Away
0—3	Aston Villa ..	.. 1—4	0—0	Manchester United ..	0—2
0—1	Blackburn Rovers	.. 1—1	1—1	Middlesbrough	.. 0—2
1—2	Bolton Wanderers	.. 1—5	1—1	Newcastle United	.. 1—3
1—1	Bradford City	.. 1—3	0—0	Notts County..	.. 1—2
0—1	Chelsea ..	.. 1—1	0—0	Oldham Athletic	.. 0—0
1—2	Derby County	.. 1—4	1—3	Sheffield United	.. 3—1
0—0	Everton ..	.. 0—3	2—5	Sheffield Wednesday	0—2
1—1	Liverpool ..	.. 0—3	1—3	Sunderland ..	.. 1—4
0—4	Manchester City	.. 1—0	0—3	Tottenham Hotspur ..	1—1
		1—0 West Bromwich Albion .. 1—2			

51

LEAGUE APPEARANCES (30 PLAYERS)

Burrell, G. ..	.. 17	Grant, G.	.. 13	Payne, C. ..	.. 3
Common, A.	.. 12	Greenaway, D.	27	Peart, J. G.	.. 16
Crawford, H. S.	.. 19	Groves, F. W.	3	Randall, C. E.	.. 15
Devine, A. ..	.. 11	Hanks, E.	.. 4	Sands, P. ..	.. 28
Duncan, D. ..	.. 3	King, E.	.. 11	Shaw, J. ..	.. 38
Evans, R. ..	.. 1	Lewis, C.	.. 24	Spittle, W.	.. 6
Fidler, J. ..	.. 13	McDonald, H.	18	Stonley, S.	.. 10
Flannagan, J.	.. 22	McEachrane, R. J.	7	Thomson, M.	.. 25
Ford, G. E. ..	.. 3	McKinnon, A.	29	Wilson, O.	.. 1
Graham, A.	.. 12	McLoughlin, J.	13	Winship, T.	.. 14

LEAGUE GOAL-SCORERS

Randall, C. E.	.. 4	Graham, A.	.. 2	Duncan, D.	.. 1
Flannagan, J.	.. 3	Grant, G.	.. 2	Sands, P. ..	.. 1
McLoughlin, J.	.. 3	Hanks, E.	.. 2	Stonley, S.	.. 1
Burrell, G. ..	.. 2	Lewis, C.	.. 2	Winship, T.	.. 1
Devine, A. ..	.. 2			Total	26

F.A. CUP COMPETITION

1st Rd. *v.* Croydon Common .. (a) 0—0
Replay *v.* Croydon Common .. (h) 2—1
2nd Rd. *v.* Liverpool .. .. (h) 1—4

LONGEST RUN WITHOUT A VICTORY

Twenty-three matches from 28th September 1912 to 1st March 1913.

Season 1913–14

Football League—Division II

P.38 W.20 D.9 L.9 Goals 54—38 Pts.49 3rd

Back in Division II, the Club dropped the title 'Woolwich' and became known as Arsenal F.C. In addition, it severed its connections with Plumstead and opened a new ground in North London at Highbury, where Leicester Fosse were the first visitors on 6th September 1913. Arsenal set off with a 2—1 victory; Jobey and Devine (pen.) scored for the winners and Benfield for the Fosse. The teams in this first match at Highbury were: *Arsenal:* Lievesley; Shaw, Fidler; Grant, Sands, McKinnon; Greenaway, Hardinge, Jobey, Devine, Winship. *Leicester Fosse:* R. G. Brebner; Clay, Bunton; D. McWhirter, Harrold, King; Douglas, Mills, Sparrow, Benfield, Waterall.

Arsenal narrowly missed promotion at the first attempt. On the last day of the season they were level with Bradford in second place, with Notts County, six points ahead, assured of the Division II title. Arsenal duly won at Glossop 2—0, but Bradford, with a 4—1 home victory over Blackpool, edged the Londoners into third place by virtue of a goal average ·09 of a goal the superior.

The composition of Division II had changed considerably during the nine-year interval when Arsenal claimed First Division status. Burton United, Gainsborough Trinity and Burslem Port Vale had all disappeared from the Football League, while newcomers whom Arsenal met for the first time in League football this season were Bradford (P.A.), Clapton Orient, Fulham, Huddersfield, Hull City and Leeds City.

FOOTBALL LEAGUE RESULTS

Home	Opponents	Away	Home	Opponents	Away
1—0	Barnsley	0—1	2—0	Grimsby Town	1—1
1—0	Birmingham	0—2	0—1	Huddersfield	2—1
2—1	Blackpool	1—1	0—0	Hull City	2—1
2—0	Bradford P.A.	3—2	1—0	Leeds City	0—0
1—1	Bristol City	1—1	2—1	Leicester Fosse	2—1
0—1	Bury	1—1	3—0	Lincoln City	2—5
2—2	Clapton Orient	0—1	3—0	Notts County	0—1
2—0	Fulham	1—6	3—2	Notts Forest	0—0
2—0	Glossop	2—0	4—0	Stockport County	0—2
		3—1	Wolverhampton W.	2—1	

53

LEAGUE APPEARANCES (27 PLAYERS)

Bell, C.	..	1	Greenaway, D.	8	Randall, C. E.	.. 1
Benson, R.	..	25	Groves, F. W.	3	Rutherford, J.	.. 21
Burrell, G.	..	6	Hardinge, H. W.	29	Sands, P.	.. 33
Caldwell, J. H.	..	3	Jobey, G.	.. 28	Shaw, J. ..	.. 36
Devine, A.	..	13	Lewis, C.	.. 26	Slade, D.	.. 12
Fidler, J.	..	11	Lievesley, J.	.. 35	Spittle, W. A.	.. 1
Flannagan, J.		24	McEachrane, R. J.	2	Stonley, S.	.. 28
Graham, A.		13	McKinnon, A,	24	Thomson, M.	.. 7
Grant, G.	..	12	Peart, J. G.	.. 1	Winship, T.	.. 15

LEAGUE GOAL-SCORERS

Stonley, S.	 13	Devine, A.	.. 3	Winship, T.	.. 2
Flannagan, J.	.. 11	Jobey, G.	.. 3	Burrell, G.	.. 1
Rutherford, J.	.. 6	Bell, C.	.. 2	Stapley (Glossop)	1
Hardinge, H. W.	.. 4	Benson, R.	.. 2	Total 54
Slade, D.	 4	Grant, G.	.. 2	

F.A. CUP COMPETITION

1st Rd. *v.* Bradford City   .. (a) o—2

Season 1914–15

Football League—Division II

P.38 W.19 D.5 L.14 Goals 69—41 Pts.43 6th

After the débâcle of 1912–13, Arsenal attempted to regain Division I status by extensive team rebuilding, during which several well-known players were drafted to Highbury. For the opening of the 1913–14 season they signed Sheffield United's goalkeeper, Lievesley, who played for the F.A. in the tour of South Africa in 1910, and, a few weeks later, obtained another United player—full-back Benson, an English international *v.* Ireland during the previous season. In addition, the attack was strengthened by the acquisition of the famous Newcastle right-winger, Rutherford.

During this season, Buckley, signed from Aston Villa, took over the centre-half berth from the veteran Sands and Blyth (ex-Manchester City) made his first of many appearances in the League side.

The football season opened early in September under the cloud of the initial phases of the First World War, and as it closed, the general public, concerned with the events around Ypres, had little heart for less urgent matters such as football. After this season competitive football was abandoned until 1919.

For the record, Arsenal's challenge in this campaign did not materialize, because their harvest on away terrain was only four victories, and they slipped back to sixth position. At home it was a vastly different story. Of the first nine teams to visit Highbury, only Lincoln City managed to collect a point.

FOOTBALL LEAGUE RESULTS

Home	Opponents	Away	Home	Opponents	Away
1—0	Barnsley	0—1	6—0	Grimsby Town	0—1
1—0	Birmingham	0—3	0—3	Huddersfield	0—3
2—0	Blackpool	2—0	2—1	Hull City	0—1
3—0	Bristol City	1—1	2—0	Leeds City	2—2
3—1	Bury	1—3	6—0	Leicester Fosse	4—1
2—1	Clapton Orient	0—1	1—1	Lincoln City	0—1
1—2	Derby County	0—4	7—0	Notts Forest	1—1
3—0	Fulham	1—0	1—2	Preston North End	0—3
3—0	Glossop	4—0	3—1	Stockport County	1—1
		5—1	Wolverhampton W.	0—1	

55

LEAGUE APPEARANCES (22 PLAYERS)

Benson, R. W.	.. 27	Grant, G.	.. 28	McKinnon, A.	.. 21
Blyth, W. ..	.. 12	Greenaway, D.	6	Norman, J.	.. 4
Bradshaw, F.	.. 29	Groves, F. ..	2	Rutherford, J.	.. 26
Buckley, C. S.	.. 29	Hardinge, H. W.	12	Sands, P. ..	.. 10
Flannagan, J.	.. 26	King, H.	.. 37	Shaw, J. ..	.. 38
Fletcher, A. ..	.. 3	Lewis, C.	.. 24	Winship, T.	.. 12
Ford, G. ..	.. 6	Liddell, E.	.. 2		
Graham, A.	.. 26	Lievesley, J.	.. 38		

LEAGUE GOAL-SCORERS

King, H. ..	.. 26	Benson, R. W.	5	McKinnon, A.	.. 2
Bradshaw, F.	.. 10	Lewis, C.	.. 4	Winship, T.	.. 2
Hardinge, H. W.	.. 7	Rutherford, J. ..	3	Buckley, C. S.	.. 1
Flannagan, J.	.. 6	Blyth, W.	.. 2	Grant, G.	.. 1

Total 69

F.A. CUP COMPETITION

1st Rd. *v.* Merthyr T. .. .. (h) 3—0
2nd Rd. *v.* Chelsea .. .. (a) 0—1

56

Football League—Division I

P.42 W.15 D.12 L.15 Goals 56—58 Pts.42 10th

London Football Combination

P.36 W.18 D.10 L.8 Goals 81—41 Pts.46 2nd

In the last full season of League football, 1914–15, Chelsea and Tottenham were relegated from Division I, while the first six places in the Second Division were made up as follows:

Derby County	.. W.23	D.7	L.8	Goals 71—33	Pts.53
Preston North End	.. W.20	D.10	L.8	Goals 61—42	Pts.50
Barnsley	.. W.22	D.3	L.13	Goals 51—51	Pts.47
Wolverhampton W.	.. W.19	D.7	L.12	Goals 77—52	Pts.45
Birmingham	.. W.17	D.9	L.12	Goals 62—39	Pts.43
Arsenal	.. W.19	D.5	L.14	Goals 69—41	Pts.43

When the League Management Comittee decided to increase the number of clubs in the First Division by two, to twenty-two, it was generally expected that Chelsea and Tottenham would fill the two vacant places—or perhaps Barnsley or Wolverhampton, next in line in Division II, might be elected.

Not so Sir Henry Norris, who had saved Arsenal from financial disaster in 1909–10 by pouring thousands of pounds into the Club and who was determined to make the Gunners the most famous side in the country. Lobbying astutely, Norris, with unmatched eloquence, persuaded the League Management Committee to elect Arsenal, along with Chelsea, to the First Division. Tottenham found themselves levered out before they realized what was happening.

Arsenal started off with a home defeat by Newcastle, followed by an away win at Liverpool. This set the pattern for the first half of the season, when points were frequently dropped at home whereas only one of the first eight away was games lost. After Christmas, however, Arsenal lost all but three of their away encounters.

	Home	*Away*
August to December	W.5 D.3 L.3 Pts.13	W.3 D.5 L.3 Pts.11
January to May	.. W.6 D.2 L.2 Pts.14	W.1 D.2 L.7 Pts.4

FOOTBALL LEAGUE RESULTS

Home	Opponents	Away	Home	Opponents	Away
0—1	Aston Villa ..	.. 1—2	2—2	Manchester City	.. 1—4
0—1	Blackburn Rovers	.. 2—2	0—3	Manchester United	.. 1—0
2—2	Bolton Wanderers	.. 2—2	2—1	Middlesbrough	.. 0—1
1—2	Bradford City	.. 1—1 ..	0—1	Newcastle United	.. 1—3
3—0	Bradford P.A.	.. 0—0	3—1	Notts County..	.. 2—2
2—0	Burnley ..	.. 1—2	3—2	Oldham Athletic	.. 0—3
1—1	Chelsea ..	.. 1—3	0—0	Preston North End	.. 1—1
1—0	Derby County ..	.. 1—2	3—0	Sheffield United	.. 0—2
1—1	Everton ..	.. 3—2	3—1	Sheffield Wednesday	2—1
1—0	Liverpool ..	.. 3—2	3—2	Sunderland ..	.. 1—1

1—0 West Bromwich Albion .. 0—1

LEAGUE APPEARANCES (27 PLAYERS)

Baker, A. ..	.. 17	Graham, A.	.. 22	Pattison, G. C.	.. 1
Blyth, W. ..	.. 29	Greenaway, D.	3	Peart, J. C.	.. 5
Bradshaw, F.	.. 33	Groves, F.	.. 29	Rutherford, J.	.. 36
Buckley, C. S.	.. 23	Hardinge, H. W.	13	Shaw, J. ..	.. 33
Burgess, D.	.. 7	Hutchins, A. V.	18	Toner, J. ..	.. 15
Butler, J. D.	.. 21	Lewis, C.	.. 5	Voysey, C. R.	.. 5
Coopland, W. E.	.. 1	McKinnon, A.	41	White, H. A.	.. 29
Counley, F. F.	.. 4	North, F. J.	.. 4	Whittaker, T. J.	.. 1
Dunn, S. ..	.. 15	Pagnam, F.	.. 25	Williamson, E. C.	26

LEAGUE GOAL-SCORERS

White, H. A.	.. 15	Hardinge, H. W.	3	Butler, J. D.	.. 1
Pagnam, F.	.. 12	Rutherford, J. ..	3	Lewis, C.	.. 1
Blyth, W. ..	.. 6	Bradshaw, F. ..	2	North, F. J.	.. 1
Graham, A.	.. 4	Burgess, D. ..	2	Toner, J. ..	.. 1
Groves, F. ..	.. 4	Buckley, C. S. ..	1	Total	56

F.A. CUP COMPETITION

1st Rd. v. Rochdale (h) (by arrangement) 4—2
2nd Rd. v. Bristol City .. .. (a) 0—1

Season 1920–1

Football League—Division I

P.42 W.15 D.14 L.13 Goals 59—63 Pts.44 9th

London Football Combination

P.36 W.12 D.4 L.20 Goals 57—63 Pts.28 9th

When Mr. Leslie Knighton was appointed manager, on the resumption of League football in 1919, he had but a small nucleus of pre-war players around which to build a team. These included McKinnon, Rutherford, Bradshaw, Blyth, Shaw, Groves, Buckley, Graham and Hardinge. Knighton then obtained Williamson and Dunn (goalkeepers); Hutchins, a full-back from Croydon; Baker, half-back from Ilkeston; inside-forward Pagnam; White, a centre-forward from Aston Villa and Toner from Ireland. These were the players from which the Arsenal team was generally chosen during the first two seasons after the war.

There is little to choose between those two campaigns as far as relative success is concerned. In the first, forty-two points placed the Club tenth in the table while, a year later, two extra points earned the ninth position.

In 1920–1 there was once again a poor start, in which only two matches were won of the first eleven and nine points gained out of a possible twenty-two. November was more profitable, however, for after drawing at Blackburn Arsenal won the return fixture and then went on to complete the double over Huddersfield Town.

Later, Arsenal also twice defeated Bradford (P.A.), Preston North End and West Bromwich Albion, but Aston Villa, Bradford City and Sunderland, on the other hand, each obtained four points at the expense of the Londoners.

Arsenal fell at the first hurdle in the F.A. Cup; their opponents, Queen's Park Rangers, were members of the newly formed Third Division (South). Finishing third in the table, the Rangers had a sound home record, where only Gillingham, Northampton and Watford managed to take away two points.

Home	Opponents	Away	Home	Opponents	Away
0—1	Aston Villa ..	.. 0—5	0—0	Liverpool ..	.. 0—3
2—0	Blackburn Rovers	.. 2—2	2—1	Manchester City	.. 1—3
0—0	Bolton Wanderers	.. 1—1	2—0	Manchester United	.. 1—1
1—2	Bradford City	.. 1—3	2—2	Middlesbrough	.. 1—2
2—1	Bradford P.A.	.. 1—0	1—1	Newcastle United	.. 0—1
1—1	Burnley ..	.. 0—1	2—2	Oldham Athletic	.. 1—1
1—1	Chelsea ..	.. 2—1	2—1	Preston North End	.. 1—0
2—0	Derby County	.. 1—1	2—6	Sheffield United	.. 1—1
1—1	Everton ..	.. 4—2	1—2	Sunderland ..	.. 1—5
2—0	Huddersfield Town	.. 4—0	3—2	Tottenham Hotspur	.. 1—2

2—1 West Bromwich Albion .. 4—3

LEAGUE APPEARANCES (28 PLAYERS)

Baker, A.	..	.. 37	Hopkins, J.	..	8	Rutherford, J.	..	32
Blyth, W.	..	.. 39	Hutchins, A. V.		39	Shaw, J.	..	28
Bradshaw, F.		.. 21	Jones	..	1	Smith, J.	..	10
Buckley, C. S.		.. 4	McKenzie, A.		5	Toner, J.	..	11
Burgess, D.		.. 4	McKinnon, A.		37	Walden, H. A.	..	2
Butler, J. D.		.. 6	North, F. J.	..	8	White, H. A.	..	27
Counley, F. F.		.. 1	Pagnam, F.	..	25	Whittaker, T. J.	..	5
Dunn, S.	..	.. 9	Paterson, J. A.		20	Williamson, E. C.		33
Graham, A.		.. 30	Pattinson, G. C.		6			
Groves, F.		.. 13	Peart, J. C.	..	1			

LEAGUE GOAL-SCORERS

Pagnam, F.	..	.. 14	Toner, J.	..	3	Buckley, C. S.	..	1
White, H. A.		.. 10	Baker, A.	..	2	Groves, F.	..	1
Blyth, W.	..	.. 7	Hopkins, J.	..	2	McKenzie, A.	..	1
Rutherford, J.		.. 7	McKinnon, A.		2	Smith, J.	..	1
Graham, A.		.. 5	North, F. J.	..	2	Walden, H. A.	..	1
						Total	..	59

F.A. CUP COMPETITION

1st Rd. *v.* Queen's Park Rangers .. (a) 0—2

HONOURS

Baker, A.: England trial.
Graham, A.: Scotland *v.* England.
Hutchins, A. V.: England trial.
Paterson, J. A.: Football League *v.* Scottish League.

Season 1921-2

Football League—Division I

P.42 W.15 D.7 L.20 Goals 47—56 Pts.37 17th

London Football Combination

P.40 W.21 D.13 L.6 Goals 67—47 Pts.55 2nd

A splendid rally at the end of the season pulled the Club out of a precarious position near the foot of the table, to finish in seventeenth place. Five points were gained from the first thirteen matches, sixteen points from the next thirteen, followed by five defeats in succession, then sixteen points from the remaining eleven games. In the Cup, Arsenal reached the last eight for the third time in their history. Such were the ups and downs of the season.

December was a peculiar month for results, because the Gunners won three of four away games and yet failed to win at home in four attempts.

In an attack which usually read Rutherford, Boreham, White, Blyth and Toner, most of the goal-scoring rested with White and the amateur from Wycombe, Boreham, who between them scored more than half of the total of forty-seven goals. The other three managed only one apiece.

FOOTBALL LEAGUE RESULTS

Home	Opponents	Away	Home	Opponents	Away
2—0	Aston Villa ..	.. 0—2	1—0	Liverpool ..	.. 0—4
5—2	Birmingham ..	.. 1—0	0—1	Manchester City	.. 0—2
1—1	Blackburn Rovers	.. 1—0	3—1	Manchester United ..	0—1
1—1	Bolton Wanderers	.. 0—1	2—2	Middlesbrough ..	2—4
1—0	Bradford City	.. 2—0	2—1	Newcastle United ..	1—3
0—0	Burnley ..	.. 0—1	0—1	Oldham Athletic ..	1—2
0—0	Cardiff City ..	.. 3—4	1—0	Preston North End ..	2—3
1—0	Chelsea ..	.. 2—0	1—2	Sheffield United ..	1—4
1—0	Everton ..	.. 1—1	1—2	Sunderland ..	.. 0—1
1—3	Huddersfield Town ..	0—2	1—0	Tottenham Hotspur ..	0—2

2—2 West Bromwich Albion .. 3—0

LEAGUE APPEARANCES (30 PLAYERS)

Baker, A.	.. 32	Graham, A. ..	21	Pattinson, G. C. ..	2
Blyth, W. ..	.. 25	Henderson, W.	5	Rutherford, J.	.. 36
Boreham, R.	.. 22	Hopkins, J. ..	11	Shaw, J. ..	.. 6
Bradshaw, F.	.. 32	Hutchins, A. V.	37	Toner, J. ..	.. 24
Burgess, D. ..	.. 2	Maxwell ..	1	Turnbull, R.	.. 5
Butler, J. D.	.. 25	Milne, W. ..	4	Voysey, C. R.	.. 1
Counley, F. F.	.. 10	McKenzie, A.	3	White, H. A.	.. 35
Creegan, W. W.	.. 5	McKinnon, A.	17	Whittaker, T. J.	.. 36
Dunn, S. ..	.. 1	North, F. J. ..	11	Williamson, E. C.	41
Earle, S. J. C.	.. 1	Paterson, J. A.	2	Young, A.	.. 9

LEAGUE GOAL-SCORERS

White, H. A.	.. 14	North, F. J. ..	3	Rutherford, J. ..	1
Boreham, R.	.. 10	Bradshaw, F. ..	2	Toner, J.	1
Baker, A. ..	.. 4	Butler, J. D. ..	2	Whittaker, T. J. ..	1
Graham, A.	.. 3	Young, A. ..	2	Total	47
Hopkins, J.	.. 3	Blyth, W. ..	1		

F.A. CUP COMPETITION

1st Rd. *v.* Queen's Park Rangers	(h)	0—0	
Replay *v.* Queen's Park Rangers	(a)	2—1	
2nd Rd. *v.* Bradford ..	(a)	3—2	
3rd Rd. *v.* Leicester City ..	(h)	3—0	White 2, Rutherford
4th Rd. *v.* Preston North End ..	(h)	1—1	
Replay *v.* Preston North End ..	(a)	1—2	(after extra time)

HONOUR

Toner, J.: Ireland *v.* Wales.

Season 1922–3

Football League—Division I

P.42 W.16 D.10 L.16 Goals 61—62 Pts.42 11th

London Football Combination

P.40 W.20 D.9 L.11 Goals 89—39 Pts.49 1st

The improved form shown in March and April, when sixteen points were gained from the final eleven matches, was not carried forward to the 1922–3 campaign. Opening at Liverpool, the champions who repeated their success this year, Arsenal were beaten 5–2, and in their next eleven away games managed to muster only four points. Furthermore, home encounters produced an average of fewer than a point per match, with the result that, at the half-way stage, Arsenal had collected only fourteen points and a goal aggregate of 26—48.

Happily, the second half of the season was a vastly different story, and much of the transformation can be traced to the success of moving Turnbull from right-back to centre-forward at Bolton on Christmas Day and to the introduction of Mackie and Kennedy at full-back. From then onwards Arsenal lost only three more games, were undefeated at home (winning eight in succession!) and gained twenty-seven points with a goal aggregate of 35—14.

Among the newcomers to the League side were Mackie and Kennedy from Ireland, John from Barry Town and Robson, while the players who made their last appearance in the first team included goalkeepers Dunn (42 apps.) and Williamson (105), who later joined Norwich; White (102 apps., 40 goals) to Blackpool; Hutchins (104); Bradshaw (132) and Hopkins.

FOOTBALL LEAGUE RESULTS

Home	Opponents	Away	Home	Opponents	Away
2—0	Aston Villa	1—1	1—2	Everton	0—1
1—0	Birmingham	2—3	1—1	Huddersfield Town	0—4
1—1	Blackburn Rovers	5—0	1—0	Liverpool	2—5
5—0	Bolton Wanderers	1—4	1—0	Manchester City	0—0
1—1	Burnley	1—4	3—0	Middlesbrough	0—2
2—1	Cardiff City	1—4	1—2	Newcastle United	1—1
3—1	Chelsea	0—0	2—0	Notts Forest	1—2

Home	Opponents	Away	Home	Opponents	Away
2—0	Oldham Athletic ..	0—0	3—0	Stoke City ..	.. 0—1
1—1	Preston North End ..	2—1	2—3	Sunderland ..	.. 3—3
2—0	Sheffield United ..	1—2	0—2	Tottenham Hotspur ..	2—1
		3—1 West Bromwich Albion .. 0—7			

LEAGUE APPEARANCES (30 PLAYERS)

Baker, A. ..	.. 29	Henderson, W.	2	Roe, A. ..	.. 4
Blyth, W. ..	.. 31	Hopkins, J.	.. 2	Rutherford, J.	.. 26
Boreham, R.	.. 27	Hutchins, A. V.	10	Toner, J. ..	.. 6
Bradshaw, F.	.. 17	John, R. F.	.. 24	Townrow, F. A.	1
Butler, J. D.	.. 18	Kennedy, A. L.	24	Turnbull, R.	.. 35
Clarke, G. B.	.. 2	Mackie, J. A.	.. 23	Voysey, C. R.	.. 18
Dunn, S. ..	.. 17	McKenzie, A.	7	White, H. A.	.. 11
Earle, S. J. C.	.. 1	Milne, W.	.. 31	Whittaker, T. J.	.. 13
Elvy, R. ..	.. 1	Paterson, J. A.	27	Williamson, E. C.	5
Graham, A.	.. 17	Robson, J. H.	20	Young, A.	.. 13

LEAGUE GOAL-SCORERS

Turnbull, R...	.. 20	Hopkins, J.	.. 2	Rutherford, J.	.. 1
Blyth, W. ..	.. 10	Earle, S. J. C.	1	White, H. A.	.. 1
Boreham, R.	.. 8	Graham, A.	.. 1	Whittaker, T. J.	.. 1
Baker, A. ..	.. 5	Hutchins, A. V.	1	Freeman	
Voysey, C. R.	.. 4	McKenzie, A.	1	(Oldham)	1
Young, A. ..	.. 3	Roe, A.	.. 1	Total	61

F.A. CUP COMPETITION

1st Rd. *v.* Liverpool .. .. (a) 0—0
Replay *v.* Liverpool .. .. (h) 1—4

HONOURS

John, R. F.: Wales *v.* Scotland, Ireland.
Kennedy, A. L.: Ireland *v.* Wales.
Mackie, J. A.: Ireland *v.* Wales.
Toner, J.: Ireland *v.* Wales.
Williamson, E. C.: England *v.* Sweden.

64

M. CHARLES   D. CLAPTON

D. COMPTON   L. COMPTON

W. COPPING

J. CRAYSTON

R. DANIEL

T. DOCHERTY

Football League—Division 1

P.42 W.12 D.9 L.21 Goals 40—63 Pts.33 19th

London Football Combination

P.44 W.16 D.11 L.17 Goals 69—66 Pts.43 6th

A home defeat by Newcastle United on the opening day of the season, immediately followed by further reverses at West Ham, Newcastle and West Bromwich, set the pattern of a struggling season for the Highbury club. The shadow of relegation, which was always near, was revealed in the play; particularly in the forward line, where the players appeared to have little confidence to shoot. Woods was the leading scorer with nine goals, and the season's aggregate was less than a goal per match.

The defence, with goalkeeper Robson the only ever-present, was more stable and generally consisted of Robson; Mackie, Kennedy; Milne, Butler and Graham.

Although, at the beginning of April, Arsenal had three games in hand over their fellow relegation candidates, their position was by no means secure. Chelsea made a spirited attempt to escape by winning their last four home games, with an aggregate of ten goals to three, but it was of no avail, because Arsenal also gained eight points from their remaining nine matches and so kept a point in front.

Among the newcomers introduced into the team were Haden, Ramsey, Neil and Woods, while Boreham (51 matches) and Graham (166), who left for Brentford, made their last League appearance for the Club during the season.

THE FOOT OF DIVISION I

On 1st April			*Final Positions*		
Preston North End	P.36	Pts.28	Preston North End	P.42	Pts.34
Notts Forest	P.36	Pts.28	Arsenal	P.42	Pts.33
Arsenal	P.33	Pts.25	Notts Forest	P.42	Pts.32
Chelsea	P.36	Pts.24	Chelsea	P.42	Pts.32
Middlesbro'	P.36	Pts.19	Middlesbro'	P.42	Pts.22

FOOTBALL LEAGUE RESULTS

Home	Opponents	Away	Home	Opponents	Away
0—1	Aston Villa ..	.. 1—2	1—2	Manchester City	.. 0—1
0—0	Birmingham ..	.. 2—0	2—1	Middlesbro'	.. 0—0
2—2	Blackburn Rovers	.. 0—2	1—4	Newcastle United	.. 0—1
0—0	Bolton Wanderers	.. 2—1	0—0	Notts County..	.. 2—1
2—0	Burnley ..	.. 1—4	1—0	Notts Forest	.. 1—2
1—2	Cardiff City ..	.. 0—4	1—2	Preston North End	.. 2—0
1—0	Chelsea ..	.. 0—0	1—3	Sheffield United	.. 1—3
0—1	Everton ..	.. 1—3	2—0	Sunderland ..	.. 1—1
1—3	Huddersfield Town ..	1—6	1—1	Tottenham Hotspur ..	0—3
3—1	Liverpool ..	.. 0—0	1—0	West Bromwich Albion	0—4
	4—1	West Ham United ..	0—1		

LEAGUE APPEARANCES (26 PLAYERS)

Baker, A. ..	.. 21	Jones, F. J.	.. 2	Toner, J. ..	.. 3
Blyth, W. ..	.. 27	Kennedy, A. L.	29	Townrow, F. A.	7
Boreham, R.	.. 2	Mackie, J. A.	.. 31	Turnbull, R.	.. 18
Butler, J. D.	.. 24	Milne, W.	.. 36	Voysey, C. R.	.. 10
Clark, J. ..	.. 2	Neil, A.	.. 11	Wallington, E. E.	1
Earle, S. J. C.	.. 2	Paterson, J. A.	21	Woods, H.	.. 36
Graham, A.	.. 25	Ramsey, J. H. ..	11	Young, A.	.. 25
Haden, S. ..	.. 31	Robson, J. H. ..	42	Whittaker, T. J. ..	8
John, R. F.	.. 15	Rutherford, J. ..	22		

LEAGUE GOAL-SCORERS

Woods, H. ..	.. 9	Earle, S. J. C.	2	Young, A.	.. 2
Turnbull, R.	.. 6	Neil, A.	2	Baker, A. ..	.. 1
Blyth, W. ..	.. 3	Rutherford, J. ..	2	Graham, A.	.. 1
Haden, S. ..	.. 3	Townrow, F. A.	2	Milne, W.	.. 1
Ramsey, J. H.	.. 3	Voysey, C. R. ..	2	McIntyre	
				(Blackburn) o.g.	1
					Total 40

F.A. CUP COMPETITION

1st Rd. *v.* Luton Town .. (h) 4—1
2nd Rd. *v.* Cardiff City .. (a) 0—1

HONOURS

Baker, A.: Professionals *v.* Amateurs (F.A. Charity Shield).
Paterson, J. A.: England trial.
Toner, J.: Ireland *v.* England & Wales.

66

Season 1924–5

Football League—Division I

P.42   W.14   D.5   L.23   Goals 46—58   Pts.33   20th

London Football Combination

P.44   W.17   A.12   L.15   Goals 62—54   Pts.46   6th

Arsenal began the season by indicating that something better than the nineteenth position would be attained. In fact, they set off with three successive victories and, with eleven points out of a possible sixteen by the beginning of October, relegation worries seemed far from the precincts of Highbury.

Unfortunately, the early promise was not fulfilled, and after drawing at Cardiff on 29th November the team failed to gain a single point away from home during the remainder of the season. Furthermore, a run of six successive defeats, from 3rd January to 28th February, which is the worst in the history of the Club, sent them sliding down the League table, and it was only the even poorer records of Preston and Notts Forest which kept Arsenal out of the bottom two places. Relegation was not a serious threat to the London club, however, because both of these clubs were always about ten points inferior to Arsenal.

This season saw the last League appearance for Arsenal of both Whittaker and Turnbull. Twenty-four players were called upon, amongst whom were newcomers Cock and Hoar.

In the first round of the F.A. Cup there were five attempts to reach a decision. Twice the game was postponed because of fog, then a 0—0 draw resulted at West Ham, followed by another draw, 2—2, after extra time at Highbury. Finally, in the second replay at Stamford Bridge, West Ham won by an orphan goal. Milne was out of this game with a broken leg.

FOOTBALL LEAGUE RESULTS

Home	Opponents	Away	Home	Opponents	Away
1—1	Aston Villa ..	.. 0—4	3—1	Everton ..	.. 3—2
0—1	Birmingham ..	.. 1—2	0—5	Huddersfield Town	.. 0—4
1—0	Blackburn Rovers	.. 0—1	6—1	Leeds United	.. 0—1

67

Home	Opponents	Away	Home	Opponents	Away
1—0	Bolton Wanderers ..	1—4	2—0	Liverpool ..	.. 1—2
5—0	Burnley ..	.. 0—1	1—0	Manchester City	.. 0—2
0—1	Bury	.. 0—2	0—2	Newcastle United	.. 2—2
1—1	Cardiff City ..	.. 1—1	0—1	Notts County..	.. 1—2
2—1	Notts Forest	.. 2—0	0—0	Sunderland ..	.. 0—2
4—0	Preston North End	.. 0—2	1—0	Tottenham Hotspur ..	0—2
2—0	Sheffield United	.. 1—2	2—0	West Bromwich Albion	0—2
		1—2	West Ham United	.. 0—1	

LEAGUE APPEARANCES (24 PLAYERS)

Baker, A.	..	.. 32	Hughes, J.	.. 1	Robson, J. H.	.. 26
Blyth, W.	..	.. 17	John, R. F.	.. 39	Roe, A. ..	.. 1
Brain, J.	..	.. 28	Kennedy, A. L.	40	Rutherford, J.	.. 21
Butler, J. D.		.. 39	Lewis, D.	.. 16	Toner, J. ..	.. 26
Clark, J.	..	.. 2	Mackie, J. A.	.. 19	Turnbull, R.	.. 1
Cock, J. D.		.. 2	Milne, W.	.. 32	Whittaker, T. J.	.. 1
Haden, S.	..	.. 15	Neil, A.	.. 16	Woods, H.	.. 32
Hoar, S.	..	.. 18	Ramsey, J. H.	.. 30	Young, A.	.. 8

LEAGUE GOAL-SCORERS

Brain, J.	..	.. 12	Neil, A.	.. 2	Hoar, S. ..	.. 1
Woods, H.	..	.. 12	Rutherford, J. ..	2	John, R. F.	.. 1
Ramsey, J. H.	.. 6	Young, A.	.. 2	Toner, J. ..	.. 1
Butler, J. D.	.. 3	Blyth, W.	.. 1		Total 46
Baker, A.	..	.. 2	Haden, S.	.. 1		

F.A. CUP COMPETITION

1st Rd. *v.* West Ham United .. (a) 0—0 (after two postponements through fog)

Replay *v.* West Ham United .. (h) 2—2 (after extra time)

2nd Replay *v.* West Ham United   0—1 (at Stamford Bridge)

HONOURS

Baker, A.: Football League *v.* Irish League; England trial.
Butler, J. D.: England *v.* Belgium.
Hoar, S.: England trial.
John, R. F.: Wales *v.* Ireland.
Kennedy, A. L.: Ireland *v.* England.
Toner, J.: Ireland *v.* England, Scotland.
Whittaker, T. J.: F.A. Australian tour.

68

Season 1925–6

Football League—Division I

P.42 W.22 D.8 L.12 Goals 87—63 Pts.52 2nd

London Football Combination

P.44 W.20 D.6 L.18 Goals 83—68 Pts.46 5th

Herbert Chapman was appointed manager in place of Leslie Knighton, who left for Bournemouth, and Arsenal were quickly transformed from a struggling First Division club to a power in the land. Newcomer Buchan from Sunderland captained the side, while other notable signings included Hulme (Blackburn) and Parker (Southampton).

Nevertheless, apart from victories at Leicester and Manchester, the team made a poor start, culminating in a disastrous 7—0 defeat at Newcastle on 3rd October. Chapman then decided to counteract the change in the off-side law by introducing the 'third-back' game, with the centre-half policing the penalty area and an inside-forward linking the defence and the attack. With Butler often operating behind his backs, and Neil supplying the mid-field prompting, this was tried out on the following Monday at West Ham. Arsenal returned 4—0 victors and thereafter the new style reaped rich rewards.

From the nineteenth and twentieth positions of the two previous seasons, Arsenal climbed to second place, collected more points than any other London Division I club had ever done, and gained maximum points from five clubs (previous best was four points from each of three clubs in a season). In addition, Brain broke the club individual-scoring record by netting thirty-four League goals.

FOOTBALL LEAGUE RESULTS

Home	Opponents	Away	Home	Opponents	Away
2—0	Aston Villa ..	.. 0—3	5—0	Cardiff City ..	.. 0—0
3—0	Birmingham ..	.. 0—1	4—1	Everton ..	.. 3—2
4—2	Blackburn Rovers	.. 3—2	3—1	Huddersfield Town	.. 2—2
2—3	Bolton Wanderers	.. 1—1	4—1	Leeds United	.. 2—4
1—2	Burnley ..	.. 2—2	2—2	Leicester City..	.. 1—0
6—1	Bury	.. 2—2	1—1	Liverpool ..	.. 0—3

Home	Opponents	Away	Home	Opponents	Away
1—0	Manchester City ..	5—2	4—0	Sheffield United ..	0—4
3—2	Manchester United ..	1—0	2—0	Sunderland	1—2
3—0	Newcastle United ..	0—7	0—1	Tottenham Hotspur	1—1
3—0	Notts County.. ..	1—4	1—0	West Bromwich Albion	1—2
			3—2	West Ham United ..	4—0

LEAGUE APPEARANCES (28 PLAYERS)

Baker, A. ..	.. 31	John, R. F.	.. 29	Robson, J. H.	.. 9
Blyth, W. ..	.. 40	Kennedy, A. L.	16	Rutherford, J.	.. 3
Brain, J. ..	.. 41	Lawson, H.	.. 13	Rutherford, J. J.	1
Buchan, C. M.	.. 39	Lewis, D.	.. 14	Seddon, W. C.	.. 1
Butler, J. D.	.. 41	Mackie, J. A.	.. 35	Toner, J. ..	.. 2
Cock, D. J.	.. 1	Milne, W.	.. 5	Voysey, C. R.	.. 1
Haden, S. ..	.. 25	Neil, A.	.. 27	Woods, H.	.. 2
Harper, W. ..	.. 19	Parker, T. R.	.. 7	Young, A.	.. 7
Hoar, S. ..	.. 21	Paterson, J. A.	1		
Hulme, J. H. A.	.. 15	Ramsey, J. H.	.. 16		

LEAGUE GOAL-SCORERS

Brain, J. ..	.. 34	Hoar, S.	.. 3	Paterson, J. A.	.. 2
Buchan, C. M.	.. 19	Parker, T. R.	.. 3	Johnson (Leeds)	1
Blyth, W. ..	.. 7	Haden, S.	.. 2	Rollo (Blackburn)	1
Baker, A. ..	.. 5	Hulme, J. H. A.	2	Watson (Leicester)	1
Neil, A. ..	.. 5	Lawson, H.	.. 2	Total	87

F.A. CUP COMPETITION

3rd Rd. *v.* Wolverhampton Wanderers (a) 1—1
Replay *v.* Wolverhampton Wanderers (h) 1—0 Baker
4th Rd. *v.* Blackburn Rovers .. (h) 3—1
5th Rd. *v.* Aston Villa .. .. (a) 1—1
Replay *v.* Aston Villa .. .. (h) 2—0 Paterson, Brain
6th Rd. *v.* Swansea Town .. .. (a) 1—2

HONOURS

Baker, A.: Football League *v.* Irish League; England trial (2).
Brain, J.: England trial.
Buchan, C. M.: Football League *v.* Army.
Butler, J. D.: England trial.
Harper, D.: Scotland *v.* England, Ireland.
Hulme, J. H. A.: England *v.* Wales; Football League *v.* Army.
John, R. F.: Wales *v.* England.

Season 1926-7

Football League—Division I

P.42   W.17   D.9   L.16   Goals 77—86   Pts.43   11th

London Football Combination

P.42   W.30   D.4   L.8   Goals 125—45   Pts.64   1st

After the exalted runners-up position in 1925-6, this season found Arsenal in a mid-table place for much of the time. Although, during the Club's victorious path to Wembley, an inexplicable loss of form in the League (six defeats with the shocking goal aggregate of 5—26) led to a dangerously low position in the table. This was counterbalanced, however, in the ensuing seven matches in which the team collected twelve points and, in an Easter maximum, registered its first-ever double over Aston Villa.

Right-back Parker had an unfortunate game at Port Vale in the fourth round of the Cup, which nearly led to the Gunners' exit. He first put the ball into his own goal, which Buchan neutralized, and then conceded a penalty. There were only two minutes left to play when Brain scored a second goal to earn a replay.

Among the players who made their League début for Arsenal during the season were Cope, Lambert and Roberts.

CUP FINAL, WEMBLEY 1926-7

Arsenal 0 v. Cardiff City 1

This was Arsenal's first appearance in the F.A. Cup final. For Cardiff City, their opponents, however, it was the second final in three years. Not that the Welsh side gained much advantage by their previous appearance at Wembley, because only four of that eleven remained in 1927. The forward line was completely new, and, in the defence, only Farquharson, Nelson, Hardy and Keenor had played in the losing final against Sheffield United two years previously.

Cardiff, of course, were then at the pinnacle of their history, for, besides taking part in the two Cup finals already mentioned, in 1923-4 they were runners-up in Division I. And, furthermore, were

71

only beaten for the championship title by Huddersfield on goal average. Two years after their final against Arsenal, however, the club was caught in a disastrous slide which culminated in its applying for re-election to the Football League in 1934.

In complete contrast, the 1927 final was the curtain-raiser for many honours to be won by Arsenal and which were to make the club known the world over. The famous Arsenal plan, devised during the previous season by Herbert Chapman—the plan of the 'third full-back' and roving inside-forward—was already beginning to reap rich rewards.

Although the 1927 final, the fifth at Wembley, contained a galaxy of international players—Cardiff fielded eight while Arsenal boasted of five—it was not the exhibition of classical football which one would expect from such a talented set of players.

While the forwards shared much of the enjoyment, at least up to the penalty area, the real honours of the game went to the defenders. The City's main strength lay in the half-back line where the much-capped Keenor was, once again, peerless in leading his men.

Joe Hulme, with lightning dashes along the touchline, and captain Charlie Buchan formed an enterprising right-wing for Arsenal, while Curtis was the most dangerous Cardiff forward. Nevertheless, with both defences covering well, there seemed little chance of a goal being scored—until the unexpected happened a quarter of an hour before time.

In collecting the ball from a throw-in, the Cardiff centre-forward, Ferguson, tried a long and low diagonal shot. Danny Lewis, in the Arsenal goal, appeared to field the ball comfortably, but, on being harassed by Irving and Davies, allowed it to twist over his arms into the net. It was a real tragedy for Arsenal and this one unfortunate slip gave the Cup to Cardiff, who had thus amply atoned for their disappointment of 1925. History had been created, in that the F.A. Cup had been taken out of England for the first time.

It is a coincidence that Cardiff's Scottish international right-back, Nelson, appeared against Arsenal at Wembley five years later when in the colours of Newcastle United.

Cardiff City: Farquharson; Nelson, Watson; Keenor, Sloan, Hardy; Curtis, Irving, Ferguson, Davies (L.), McLachlan.

Arsenal: Lewis; Parker, Kennedy; Baker, Butler, John; Hulme, Buchan, Brain, Blyth, Hoar.

FOOTBALL LEAGUE RESULTS

Home	Opponents	Away	Home	Opponents	Away
2—1	Aston Villa ..	.. 3—2	1—0	Leeds United	.. 1—4
3—0	Birmingham ..	.. 0—0	2—2	Leicester City	.. 1—2
2—2	Blackburn Rovers	.. 2—1	2—0	Liverpool ..	.. 0—3
2—1	Bolton Wanderers	.. 2—2	1—0	Manchester United	.. 2—2
6—2	Burnley ..	.. 0—2	2—2	Newcastle United	.. 1—6
1—0	Bury	.. 2—3	1—1	Sheffield United	.. 0—4
3—2	Cardiff City ..	.. 0—2	6—2	Sheffield Wednesday	2—4
2—1	Derby County ..	.. 2—0	2—3	Sunderland ..	.. 1—5
1—2	Everton ..	.. 1—3	2—4	Tottenham Hotspur ..	4—0
0—2	Huddersfield Town ..	3—3	4—1	West Bromwich Albion	3—1
		2—2	West Ham United	.. 0—7	

LEAGUE APPEARANCES (27 PLAYERS)

Baker, A. ..	.. 24	Harper, W.	.. 23	Moody, J...	.. 2
Barley, J. C.	.. 3	Hoar, S.	.. 16	Parker, T. R.	.. 42
Blyth, W. ..	.. 33	Hulme, J. H. A.	37	Peel, H. ..	.. 9
Bowen, E. ..	.. 1	John, R. F.	.. 41	Ramsey, J. H.	.. 12
Brain, J. ..	.. 37	Kennedy, A. L.	11	Roberts, H.	.. 2
Buchan, C. M.	.. 33	Lambert, J.	.. 16	Seddon, W. C.	.. 17
Butler, J. D.	.. 30	Lee, J. H.	.. 7	Shaw, J. ..	.. 5
Cope, H. ..	.. 11	Lewis, D.	.. 17	Tricker, R. W.	.. 4
Haden, S. ..	.. 17	Milne, W.	.. 6	Young, A.	.. 6

LEAGUE GOAL-SCORERS

Brain, J. ..	.. 30	Hoar, S. ..	3	Barley, J. C.	.. 1
Buchan, C. M.	.. 14	John, R. F. ..	3	Butler, J. D.	.. 1
Hulme, J. H. A.	.. 8	Tricker, R. W.	3	Lambert, J.	.. 1
Haden, S. ..	.. 4	Blyth, W. ..	2	Shaw, J. ..	.. 1
Parker, T. R.	.. 4	Ramsey, J. H...	2	Total	77

3rd Rd. *v.* Sheffield United ..	.. (a)	3—2	Hulme, Brain, Buchan
4th Rd. *v.* Port Vale ..	.. (a)	2—2	Buchan, Brain
Replay *v.* Port Vale	.. (h)	1—0	Buchan
5th Rd. *v.* Liverpool	.. (h)	2—0	Brain, Buchan
6th Rd. *v.* Wolverhampton W.	.. (h)	2—1	Butler, Blyth
S.F. *v.* Southampton (at Chelsea) ..		2—1	Hulme, Buchan
Final *v.* Cardiff City ..	..	0—1	

HONOURS

Cope, H. and Parker, T. R.: England trial.
Hulme, J. H. A.: England *v.* Scotland, Belgium, France; England trial.
John, R. F.: Wales *v.* England.
Lewis, D.: Wales *v.* England.

Season 1927–8

Football League—Division I

P.42 W.13 D.15 L.14 Goals 82—86 Pts.41 10th

London Football Combination

P.42 W.27 D.7 L.8 Goals 105—46 Pts.61 1st

The goal aggregate of 82—86 gives the clue to a season of high-scoring games; in fact, eighty-two goals had been surpassed only once previously by the Club in Division I, but, on the other hand, eighty-six goals against equalled their worst record.

Opening the season with a 5—1 defeat at Bury, Arsenal recovered sufficiently in the following home games to win 4—1 and 6—1 against Burnley and Sheffield United respectively. The return match against the latter club at Bramall Lane was an exciting free-scoring encounter. Within seventeen minutes the United had scored four times, but Arsenal rallied to make the score 4—3 just after the interval. The result, however, was 6—4 in Sheffield's favour.

Derby County twice scored four goals against Arsenal, and Manchester United also gained four points at their expense. These fruitless games were balanced by Arsenal doubles over Burnley and Liverpool.

The last game of the season at Goodison Park, where Arsenal were the visitors, provided the great talking point: 'Would Dean score three goals to beat the individual scoring record of fifty-nine goals set up by Camsell of Middlesbrough during the previous season?' It was quite a tall order—even for Dean—but he managed to put the ball into the net three times, despite the close attentions of Arsenal's centre-half. The first goal came early in the game, the second from the penalty spot and the third was banged in with only three minutes to spare.

Arsenal's team during the season generally consisted of: Lewis; Parker, Cope; Baker, Butler, John; Hulme, Buchan, Brain, Blyth, Hoar. Welsh-international-goalkeeper Lewis regained a regular place in the League side when Harper emigrated to the United States, and played in all but nine of the matches. Patterson was the custodian in five, while Moody, who was transferred to Bradford during the

75

season, played in the remaining four. Among the four players who made their League début for Arsenal in this campaign was the young and promising full-back from Kettering, Hapgood.

FOOTBALL LEAGUE RESULTS

Home	Opponents	Away	Home	Opponents	Away
0—3	Aston Villa	2—2	2—2	Leicester City.. ..	2—3
2—2	Birmingham	1—1	6—3	Liverpool	2—0
3—2	Blackburn Rovers ..	1—4	0—1	Manchester United ..	1—4
1—2	Bolton Wanderers	1—1	3—1	Middlesbrough ..	2—2
4—1	Burnley	2—1	4—1	Newcastle United ..	1—1
3—1	Bury	1—5	0—2	Portsmouth	3—2
3—0	Cardiff City	2—2	6—1	Sheffield United ..	4—6
3—4	Derby County	0—4	1—1	Sheffield Wednesday	1—1
3—2	Everton	3—3	2—1	Sunderland	1—5
0—0	Huddersfield Town ..	1—2	1—1	Tottenham Hotspur	0—2
			2—2	West Ham United ..	2—2

LEAGUE APPEARANCES (24 PLAYERS)

Baker, A.	..	.. 37	Hapgood, E. A.	3	Parker, T. R.	.. 42
Barley, J. C.	..	.. 2	Hoar, S.	.. 38	Patterson, W.	.. 5
Blyth, W.	..	.. 39	Hulme, J. H. A.	36	Peel, H. ..	.. 13
Brain, J.	..	.. 39	John, R. F.	.. 39	Roberts, H.	.. 3
Buchan, C. M.	..	30	Kennedy, A. L.	2	Seddon, W. C.	.. 4
Butler, J. D.	..	38	Lambert, J.	.. 16	Shaw, J. ..	.. 6
Clark, W.	..	.. 1	Lewis, D.	.. 33	Thompson, L.	.. 1
Cope, H.	..	.. 24	Moody, J.	.. 4	Tricker, R. W.	.. 7

LEAGUE GOAL-SCORERS

Brain, J.	..	.. 22	Parker, T. R.	.. 4	John, R. F.	.. 1
Buchan, C. M.	..	16	Lambert, J.	.. 3	Collins (West Ham)	1
Hoar, S.	..	.. 10	Shaw, J.	.. 3	O'Donnell (Everton)	1
Hulme, J. H. A.	..	9	Baker, A.	.. 2	Wilson (Man. Utd.)	1
Blyth, W.	..	.. 7	Tricker, R. W.	2	Total	82

F.A. CUP COMPETITION

3rd Rd. v. West Bromwich Albion ..	(h) 2—0
4th Rd. v. Everton	(h) 4—3
5th Rd. v. Aston Villa	(h) 4—1
6th Rd. v. Stoke City	(h) 4—1
S.F. v. Blackburn Rovers	0—1 (at Leicester)

HONOURS

Baker, A.: England *v.* Wales.
Hulme, J. H. A.: England *v.* Scotland, Ireland; Football
League *v.* Scottish League, Irish League; England trial (2).
John, R. F.: Wales *v.* England, Ireland.
Lewis, D.: Wales *v.* Ireland.

77

Season 1928-9

Football League—Division I

P.42 W.16 D.13 L.13 Goals 77—72 Pts.45 9th

London Football Combination

P. 42 W.26 D.7 L.9 Goals 108—42 Pts.59 1st

This season witnessed the change-over at inside-right of two very great names—Charles Buchan, who retired during the summer of 1928, and the transfer from Bolton of David Jack, whose graceful ball control was to help the team to great heights in the years ahead. Jack made his début for Arsenal at Highbury in an exciting game against Liverpool. A hat-trick by their South African centre-forward Hodgson put Arsenal two goals in arrears, but, despite an injury to Roberts, the Gunners managed to draw level at four all.

After a poor start to the season, when only four victories were recorded in the first seventeen matches, the tide began to turn in December with two wins and four draws in seven encounters. In the new year further progress was made and a splendid run of eleven games without defeat enabled the Club to finish in ninth position.

On 6th October 1928 Parker made his one-hundredth consecutive appearance for Arsenal, in a League game at Everton which the home side won 4—2. Parker had played in every match since moving from Southampton.

In the fourth round of the F.A. Cup Arsenal met the Midland League club Mansfield Town, who had in the previous round knocked out Wolverhampton Wanderers at Molineux. Arsenal had some luck on that day, for, not only did the Town's inside-right Stansfield miss a penalty kick in the first half, but in addition the famous Arsenal forwards were unable to penetrate the stubborn Mansfield defence until ten minutes from time—this at Highbury too!

The Club, nevertheless, once again reached the last eight; finally succumbing to Aston Villa at Birmingham. It was a lively battle in which Arsenal's rearguard withstood the powerful onslaughts of the Villa's attack until a few minutes from the end. A dramatic victory went to the Midland side when Parker unluckily deflected a shot from Waring into his own net.

FOOTBALL LEAGUE RESULTS

Home	Opponents	Away	Home	Opponents	Away
2—5	Aston Villa ..	.. 2—4	1—0	Leeds United	.. 1—1
0—0	Birmingham ..	.. 1—1	1—1	Leicester City..	.. 1—1
1—0	Blackburn Rovers	.. 2—5	4—4	Liverpool ..	.. 4—2
2—0	Bolton Wanderers	.. 2—1	0—0	Manchester City	.. 1—4
3—1	Burnley ..	.. 3—3	3—1	Manchester United	.. 1—4
7—1	Bury	.. 0—1	1—2	Newcastle United	.. 3—0
2—1	Cardiff City ..	.. 1—1	4—0	Portsmouth ..	.. 0—2
1—3	Derby County	.. 0—0	2—2	Sheffield Wednesday	2—3
2—0	Everton ..	.. 2—4	2—0	Sheffield United	.. 2—2
2—0	Huddersfield Town ..	1—0	1—1	Sunderland ..	.. 1—5
	2—3	West Ham United	.. 4—3		

LEAGUE APPEARANCES (21 PLAYERS)

Baker, A. ..	.. 31	Hoar, S.	.. 6	Parker, T. R.	.. 42
Barley, J. C.	.. 3	Hulme, J. H. A.	41	Parkin, R.	.. 5
Blyth, W. ..	.. 21	Jack, D. B. N.	31	Patterson, W.	.. 10
Brain, J. ..	.. 37	John, R. F.	.. 34	Peel, H. ..	.. 24
Butler, J. D.	.. 22	Jones, C.	.. 39	Roberts, H.	.. 20
Cope, H. ..	.. 23	Lambert, J.	.. 6	Thompson, L.	.. 17
Hapgood, E. A.	.. 17	Lewis, D.	.. 32	Tricker, R. W.	.. 1

LEAGUE GOAL-SCORERS

Jack, D. B. N.	.. 23	Thompson, L. ..	5	John, R. F.	.. 1
Brain, J. ..	.. 21	Parker, T. R. ..	3	Lambert, J.	.. 1
Hulme, J. H. A.	.. 6	Parkin, R. ..	3	Davidson (L'pool)	1
Jones, C. ..	.. 6	Blyth, W. ..	1	Total	77
Peel, H. ..	.. 5	Hoar, S. ..	1		

F.A. CUP COMPETITION

3rd Rd.	v. Stoke City ..	.. (h)	2—1
4th Rd.	v. Mansfield Town ..	.. (h)	2—0
5th Rd.	v. Swindon Town ..	.. (a)	0—0
Replay	v. Swindon Town ..	.. (h)	1—0
6th Rd.	v. Aston Villa ..	.. (a)	0—1

HONOURS

Hulme, J. H. A.: England v. Wales, Ireland; Football
League v. Scottish League; England trial (2).
Williams, J. J.: Professionals v. Amateurs (Charity Shield).

Season 1929–30

Football League Division I

P.42 W.14 D.11 L.17 Goals 78—66 Pts.39 14th

London Football Combination

P.42 W.30 D.5 L.7 Goals 132—55 Pts.65 1st

Arsenal started the season in fine style, gaining five victories in the first six matches. A serious slump followed, however, because the forwards particularly were out of touch. Halliday was obtained from Sunderland, but even then the costly attack of Hulme, Jack, Halliday, James and Jones could not produce the goals. James was dropped for a time, Bastin came in for Jones and Lambert replaced Halliday in various combinations to find a settled line.

With nothing to gain in the League, Arsenal made a concerted effort in the Cup, and by the time the semi-final was reached the forward line of Hulme, Jack, Lambert, James and Bastin was established as one of the best the club ever had. In beating Huddersfield in the Cup final at Wembley the Gunners won their first major trophy.

On the Monday before the final Arsenal took part in a record drawn game of 6—6 at Leicester. Losing 1—3 at half-time, Arsenal managed to equalize and then each team scored in turn up to the final score 6—6. Halliday (4) and Bastin (2) scored for the Londoners while Leicester City's marksmen were Adcock (2), Hine, Lockhead (2) and Chandler.

CUP FINAL, WEMBLEY, 1929–30

Arsenal 2 v. Huddersfield Town 0

It was a strange coincidence that the late Herbert Chapman, then manager of Arsenal, had also served their Cup-final opponents in the same capacity before his arrival at Highbury. In fact, much of the credit for building the successful Huddersfield team of the 1920's can be attributed to his shrewd managership.

The final can be divided into two distinct phases. The first belonged to Arsenal. In the first fifteen minutes the Huddersfield goal survived narrow escapes when Bastin headed against the bar; when

E. DRAKE

G. EASTHAM

A. FORBES

V. GROVES

E. HAPGOOD

J. HENDERSON

D. HERD

J. HULME

Lambert's shot rebounded off the goalkeeper; and when, after a corner, full-back Goodall headed clear with his goalkeeper beaten by a shot from Jack.

Huddersfield earned a brief respite when Smith, on the left-wing, outstripped Arsenal's defence, but Jackson turned his centre just wide of the post. Soon afterwards Arsenal gained the lead they so richly deserved. And it was ironical that, in a game containing only half a dozen fouls throughout, a free kick should pave the way for the first goal. Goodall charged James unfairly and the wee Scot quickly slipped the ball to Bastin, took the return pass in his stride and banged the ball into the net.

Arsenal continued to attack with Lambert, in characteristic bursts down the middle, unsettling the Town defence. James, easily the best inside-forward of the day, was a brilliant tactician, and his defence-splitting passes were uncanny in their accuracy. Bastin, too, was very dangerous, but in Goodall he had a difficult man to beat. In comparison, the right-wing pair, Hulme and Jack, were fairly quiet. Once Lambert found himself clear of the defence, but as the goalkeeper advanced he pulled his shot just outside the up-right. Although Arsenal were still in command during the remainder of the first half, they were not able to increase their slender lead.

After the interval, however, came a transformation. Huddersfield's half-back line of Naylor, Wilson and Campbell began to dominate the mid-field and the wingers, Jackson and Smith, became powerful spearheads in a revitalized Town attack. Arsenal, instead of *making* the running, were then compelled to *do* the running. If only the Huddersfield inside-forwards could have produced a few worthwhile shots the result of the match would have been a vastly different one. But no, they did not appear to have the confidence, and looked to Jackson, who had netted nine of the eleven goals en route to the final, to do the scoring. Hapgood, however, polished and cool throughout, gave Jackson few chances to manœuvre into a good shooting position.

Nevertheless, other Huddersfield forwards had numerous chances until a left-wing movement by John, James and Bastin led to an unexpected second goal for Arsenal. The opportunist Lambert raced between the backs to hit the ball past the helpless Turner. Huddersfield, who had striven so hard for an equalizing goal, were then a well-beaten side.

The Arsenal half-back line never quite attained the brilliance of the Huddersfield trio, but, in taking the whole ninety minutes, there was very little to choose between the two teams. Arsenal's advantage lay mainly in the inside-forwards, and one is left wondering if the move of dropping Lewis, the regular leader, in favour of Davies at centre-forward in the Huddersfield side was a wise one. This final gave Huddersfield's Wilson and Arsenal's Jack two strangely contrasting records. For both this was the third Cup-final appearance. In Wilson's case it was his third on the losing side, whereas David Jack had been successful in each.

CUP FINAL TEAMS

Arsenal: Preedy; Parker, Hapgood; Baker, Seddon, John; Hulme, Jack, Lambert, James, Bastin.
Huddersfield Town: Turner; Goodall, Spence; Naylor, Wilson, Campbell; Jackson (A.), Kelly, Davies, Raw, Smith (W. H.).

FOOTBALL LEAGUE RESULTS

Home	Opponents	Away	Home	Opponents	Away
2—4	Aston Villa	2—5	1—1	Leicester City.. ..	6—6
1—0	Birmingham	3—2	0—1	Liverpool	0—1
4—0	Blackburn Rovers ..	1—1	3—2	Manchester City ..	1—3
1—2	Bolton Wanderers ..	0—0	4—2	Manchester United ..	0—1
6—1	Burnley	2—2	1—2	Middlesbrough ..	1—1
1—1	Derby County ..	1—4	0—1	Newcastle United ..	1—1
4—0	Everton	1—1	1—2	Portsmouth	1—0
4—1	Grimsby Town ..	1—1	8—1	Sheffield United ..	1—4
2—0	Huddersfield Town ..	2—2	2—3	Sheffield Wednesday	2—0
4—0	Leeds United ..	0—2	0—1	Sunderland	1—0
	0—1 West Ham United .. 2—3				

LEAGUE APPEARANCES (24 PLAYERS)

Baker, A.	19	Hulme, J. H. A.	37	Lewis, D.	30
Bastin, C. S... ..	21	Humpish, E. ..	3	Parker, T. R. ..	41
Brain, J.	6	Jack, D. B. N.	33	Peel, H.	1
Butler, J. D. ..	2	James, A. ..	31	Preedy, C. J. ..	12
Cope, H.	1	John, R. F. ..	34	Roberts, H. ..	26
Halliday, D. ..	15	Johnstone, W.	7	Seddon, W. C. ..	24
Hapgood, E. A. ..	38	Jones, C. ..	31	Thompson, L. ..	5
Haynes, A. E. ..	13	Lambert, J. ..	20	Williams, J. J. ..	12

82

Lambert, J.	.. 18	Bastin, C. S.	.. 7	Williams, J. J.	.. 3
Hulme, J. H. A.	.. 14	James, A.	.. 6	Jones, C.	.. 1
Jack, D. B. N.	.. 13	Johnstone, W.	3	Thompson, L.	.. 1
Halliday, D.	.. 8	Parker, T. R.	.. 3	Waterfield (Burnley)	1

Total 78

F.A. CUP COMPETITION

3rd Rd. *v.* Chelsea	..	.. .. (h)	2—0	Lambert, Bastin
4th Rd. *v.* Birmingham	..	.. (h)	2—2	Bastin, Jack
Replay *v.* Birmingham	..	.. (a)	1—0	Baker
5th Rd. *v.* Middlesbrough	..	.. (a)	2—0	Lambert, Bastin
6th Rd. *v.* West Ham United	..	(a)	3—0	Lambert 2, Baker
S.F. *v.* Hull City (at Leeds)	..		2—2	Jack, Bastin
Replay *v.* Hull City (at Villa Park)	..		1—0	Jack
Final *v.* Huddersfield Town	..		2—0	James, Lambert

HONOURS

Hapgood, E. A.: England trial.
Jack, D. B. N.: England *v.* Scotland, Austria and Germany;
  Football League *v.* Scottish League; England trial.
James, A.: Scotland *v.* England, Wales and Ireland.
John, R. F.: Wales *v.* England and Scotland.
Jones, C.: Wales *v.* England and Scotland.
Lewis, D.: Wales *v.* England.

Season 1930–1

Football League—Division I

P.42 W.28 D.10 L.4 Goals 127—59 Pts.66 1st

London Football Combination

P.42 W.28 D.6 L.8 Goals 120—48 Pts.62 1st

Arsenal's peak season! In which, when winning the League championship for the first time, the team set up several club and Division I records. Under the captaincy of Parker, Arsenal collected a record total of sixty-six points, half of which were gained away from home —a figure which exceeded by three the previous best made by Huddersfield in 1925.

Twenty-eight victories equalled the record credited to West Bromwich Albion in 1920, and the four defeats has only been bettered in Division I by Preston in the first season of the League (1889) when the North End remained undefeated. In addition, a club record was created with a total of 127 goals—this figure beat the previous best in Division I, too, but Aston Villa, who were runners-up seven points behind Arsenal, scored 128 goals during the season to set up a new record. Lambert, who netted thirty-eight times in League games, broke the Club's individual scoring record previously held by Brain (thirty-four in season 1925–6).

As holders of the F.A. Cup, Arsenal took the trophy to Blackpool to open the season there. It was, incidentally, the début of the unorthodox Dutch goalkeeper Keyser, and Arsenal returned winners by 4—1. In the corresponding game at Highbury Male made his début, and Brain and Jack each gained hat-tricks in a 7—1 victory— four goals came from corners in the game. There was also a memorable encounter at Chelsea where thirty minutes from time the home side was leading 1—0 by a penalty scored by Law. Arsenal then applied the pressure and scored five in quick time—Jack again getting three of them.

FOOTBALL LEAGUE RESULTS

Home	Opponents	Away	Home	Opponents	Away
5—2	Aston Villa ..	.. 1—5	3—2	Blackburn Rovers	.. 2—2
1—1	Birmingham ..	.. 4—2	7—1	Blackpool ..	.. 4—1

84

Home	Opponents	Away	Home	Opponents	Away
5—0	Bolton Wanderers ..	4—1	3—1	Manchester City ..	4—1
2—1	Chelsea	5—1	4—1	Manchester United ..	2—1
6—3	Derby County ..	2—4	5—3	Middlesbrough ..	5—2
9—1	Grimsby Town ..	1—0	1—2	Newcastle United ..	3—1
0—0	Huddersfield Town ..	1—1	1—1	Portsmouth	1—1
3—1	Leeds United ..	2—1	1—1	Sheffield United ..	1—1
4—1	Leicester City.. ..	7—2	2—0	Sheffield Wednesday	2—1
3—1	Liverpool	1—1	1—3	Sunderland	4—1
	1—1 West Ham United .. 4—2				

LEAGUE APPEARANCES (22 PLAYERS)

Baker, A. ..	..	1	Jack, D. B. N.	35	Parker, T. R.	..	41
Bastin, C. S.	..	42	James, A.	.. 40	Preedy, C. J.	..	11
Brain, J. ..	..	16	John, R. F.	.. 40	Roberts, H.	..	40
Cope, H. ..	..	1	Johnstone, W.	2	Seddon, W. C.	..	18
Hapgood, E. A.	..	38	Jones, C.	.. 24	Thompson, L.	..	2
Harper, W. ..	..	19	Keyser, G. P.	.. 12	Williams, J. J.	..	9
Haynes, A. E.	..	2	Lambert, J.	.. 34			
Hulme, J. H. A.	..	32	Male, G.	.. 3			

LEAGUE GOAL-SCORERS

Lambert, J.	..	38	James, A.	.. 5	Johnstone, W.	..	1
Jack, D. B. N.	..	31	Brain, J.	.. 4	Jones, C. ..	..	1
Bastin, C. S.	..	28	John, R. F.	.. 2	Roberts, H.	..	1
Hulme, J. H. A.	..	14	Williams, J. J. ..	2	Total 127		

F.A. CUP COMPETITION

3rd Rd. v. Aston Villa	..	.. (h)	2—2	Lambert, Jack
Replay v. Aston Villa	..	.. (a)	3—1	Hulme 2, Jack
4th Rd. v. Chelsea	..	.. (a)	1—2	Bastin

HONOURS

Bastin, C. S.: England trial.
Hapgood, E. A.: Football League v. Irish League.
Jack, D. B. N.: Football League v. Irish League.
Roberts, H.: England v. Scotland.

Season 1931–2

Football League—Division I

P.42 W.22 D.10 L.10 Goals 90—48 Pts.54 2nd

London Football Combination

P.42 W.27 D.8 L.7 Goals 111—43 Pts.62 2nd

A remarkable season, because the Club did splendidly but won nothing except the F.A. Charity Shield. For a long time it looked as if the team would capture the 'double' but, in the end, both honours were just out of their reach, being beaten by Newcastle United in the Cup final and being second to Everton in the League.

The results in the League were not particularly promising in the first half of the season (three defeats in the Christmas games!), but successes in the Cup competition bred confidence in the ensuing League encounters. Arsenal climbed rapidly up the table and, just before the semi-final, were only three points behind Everton. Although the Gunners finished the season by gaining seven points from the last four matches, Everton still remained two points ahead to win the championship.

On the way to the final Arsenal had two very narrow victories. In the first, Roberts forsook his usual defensive role for one moment to head the goal which beat Huddersfield in the sixth round, and in the semi-final Bastin scored the only goal after intense Manchester City pressure with the last kick of the game.

CUP FINAL, WEMBLEY, 1931–2

Arsenal 1 v. Newcastle United 2

For their third Cup final Arsenal were matched against Newcastle United in a great North v. South battle. The line-up of the Arsenal eleven was not settled until the day before the game. The fitness of both Hulme and James was doubtful, due to injuries sustained in earlier League encounters. Hulme subsequently passed the fitness test but James, unfortunately, broke down. As a result, Bastin was moved to inside-left with the versatile John as his wing partner, and

Male was brought in at left-half to play his first cup-tie in a Wembley final.

Nelson, the Newcastle right-back and captain, who opposed the Gunners in the 1927 final while a Cardiff player, lost the toss and Parker chose to play with the slight breeze. The first thrill came when the Newcastle goalkeeper McInroy just got to the ball before Lambert rushed in. Then Bastin manœuvred cleverly and put in a hard shot which McInroy punched over the bar. The corner was cleared and for some minutes the situation looked serious for Arsenal, with the ball bobbing about near the Londoners' goal. Roberts eventually came to the rescue, and sent a long pass out to Hulme who beat Fairhurst and centred. McInroy and Nelson both misjudged the cross and John, closing in from the wing, was able to score an easy goal. McInroy was not always safe in handling the ball, and once dropped it in fielding a long shot from Jones. Luckily for the United, Nelson dashed across to complete the clearance.

Newcastle's left-winger, Lang, who was often too fast for Parker, caused the Arsenal defence a lot of trouble, and several times only excellent interceptions on the part of Roberts and Hapgood prevented the winger from getting through. Allen, however, was almost completely blotted out by the policeman tactics of Roberts. The United equalized seven minutes before the interval when Allen 'lost' Roberts for once and headed through a centre from Richardson. This has since become known as the 'over-the-line' goal. Photographs show that the ball had run over the line before Richardson was able to hook it into the centre. It was the turning point of the game because Newcastle, spurred on by the goal, became the more dangerous side. In point of fact, they fully deserved to be on level terms at the interval.

On the resumption, Moss was brought into action several times and made some brilliant saves, particularly in going full length to stop shots from Boyd and Allen. Arsenal's attack, on the other hand, was less effective than in the first forty-five minutes, although one shot from Hulme was only inches wide of the mark. After twenty-seven minutes Newcastle went ahead when Allen, taking full advantage of a miskick by Roberts, found that he had only Moss to beat. This he did with a fine shot into the top left-hand corner of the net.

In an effort to equalize Arsenal switched the forwards, Jack moving to the centre, with Bastin on his right and Lambert on the left. John twice shot wide when well placed and Jack, too, had a good chance to put Arsenal on level terms again. The final whistle came with Newcastle still displaying the better team-work and the more purpose in their raids. Although they were fortunate to equalize John's early goal, Newcastle were the worthy winners of a great battle.

For Arsenal, Moss played brilliantly, and Hulme was easily the fastest player on the field. Roberts, except for that one fatal slip, was in complete command in his own penalty area, and Male, in his first cup-tie, was quietly effective.

CUP FINAL TEAMS

Arsenal: Moss; Parker, Hapgood; Jones (C.), Roberts, Male; Hulme, Jack, Lambert, Bastin, John.

Newcastle United: McInroy; Nelson, Fairhurst; McKenzie, Davison, Weaver; Boyd, Richardson, Allen, McMenemy, Lang.

FOOTBALL LEAGUE RESULTS

Home	Opponents	Away	Home	Opponents	Away
1—1	Aston Villa	1—1	2—1	Leicester City.. ..	2—1
3—0	Birmingham	2—2	6—0	Liverpool	1—2
4—0	Blackburn Rovers ..	1—1	4—0	Manchester City ..	3—1
2—0	Blackpool	5—1	5—0	Middlesbrough ..	5—2
1—1	Bolton Wanderers ..	0—1	1—0	Newcastle United ..	2—3
1—1	Chelsea	1—2	3—3	Portsmouth	3—0
2—1	Derby County ..	1—1	0—2	Sheffield United ..	1—4
3—2	Everton	3—1	3—1	Sheffield Wednesday	3—1
4—0	Grimsby Town ..	1—3	2—0	Sunderland	0—2
1—1	Huddersfield Town ..	2—1	0—1	West Bromwich Albion	0—1
	4—1 West Ham United .. 1—1				

LEAGUE APPEARANCES (24 PLAYERS)

Bastin, C. S.	.. 40	Hulme, J. H. A.	40	Parker, T. R.	.. 38
Beasley, A. ..	.. 3	Jack, D. B. N.	34	Parkin, R.	.. 9
Coleman, E.	.. 6	James, A.	.. 32	Preedy, C. J.	.. 13
Compton, L. H.	.. 4	John, R. F.	.. 38	Roberts, H.	.. 35
Cope, H. ..	.. 1	Jones, C.	.. 37	Seddon, W. C.	.. 5
Hapgood, E. A.	.. 41	Lambert, J.	.. 36	Stockhill, R.	.. 3
Harper, W. ..	.. 2	Male, G.	.. 9	Thompson, L.	.. 1
Haynes, A. E.	.. 7	Moss, F.	.. 27	Williams, J. J.	.. 1

LEAGUE GOAL-SCORERS

Lambert, J.	.. 22	John, R. F.	.. 3	Hutton (Blackb'n)	1
Jack, D. B. N.	.. 20	James, A.	.. 2	McLaren (Leics.)	1
Bastin, C. S.	.. 15	Coleman, E.	.. 1	Osborne (Leics.)	1
Hulme, J. H. A.	.. 14	Stockhill, R.	.. 1	Webster (Midd'bro)	1
Parkin, R.	.. 7	Hooton (Birm'ham)	1	Total 90	

F.A. CUP COMPETITION

3rd Rd. *v.* Darwen .. .. .. (h) 11—1 Bastin 4, Jack 3,
Lambert 2, Hulme 2
4th Rd. *v.* Plymouth Argyle .. (h) 4—2 Lambert 2, Hulme, o.g.
5th Rd. *v.* Portsmouth .. .. (a) 2—0 Bastin, Hulme
6th Rd. *v.* Huddersfield Town .. (a) 1—0 Roberts
S.F. *v.* Manchester C. (at Villa Park) 1—0 Bastin
Final *v.* Newcastle United .. .. 1—2 John

HONOURS

Bastin, C. S.: England *v.* Wales; Football League *v.* Scottish
League; England trial.
Hapgood, E. A.: England trial.
Hulme, J. H. A.: Football League *v.* Irish League; England trial.
John, R. F.: Wales *v.* England.
Jones, C.: Wales *v.* England.

89

Football League—Division I

P.42 W.25 D.8 L.9 Goals 118—61 Pts.58 1st

London Football Combination

P.46 W.31 D.5 L.10 Goals 145—57 Pts.67 3rd

After so narrowly failing to win both the League and the Cup in the previous season, Arsenal succeeded in bringing the championship trophy back to Highbury for the second time in three years.

In the first half of the season the Gunners conceded only six points, and as the Christmas games came along were in the happy position at the head of the table with a lead of six points. During this period, splendid victories were recorded at home over Leicester (8—2) and Sheffield United (9—2) and at Wolverhampton, where Jack (3), Lambert (2) and (Bastin (2) scored in a fine 7—1 win.

The home match against Derby was a memorable one for the fact that a seemingly comfortable Arsenal victory was suddenly turned into a draw. Coleman (2) and Hulme had given Arsenal a 3—1 half-time lead and then Roberts had the cruel luck to turn two centres from left-winger Duncan into his own goal within the space of a minute.

After gaining three points from the Christmas matches, Arsenal's form became rather unpredictable and, coupled with the surprise cup-tie defeat at Walsall, one wondered if the team would fade. Aston Villa, Sheffield Wednesday and Newcastle were all in a good position to challenge should Arsenal crack. Five victories in successive matches, which included the defeats of rivals Aston Villa (5—0) and Sheffield Wednesday (4—2), nevertheless put the issue beyond doubt with two games to play. Hulme, who scored his only hat-trick in Division I, *v.* Sunderland, during the season, also scored three for the Football League *v.* Scottish League at Ibrox.

FOOTBALL LEAGUE RESULTS

Home	Opponents	Away	Home	Opponents	Away
5—0	Aston Villa ..	.. 3—5	1—1	Blackpool ..	.. 2—1
3—0	Birmingham ..	.. 1—0	3—2	Bolton Wanderers	.. 4—0
8—0	Blackburn Rovers	.. 3—2	4—1	Chelsea ..	.. 3—1

Home	Opponents	Away	Home	Opponents	Away
3—3	Derby County	.. 2—2	4—2	Middlesbrough	.. 4—3
3—1	Everton ..	.. 1—1	1—0	Newcastle United	.. 1—2
2—2	Huddersfield Town	.. 1—0	2—0	Portsmouth ..	.. 3—1
1—2	Leeds United	.. 0—0	9—2	Sheffield United	.. 1—3
8—2	Leicester City..	.. 1—1	4—2	Sheffield Wednesday	2—3
0—1	Liverpool ..	.. 3—2	6—1	Sunderland ..	.. 2—3
2—1	Manchester City	.. 3—2	1—2	West Bromwich Albion	1—1
	1—2 Wolverhampton Wanderers		.. 7—1		

LEAGUE APPEARANCES (22 PLAYERS)

Bastin, C. S.	.. 42	Hulme, J. H. A.	40	Parker, T. R.	.. 5
Bowden, E. R.	.. 7	Jack, D. B. N.	34	Parkin, R.	.. 5
Coleman, E.	.. 27	James, A.	.. 40	Preedy, C. J.	.. 1
Compton, L. H.	.. 4	John, R. F.	.. 37	Roberts, H.	36
Cope, H. ..	.. 4	Jones, C.	.. 16	Sidey, N.	.. 2
Hapgood, E. A.	.. 38	Lambert, J.	.. 12	Stockhill, R.	.. 4
Haynes, A. E.	.. 6	Male, G.	.. 35		
Hill, F. ..	.. 26	Moss, F.	.. 41		

LEAGUE GOAL-SCORERS

Bastin, C. S.	.. 33	Jack, D. B. N.	18	Stockhill, R.	.. 3
Coleman, E.	.. 24	Lambert, J.	.. 14	Bowden, E. R.	.. 2
Hulme, J. H. A.	.. 20	James, A.	.. 3	Hill, F. ..	.. 1

Total 118

F.A. CUP COMPETITION

3rd Rd. v. Walsall .. .. .. (a) 0—2

HONOURS

Bastin, C. S.: England v. Italy, Switzerland; England trial.
Coleman, E.: England trial.
Hapgood, E. A.: England v. Italy, Switzerland; England trial.
Hulme, J. H. A.: England v. Scotland; Football League v.
Scottish League; England trial.
Jack, D. B. N.: England v. Wales, Austria.
James, A.: Scotland v. Wales.
John, R. F.: Wales v. Ireland, France.
Jones, C.: Wales v. France.
Male, G.: England trial.
Moss, F.: Football League v. Irish League; England trial.

Season 1933–4

Football League—Division I

P.42 W.25 D.9 L.8 Goals 75—47 Pts.59 1st

London Football Combination

P.46 W.32 D.5 L.9 Goals 129—44 Pts.69 1st

Another splendid season in which the League championship and the F.A. Charity Shield were won, while in the F.A. Cup Arsenal were one of the last eight. The success of the season, however, was marred by the sudden death of Mr. Herbert Chapman. It was a sad blow, felt by all departments of the Club, but, with commendable determination, Mr. Chapman's good work was carried on with Joe Shaw as acting manager.

The attendance record at Highbury was broken twice during the season. A total of 68,828 spectators watched a mid-week game against the Spurs, when Hapgood conceded a penalty, John miskicked to let in number two and Spurs' left-winger Evans robbed Male to put the visitors three up. Arsenal rallied in brilliant fashion but Nichols, in the Spurs goal, saved his side in spite of some wonderful shots from Bowden and Dunne.

The visit on Good Friday of Derby County attracted another record 'gate' (69,070), and the home victory put Arsenal on top of the table. Huddersfield, the main challengers, regained the lead on Easter Saturday in beating Manchester City 1—0 but, at the same time, suffered a severe blow when McLean, their scheming forward, broke a leg. Five points from the Easter games (Huddersfield gained only three!) put Arsenal in the lead again where they remained until the end of the season. Among the newcomers in the team were centre-forwards Dunne, an Irish international from Sheffield United, and Drake, from Southampton.

FOOTBALL LEAGUE RESULTS

Home	Opponents	Away	Home	Opponents	Away
3—2	Aston Villa	3—2	1—0	Derby County	4—2
1—1	Birmingham	0—0	1—2	Everton	1—3
2—1	Blackburn Rovers	2—2	3—1	Huddersfield Town	1—0
2—1	Chelsea	2—2	2—0	Leeds United	1—0

Home	Opponents	Away	Home	Opponents	Away
2—0	Leicester City..	..1—4	2—0	Sheffield United	..3—1
2—1	Liverpool ..	..3—2	1—1	Sheffield Wednesday	2—1
1—1	Manchester City	..1—2	3—0	Stoke City ..	..1—1
6—0	Middlesbrough ..	..2—0	2—1	Sunderland ..	..0—3
3—0	Newcastle United	..1—0	1—3	Tottenham Hotspur ..	1—1
1—1	Portsmouth ..	..0—1	3—1	West Bromwich Albion	0—1
		3—2	Wolverhampton Wanderers	..1—0	

LEAGUE APPEARANCES (24 PLAYERS)

Bastin, C. S.	..38	Dunne, J.	..21	Jones, C. ..	..29
Beasley, A. ..	..23	Hapgood, E. A.	40	Lambert, J.	..3
Birkett, R. ..	..15	Haynes, A. E. ..	1	Male, G. ..	..42
Bowden, E. R.	..32	Hill, F. ..	..25	Moss, F. ..	..37
Coleman, E.	..12	Hulme, J. H. A.	8	Parkin, R.	..5
Cox, G. ..	..2	Jack, D. B. N.	14	Roberts, H.	..30
Dougall, J. ..	..5	James, A.	..22	Sidey, N.	..12
Drake, E. ..	..10	John, R. F.	..31	Wilson, A.	..5

LEAGUE GOAL-SCORERS

Bastin, C. S.	..13	Birkett, R.	..5	John, R. F.	..1
Bowden, E. R.	..13	Hulme, J. H. A.	5	Lambert, J.	..1
Beasley, A. ..	..10	Jack, D. B. N.	5	Roberts, H.	..1
Dunne, J. ..	..9	James, A.	..3	Fairhurst	
Drake, E. ..	..7	Coleman, E. ..	1	(Newcastle) ..	1
					Total 75

F.A. CUP COMPETITION

3rd Rd. v. Luton Town ..	..(a)	1—0	Dunne
4th Rd. v. Crystal Palace ..	..(h)	7—0	Dunne 2, Bastin 2, Beasley 2, Birkett
5th Rd. v. Derby County ..	..(h)	1—0	Jack
6th Rd. v. Aston Villa ..	..(h)	1—2	Dougall

HONOURS

Bastin, C. S.: England v. Scotland, Wales, Ireland, Hungary, Czechoslovakia; Football League v. Scottish League, Irish League; England trial.

Hapgood, E. A.: England v. Scotland, Wales, Ireland, Hungary, Czechoslovakia; England trial.

Moss, F.: England v. Scotland, Hungary, Czechoslovakia.

93

Season 1934-5

Football League—Division I

P.42 W.23 D.12 L.7 Goals 115—46 Pts.58 1st

London Football Combination

P.46 W.33 D.5 L.8 Goals 131—50 Pts.71 1st

With Mr. George Allison at the helm, some new faces were seen at Highbury to replace the older stars who had brought Arsenal to the pinnacle of fame. Lambert, Jack, Jones and Coleman all gave way to younger players, amongst whom were wing-halves Crayston (Bradford) and Copping (Leeds) and forwards Kirchen (Norwich) and Davidson (St. Johnstone).

Having won the championship in two successive seasons, Arsenal set out to equal Huddersfield's record of three wins in the years 1924-5-6, and this prodigious feat was in fact achieved. In recognition of this great achievement the Football League presented the Club with a magnificent silver shield.

At the beginning of April, Arsenal, with forty-eight points, were four ahead of Manchester City, while Sunderland and Sheffield Wednesday had forty-three and forty-two points in third and fourth places respectively. The City's challenge, however, faded, for they won only the last of their eight remaining games. Arsenal, on the other hand, marched on relentlessly, collecting six points during Easter (including an 8—0 victory over Middlesbrough, whose team included ex-Arsenal players Coleman and Birkett) and dropping only four points in the last seven games. Although both Sunderland and Sheffield were undefeated throughout April, Arsenal set such a standard that the Londoners won the title comfortably.

FOOTBALL LEAGUE RESULTS

Home	Opponents	Away	Home	Opponents	Away
1—2	Aston Villa	3—1	1—1	Grimsby Town	2—2
5—1	Birmingham	0—3	1—0	Huddersfield Town	1—1
4—0	Blackburn Rovers	0—2	3—0	Leeds United	1—1
2—2	Chelsea	5—2	8—0	Leicester City	5—3
0—1	Derby County	1—3	8—1	Liverpool	2—0
2—0	Everton	2—0	3—0	Manchester City	1—1

Home	Opponents	Away	Home	Opponents	Away
8—0	Middlesbrough ..	1—0	2—0	Stoke City	2—2
1—1	Portsmouth	3—3	0—0	Sunderland	1—2
5—3	Preston North End ..	1—2	5—1	Tottenham Hotspur ..	6—0
4—1	Sheffield Wednesday	0—0	4—3	West Bromwich Albion	3—0
	7—0	Wolverhampton Wanderers ..	1—1		

LEAGUE APPEARANCES (25 PLAYERS)

Bastin, C. S.	..	36	Drake, E.	..	41	Marshall, J.	..	4
Beasley, A. ..	..	20	Dunne, J.	..	1	Moss, F. ..	..	33
Birkett, R. ..	..	4	Hapgood, E. A.		34	Roberts, H.	..	36
Bowden, E. R.	..	24	Hill, F. ..	..	15	Rogers, E.	..	5
Compton, L. H.	..	5	Hulme, J. H. A.		16	Sidey, N.	..	6
Copping, W.	..	31	James, A.	..	30	Trim, R. ..	..	1
Crayston, W. J.	..	37	John, R. F.	..	9	Wilson, A.	..	9
Davidson, R.	..	11	Kirchen, A.	..	7			
Dougall, J. ..	..	8	Male, G.	..	39			

LEAGUE GOAL-SCORERS

Drake, E. ..	..	42	Hill, F. ..	..	3	Hapgood, E. A. ..		1
Bastin, C. S.	..	20	Birkett, R.	..	2	Moss, F. ..	..	1
Bowden, E. R.	..	14	Davidson, R.	..	2	Evans (Spurs)	..	1
Hulme, J. H. A.	..	8	Kirchen, A.	..	2	Roughton		
Beasley, A. ..	..	6	Rogers, E.	..	2	(Huddersfield)		1
James, A. ..	..	4	Compton, L. H.		1	Hough (Preston) ..		1
Crayston, W. J.	..	3	Dougall, J.	..	1	Total		115

F.A. CUP COMPETITION

3rd Rd. *v.* Brighton & Hove Albion .. (a) 2—0 Hulme, Drake
4th Rd. *v.* Leicester City .. .. (a) 1—0 Hulme
5th Rd. *v.* Reading .. .. .. (a) 1—0 Bastin
6th Rd. *v.* Sheffield Wednesday .. (a) 1—2 Catlin (o.g.)

HONOURS

Bastin, C. S.: England *v.* Scotland, Ireland, Italy; England trial.
Bowden, E. R.: England *v.* Wales, Italy; Football League *v.* S.L.
Copping, W.: England *v.* Ireland, Italy.
Drake, E.: England *v.* Ireland, Italy; England trial.
Hapgood, E. A.: England *v.* Scotland, Wales, Ireland, Italy,
Netherlands; Football League *v.* Scottish League.
John, R. F.: Wales *v.* Ireland.
Male, G.: England *v.* Scotland, Ireland, Italy, Netherlands.
Moss, F.: England *v.* Italy; Football League *v.* Scottish League.

Football League—Division I

P.42 W.15 D.15 L.12 Goals 78—48 Pts.45 6th

London Football Combination

P.46 W.29 D.5 L.12 Goals 117—55 Pts.63 3rd

The results in the League came as an anticlimax after the all-conquering previous three seasons, for in this campaign Arsenal were often struggling and unconvincing on the field. Attendances at Highbury, nevertheless, topped the million mark for the whole season and a new record for the League was set up when Arsenal's visit to Stamford Bridge attracted 82,905 spectators.

In one of the few purple patches, Drake equalled the individual goal-scoring record in the First Division by netting all of the Gunners' seven against Aston Villa at Villa Park. He scored with each of his first six shots.

Sunderland, the eventual champions, provided the opposition in two exciting matches. On the opening day of the season, at Highbury, Gurney quickly put the visitors in front, but Arsenal rallied with goals from Drake (2) and Bastin, to win 3—1, while, in the return encounter, Sunderland were in irresistible form and led 4—1 at half-time. Goals by Drake and Bowden put Arsenal back in the game before Conner added a fifth, to which Bowden replied with another for the Londoners. It was at this score, 5—4, that this pulsating game ended and, incidentally, finally crushed Arsenal's hopes of staying in the championship race.

CUP FINAL, WEMBLEY, 1935-6

Arsenal 1 v. Sheffield United 0

At Wembley again, for the fourth time in ten years, Arsenal met in 1936 the promotion-seeking Second Division team, Sheffield United. Arsenal were pronounced clear favourites, of course, but in the long history of these finals there is record of many a fallen favourite. Indeed, in this match the London side found the United no mean opponents, and the Gunners owed much to their experience of the

D. B. N. JACK

A. JAMES

R. JOHN

C. JONES

B. JOY

R. LEWIS

D. LISHMAN

J. LOGIE

big occasion and to their compact defensive system to pull them through.

Sheffield's strength was in their attack, and in Barclay and Pickering they had two of the finest constructive inside-forwards of those days, while the burly Dodds was the centre-forward discovery of the season. It was interesting to note that only two years previously Dodds had been given a free transfer by Huddersfield Town. Whereas several of the Sheffield players were local-born, and had only recently gained a regular place in the team, the majority of the Arsenal men were rich in experience. Six of them had played in an earlier Cup final, and Male, Hapgood, Crayston and Bastin had appeared on the Wembley turf only three weeks previously in the international against Scotland.

Arsenal were slow to settle down, and for some minutes the United earned all the cheers. Barton and Barclay formed a scintillating right-wing, which gave Copping a gruelling time. Dodds dashed through and was finally stopped by a timely tackle from Male. The Gunners' right-back, incidentally, gave as perfect an exhibition as anyone would wish to see, with the result that Williams, the Sheffield winger, was completely blotted out of the game. Wilson, in the Arsenal goal, caused some gasps when he dropped the ball in fielding a shot from Pickering, but he recovered miraculously.

After twenty minutes the Arsenal attack came more into the picture. Bowden missed an easy chance following a centre from Bastin, and then Hulme, as speedy as ever, and Bastin began to cause a good deal of trouble to the Sheffield defence. Nevertheless, Smith, in the United goal, was impressive, and equal to the shots that came his way and so the interval arrived without any score.

Immediately on the resumption, Crayston darted through to try for a snap goal, but his grand shot was well saved by Smith. Soon afterwards the United defence was reeling under a battering by the Gunners' attack; Hulme thrived with some beautiful passes from Crayston and was repeatedly eluding Wilkinson, and during many exciting attempts to score Smith alone often saved his side. At the other end, however, a Sheffield sortie found Dodds within five yards of the Arsenal goal, but he just failed to reach the ball as it came across.

Back came the London side to score the vital goal. James slipped the ball to Bastin who took it up the wing before placing a square pass to Drake. The centre-forward manœuvred to find a shooting position and crashed in a great left-foot shot which gave even Smith no chance at all.

In the remaining sixteen minutes Sheffield twice came near to equalizing. Within a minute Dodds hit the crossbar and then Pickering had difficulty in controlling an awkwardly bouncing ball and ballooned it over the goal when well placed.

In the second half Arsenal always looked to be the eventual winners, but Sheffield were to be congratulated on the very fine quality of their play and for keeping the score to the smallest possible margin.

CUP FINAL TEAMS

Arsenal: Wilson; Male, Hapgood; Crayston, Roberts, Copping; Hulme, Bowden, Drake, James, Bastin.

Sheffield United: Smith; Hooper, Wilkinson; Jackson, Johnson, McPherson; Barton, Barclay, Dodds, Pickering, Williams.

FOOTBALL LEAGUE RESULTS

Home	Opponents	Away	Home	Opponents	Away
1—0	Aston Villa ..	.. 7—1	2—2	Leeds United	.. 1—1
1—1	Birmingham ..	.. 1—1	1—2	Liverpool ..	.. 1—0
5—1	Blackburn Rovers	.. 1—0	2—3	Manchester City	.. 0—1
1—1	Bolton Wanderers	.. 1—2	2—0	Middlesbrough	.. 2—2
1—1	Brentford ..	.. 1—2	2—3	Portsmouth ..	.. 1—2
1—1	Chelsea ..	.. 1—1	2—1	Preston North End ..	.. 0—1
1—1	Derby County	.. 4—0	2—2	Sheffield Wednesday	2—3
1—1	Everton ..	.. 2—0	1—0	Stoke City ..	.. 3—0
6—0	Grimsby Town	.. 0—1	3—1	Sunderland ..	.. 4—5
1—1	Huddersfield Town ..	.. 0—0	4—0	West Bromwich Albion	0—1
		4—0	Wolverhampton Wanderers ..	2—2	

LEAGUE APPEARANCES (29 PLAYERS)

Bastin, C. S.	.. 31	Drake, E.	.. 26	Milne, J. V.	.. 14
Beasley, A. ..	.. 26	Dunne, J.	.. 6	Moss, F. ..	.. 5
Bowden, E. R.	.. 22	Hapgood, E. A.	33	Parkin, R.	.. 1
Cartwright, S.	.. 5	Hill, F. ..	.. 10	Roberts, H.	.. 26
Compton, L. H.	.. 12	Hulme, J. H. A.	21	Rogers, E.	.. 11
Copping, W.	.. 33	James, A.	.. 17	Sidey, N.	.. 11
Cox, G. ..	.. 5	John, R. F.	.. 6	Tuckett, E. W.	.. 2
Crayston, W. J.	.. 36	Joy, B. ..	.. 2	Westcott, R.	.. 2
Davidson, R.	.. 13	Kirchen, A. J. ..	6	Wilson, A.	.. 37
Dougall, J. ..	.. 8	Male, G.	.. 35		

LEAGUE GOAL-SCORERS

Drake, E. ..	.. 23	Dougall, J.	.. 3	Cox, G. ..	.. 1
Bastin, C. S.	.. 11	Kirchen, A. J. ..	3	Dunne, J.	.. 1
Bowden, E. R.	.. 7	Rogers, E.	.. 3	Parkin, R.	.. 1
Hulme, J. H. A.	.. 6	Beasley, A.	.. 2	Roberts, H.	.. 1
Milne, J. V. ..	.. 6	James, A.	.. 2	Westcott, R.	.. 1
Crayston, W. J.	.. 5	Compton, L. H.	1	McNab (Sunderland) 1	

Total 78

F.A. CUP COMPETITION

3rd Rd. v. Bristol Rovers ..	.. (a)	5—1	Bastin 2, Drake 2, Bowden
4th Rd. v. Liverpool	.. (a)	2—0	Bowden, Hulme
5th Rd. v. Newcastle United	.. (a)	3—3	Bowden 2, Hulme
Replay v. Newcastle United	.. (h)	3—0	Bastin 2, Beasley
6th Rd. v. Barnsley	.. (h)	4—1	Beasley 2, Bowden, Bastin
S.F. v. Grimsby Town (at Huddersfield)	1—0	Bastin
Final v. Sheffield United	..	1—0	Drake

HONOURS

Bastin, C. S.: England v. Scotland, Wales, Austria and Germany.

Bowden, E. R.: England v. Wales, Ireland and Austria; F.L. v. S. L.

Copping, W.: England v. Austria and Belgium.

Crayston, W. J.: England v. Scotland, Wales, Austria and Belgium; Football League v. Irish League.

Drake, E.: England v. Wales.

Dunne, J.: Eire v. Hungary and Switzerland.

Hapgood, E. A.: England v. Scotland, Wales, Ireland, Austria, Belgium and Germany; Football League v. Scottish League.

John, R. F.: Wales v. Scotland.

Male, G.: England v. Scotland, Wales, Ireland, Austria, Belgium and Germany; Football League v. Scottish League.

B. Joy: England v. Belgium.

99

Season 1936–7

Football League—Division I

P.42 W.18 D.16 L.8 Goals 80—49 Pts.52 3rd

London Football Combination

P.46 W.30 D.8 L.8 Goals 139—39 Pts.68 1st

For the first time since 1929–30 the championship, the Cup and the F.A. Charity Shield were all beyond the grasp of Arsenal. The team, which had swept all opposition aside, was breaking up—Moss, who had to give up football after a recurring injury at Blackburn in the previous season, was replaced by Wilson, Swindin and Boulton in turn; on the other hand, Male had become captain of England, but Hapgood lost form and gave way for a time to Compton, L. Wing-halves Crayston and Copping were as good as any Arsenal ever had; indeed, these new players were generally equal to the Gunners' tradition, but the key to the problem was the difficulty in adequately replacing James, who was then in the twilight of his League career.

No, Arsenal were not quite the force of old, although, after being seventeenth in the League at the end of October (their first away goal was scored in that month!), they climbed to the top in the new year —such was the small margin between the leaders and the lower clubs—and stayed there until mid-April.

The inevitable challenge came from Manchester City, who, ninth in the League at the beginning of January, dropped only four points in the remaining games. Their victory over Arsenal on 10th April settled the issue, and the Highbury club dropped back to third place.

FOOTBALL LEAGUE RESULTS

Home	Opponents	Away	Home	Opponents	Away
1—1	Birmingham ..	.. 3—1	1—0	Liverpool ..	.. 1—2
0—0	Bolton Wanderers ..	.. 5—0	1—3	Manchester City	.. 0—2
1—1	Brentford ..	.. 0—2	1—1	Manchester United ..	.. 0—2
1—1	Charlton Athletic	.. 2—0	5—3	Middlesbrough	.. 1—1
4—1	Chelsea ..	.. 0—2	4—0	Portsmouth ..	.. 5—1
2—2	Derby County	.. 4—5	4—1	Preston North End ..	.. 3—1
3—2	Everton ..	.. 1—1	1—1	Sheffield Wednesday	0—0
0—0	Grimsby Town	.. 3—1	0—0	Stoke City ..	.. 0—0
1—1	Huddersfield Town ..	.. 0—0	4—1	Sunderland ..	.. 1—1
4—1	Leeds United	.. 4—3	2—0	West Bromwich Albion	4—2

3—0 Wolverhampton Wanderers .. 0—2

LEAGUE APPEARANCES (25 PLAYERS)

Bastin, C. S.	.. 33	Crayston, W. J.	30	Male, G. ..	.. 37
Beasley, A. ..	.. 7	Davidson, R. ..	28	Milne, J. V.	.. 19
Biggs, A. ..	.. 1	Drake, E. ..	26	Nelson, D.	.. 8
Boulton, F.	.. 21	Hapgood, E. A.	32	Roberts, H.	.. 30
Bowden, E. R.	.. 28	Hulme, J. H. A.	3	Sidey, N.	.. 6
Cartwright, S.	.. 2	James, A. ..	19	Swindin, G.	.. 19
Compton, D. C. S.	14	John, R. F. ..	5	Wilson, A.	.. 2
Compton, L. H.	.. 15	Joy, B. ..	6		
Copping, W.	.. 38	Kirchen, A. J. ..	33		

LEAGUE GOAL-SCORERS

Drake, E. ..	.. 20	Bastin, C. S. ..	5	Hapgood, E. A. ..	1
Kirchen, A. J.	.. 18	Compton, D. C. S.	4	James, A. ..	1
Davidson, R.	.. 9	Nelson, D. ..	3	Roberts, H. ..	1
Milne, J. V. ..	.. 9	Beasley, A. ..	1	Howe (Derby Co.)	1
Bowden, E. R.	.. 6	Crayston, W. J.	1	Total	80

F.A. CUP COMPETITION

3rd Rd. *v.* Chesterfield .. .. (a) 5—1 Drake 2, Kirchen 2, Davidson

4th Rd. *v.* Manchester United .. (h) 5—0 Bastin, Drake, Kirchen, Davidson, Brown (o.g.)

5th Rd. *v.* Burnley .. .. .. (a) 7—1 Drake 4, Crayston, Bastin, Kirchen

6th Rd. *v.* West Bromwich Albion (a) 1—3 Bastin

HONOURS

Bastin, C. S.: England *v.* Wales, Ireland; Football League *v.* Scottish League.

Bowden, E. R.: England *v.* Hungary; England trial.

Compton, L. H.: England trial.

Copping, W.: England *v.* Finland, Norway, Sweden.

Drake, E.: England *v.* Hungary.

Hapgood, E. A.: England *v.* Finland.

John, R. F.: Wales *v.* England.

Kirchen, A. J.: England *v.* Finland, Norway, Sweden; England trial.

Male, G.: England *v.* Scotland, Ireland, Finland, Hungary, Norway, Sweden; Football League *v.* Scottish League; England trial.

B. Joy: Amateur Australasian tour.

Season 1937-8

Football League—Division I

P.42 W.21 D.10 L.11 Goals 77—44 Pts.52 1st

London Football Combination

P.46 W.28 D.15 L.3 Goals 116—42 Pts.71 1st

For the remarkably small total of fifty-two points, out of a possible eighty-four, Arsenal became champions for the fifth time in eight years. Sheffield Wednesday were successful with a similar total in 1928-9 and Chelsea in 1954-5, but the championship has never been won with fewer since the First Division has consisted of twenty-two clubs.

The race for the League title between Arsenal and Wolverhampton Wanderers was not settled until the very last day of the season. With a week to go the Wolves, having a match in hand, were a point behind Arsenal. The Londoners had one match left—a home game against Bolton—while the Wolves had a home encounter against West Bromwich and an away fixture at Sunderland.

On the Monday evening Wolverhampton duly beat their neighbours by two goals to one and so became one point up on Arsenal with one match for each left to play. The game at Sunderland was scheduled to start a quarter of an hour before the Highbury encounter. Within half an hour Arsenal were two goals up, and the half-time score-board showed that the Wolves were losing 0—1 at Roker Park. Two more goals by Arsenal and then came the welcome news that there was no further score at Sunderland and that Wolverhampton had been beaten by that orphan goal.

Among the transfers from Highbury were Bowden (Newcastle), Hulme (Huddersfield) and Milne (Middlesbrough).

FOOTBALL LEAGUE RESULTS

Home	Opponents	Away	Home	Opponents	Away
0—0	Birmingham ..	.. 2—1	2—0	Chelsea ..	.. 2—2
2—1	Blackpool ..	.. 1—2	3—0	Derby County	.. 0—2
5—0	Bolton Wanderers	.. 0—1	2—1	Everton ..	.. 4—1
0—2	Brentford ..	.. 0—3	5—1	Grimsby Town	.. 1—2
2—2	Charlton Athletic	.. 3—0	3—1	Huddersfield Town	.. 1—2

Home	Opponents	Away	Home	Opponents	Away
4—1	Leeds United	.. 1—0	1—1	Portsmouth ..	.. 0—0
3—1	Leicester City..	.. 1—1	2—0	Preston North End	.. 3—1
1—0	Liverpool ..	.. 0—2	4—0	Stoke City ..	.. 1—1
2—1	Manchester City	.. 2—1	4—1	Sunderland ..	.. 1—1
1—2	Middlesbrough	.. 1—2	1—1	West Bromwich Albion	0—0
	5—0 Wolverhampton Wanderers .. 1—3				

LEAGUE APPEARANCES (29 PLAYERS)

Bastin, C. S.	.. 38	Copping, W.	.. 38	Joy, B. ..	.. 26
Biggs, A. ..	.. 2	Crayston, W. J.	31	Kirchen, A. J.	.. 19
Boulton, F.	.. 15	Davidson, R.	.. 5	Lewis, R. ..	.. 4
Bowden, E. R.	.. 10	Drake, E.	.. 27	Male, G. ..	.. 34
Bremner, G.	.. 2	Drury, G. B.	.. 11	Milne, J. V.	.. 16
Carr, E. ..	.. 11	Griffiths, M.	.. 9	Roberts, H.	.. 13
Cartwright, S.	.. 6	Hapgood, E. A.	41	Sidey, N. ..	.. 3
Collett, E. ..	.. 5	Hulme, J. H. A.	7	Swindin, G.	.. 17
Compton, D. C. S.	7	Hunt, G.	.. 18	Wilson, A.	.. 10
Compton, L. H.	.. 9	Jones, L. J.	.. 28		

LEAGUE GOAL-SCORERS

Drake, E. ..	.. 17	Milne, J. V.	.. 4	Lewis, R. ..	.. 2
Bastin, C. S.	.. 15	Hunt, G.	.. 3	Bowden, E. R.	.. 1
Carr, E. ..	.. 7	Jones, L. J.	.. 3	Bremner, G.	.. 1
Kirchen, A. J.	.. 6	Cartwright, S.	.. 2	Compton, D. C. S.	1
Griffiths, M.	.. 5	Davidson, R.	.. 2	Compton, L. H.	1
Crayston, W. J.	.. 4	Hulme, J. H. A.	2	Ford (Charlton) ..	1
					Total 77

F.A. CUP COMPETITION

3rd Rd. v. Bolton Wanderers	.. (h)	3—1	Bastin 2, Kirchen
4th Rd. v. Wolverhampton Wand.	(a)	2—1	Drake, Kirchen
5th Rd. v. Preston North End	.. (h)	0—1	

HONOURS

Bastin, C. S.: England v. Scotland, France, Germany, Switzerland.
Copping, W.: England v. Scotland, Wales, Ireland, Czechoslovakia.
Crayston, W. J.: England v. Wales, Ireland, Czechoslovakia.
Drake, E.: England v. France.
Hapgood, E. A.: England v. Scotland, France, Germany, Switzerland.
Jones, L. J.: Wales v. England, Ireland, Scotland.
Bowden, E. R., Compton, L. H., Copping, W., Crayston, W. J., and Kirchen, A. J.: England trials.

103

Football League—Division I

P.42 W.19 D.9 L.14 Goals 55—41 Pts.47 5th

London Football Combination

P.46 W.30 D.7 L.9 Goals 139—57 Pts.67 1st

As the attack still required a first-class schemer, George Allison went into the transfer market in a big way three weeks before the season began and obtained the Welsh and Wolverhampton inside-left Bryn Jones for £14,000. This figure topped the previous record by more than £3,000, and the vast publicity it aroused was unfortunately alien to Jones' modesty and quiet demeanour. Unlike James, who excelled when in the spotlight, Jones was uneasy and felt that he had to put in something extra than his natural game.

Nevertheless, on his début for Arsenal, he scored one of the two goals which beat Portsmouth and also netted the two credited to the Gunners in the next three games. His form deteriorated, however, and the more he tried to fit into the James style the worse he became. On the other hand, during Arsenal's Scandinavian tour at the end of the season, Jones revealed his old brilliant form and helped his side win all seven games with an aggregate of 33—4. So, perhaps, but for the war, that £14,000 gamble would have paid rich dividends.

In addition to Jones, other established first-team players, such as Bastin, Crayston and Leslie Jones, lost their confidence and younger players were drafted into the team. Included among these was Cumner, a left-winger who gained three Welsh caps during the season and, along with fellow internationals Bryn and Leslie Jones, gave Arsenal a distinct Welsh flavour in the attack. In spite of the team changes and hopeful experiments, Arsenal finished in fifth place, having won five of their last six games.

FOOTBALL LEAGUE RESULTS

Home	Opponents	Away	Home	Opponents	Away
0—0	Aston Villa ..	.. 3—1	2—0	Brentford ..	.. 0—1
3—1	Birmingham ..	.. 2—1	2—0	Charlton Athletic	.. 0—1
2—1	Blackpool ..	.. 0—1	1—0	Chelsea ..	.. 2—4
3—1	Bolton Wanderers	.. 1—1	1—2	Derby County	.. 2—1

Home	Opponents	Away	Home	Opponents	Away
1—2	Everton	0—2	2—1	Manchester United	0—1
2—0	Grimsby Town	1—2	1—2	Middlesbrough	1—1
1—0	Huddersfield Town	1—1	2—0	Portsmouth	0—0
2—3	Leeds United	2—4	1—0	Preston North End	1—2
0—0	Leicester City	2—0	4—1	Stoke City	0—1
2—0	Liverpool	2—2	2—0	Sunderland	0—0
	0—0 Wolverhampton Wanderers		1—0		

LEAGUE APPEARANCES (29 PLAYERS)

Bastin, C. S.	23	Curtis, G.	2	Lewis, R.	15
Bremner, G.	13	Drake, E.	38	Male, G.	28
Carr, E.	1	Drury, G. B.	23	Marks, G.	2
Cartwright, S.	3	Farr, A. M.	2	Nelson, D.	9
Collett, E.	9	Fields, A.	3	Pryde, D.	4
Compton, D. C. S.	1	Hapgood, E. A.	38	Pugh, S. J.	1
Compton, L. H.	18	Jones, B.	30	Swindin, G.	21
Copping, W.	26	Jones, L. T.	18	Walsh, W.	3
Crayston, W. J.	34	Joy, B.	39	Wilson, A.	19
Cumner, H.	12	Kirchen, A. J.	27		

LEAGUE GOAL-SCORERS

Drake, E.	14	Crayston, W. J.	3	Beattie (P.N.E.)	1
Kirchen, A. J.	9	Drury, G. B.	3	Rochford	
Lewis, R.	7	Compton, L. H.	2	(Portsmouth)	1
Jones, B.	4	Cumner, H.	2	Winter (Bolton W.)	1
Bastin, C. S.	3	Farr, A. M.	1	Total	55
Bremner, G.	3	Nelson, D.	1		

F.A. CUP COMPETITION

3rd Rd. *v.* Chelsea .. .. .. (a) 1—2 Bastin

HONOURS

Copping, W.: England *v.* Wales, Rest of Europe.
Cumner, H.: Wales *v.* England, Scotland, Ireland.
Hapgood, E. A.: England *v.* Scotland, Wales, Ireland, Yugoslavia,
  Italy, Norway, Rest of Europe; Football League *v.* I.L.
Jones, B.: Wales *v.* England, Scotland.
Jones, L. J.: Wales *v.* England, Scotland, Ireland.
Male, G.: England *v.* Yugoslavia, Italy, Rumania.

Arsenal in War-time

(*1939–40* to *1945–6*)

After completing three League games in 1939–40 season, in which the team drew at Wolverhampton 2—2 and beat Blackburn Rovers and Sunderland 1—0 and 5—2 respectively at Highbury, the football competitions were revised into regional leagues. Arsenal competed in the South 'A' and 'C' and were champions of the former.

In the following season the Club was placed third in the Regional League South, but qualified to meet Preston in the League War Cup final at Wembley. A feature of this season was the success of Leslie Compton at centre-forward. Opening the season at Southend, he banged in four goals in a 7—1 victory, and in the return fixture on 6th October he scored another two when Arsenal won 7—0.

In 1941–2 the Gunners were champions of the London League and topped Group I of the London War Cup, but were beaten in the semi-final. They went one better in 1942–3, however, and the combination of a very potent forward line, which netted 134 goals in thirty-six matches, and a powerful defence enabled the Club to carry off both the League South championship and the League South Cup; the latter by the convincing score of seven goals to one. Arsenal finished five points ahead of Tottenham Hotspur in the League.

Lewis, who had a tally of thirty-nine goals in the League— thirteen in the Cup and a total of fifty-three for the season—enjoyed a personal triumph in the Cup final at Wembley by claiming four well-taken goals. Arsenal's attack in this game swung along in perfect rhythm, and their shooting was so deadly that the result was determined in twenty minutes, by which time they led 4—1. Bastin, at inside-left, revealed astute generalship, and the other forwards responded wonderfully to overwhelm a heroic Charlton side.

In the following season (1943–4) twenty-three points out of a possible thirty were obtained at White Hart Lane (Arsenal's war-time home); Portsmouth being the only club to take away full points. Away games were not quite so profitable, with an equal share of won, drawn and lost matches. Although fourteenth position was the order at the end of September, the tide turned to enable Arsenal to obtain fourth place, behind Tottenham, Queen's Park Rangers and West Ham. In the League South Cup Arsenal started off well with a 7—1 win over Luton (Drake 4, Compton, D., 3), but thereafter could only draw two more and failed to overhaul Reading and Q.P.R. in the Group IV qualifying table.

Arsenal reached the semi-final of the League South Cup in 1944-5 and met Millwall at Stamford Bridge. Both Hall and Mortensen failed with penalty kicks for Arsenal, and Millwall, who until 11th January had not registered a win, went on to beat the Gunners 1—0. In the League Arsenal lost at Brighton by three goals to nil, and the player who scored twice and 'made' the third goal in this game was Hodges—an Arsenal forward on loan to Brighton. In the match at Fratton Park the Gunners played a storming finish by netting three times in the last fifteen minutes to beat Portsmouth 4—2.

In the last season of war-time football, as in the earlier ones, Arsenal, handicapped by a shortage of playing staff and the lack of a reserve side and a ground, many times fielded an unfamiliar eleven. Many of their star players were overseas and, under the policy of using as few guests as possible, youngsters had to be played without having known the testing London Combination football.

Nevertheless, a fine run of success was achieved from 17th November to 2nd February, when the Gunners collected twenty-two points out of a possible twenty-six and rose from eighteenth position in the table to the sixth. But the warning of coming difficulties was there!

1939–40

Regional League—South 'A': Champions

P.18 W.13 D.1 L.4 Goals 62—22 Pts.27 1st

Regional League—South 'C': Third.

P.18 W.9 D.5 L.4 Goals 41—26 Pts.23 3rd

Football League War Cup: 1st Rd. *v.* Notts Co. 9—1*; 2nd Rd. *v.* Reading 5—0*; 3rd Rd. *v* Birmingham 1—2*.

1940–1

Football League—South: Third

P.18 W.10 D.5 L.3 Goals 65—35 Average 1·85 3rd

Football League War Cup: 1st Rd. *v.* Brighton & Hove 7—2*; 2nd Rd. *v.* Watford 9—0*; 3rd Rd. *v.* West Ham United 3—1*; 4th Rd. *v.* Tottenham H. 3—2*; S.F. *v.* Leicester City 3—1; Final *v.* Preston North End 1—1 (Compton, D.) at Wembley; Replay at Blackburn 1—2 (Gallimore o.g.)

Team: Marks; Scott, Hapgood; Crayston, B. Joy, Collett; Kirchen, Jones, L., Compton, L. (Drake at Blackburn), Bastin, Compton, D.

* aggregate of games played at home and away.

1941-2

London League: Champions

P.30 W.23 D.2 L.5 Goals 108—43 Pts.48 1st

London War Cup—Group I: First

P.6 W.5 D.0 L.1 Goals 19—7 Pts.10 1st

1942-3

Football League—South: Champions

P.28 W.21 D.1 L.6 Goals 102—40 Pts.43 1st

Football League—South Cup—Group I: First

v. Brighton & Hove (h) 5—0; (a) 5—1
v. Watford .. (h) 4—1; (a) 1—1
v. West Ham Utd. (h) 3—1; (a) 3—1

P.6 W.5 D.1 L.0 Goals 21—5 Pts.11 1st

S.F. *v.* Q.P.R. at Stamford Bridge 4—1 (Briscoe, Lewis, Bastin, Compton, D.)

Final *v.* Charlton Athletic 7—1 at Wembley (Lewis 4, Drake 2, Compton, D.)

Team: Marks; Scott, Compton, L; Crayston, B. Joy, Male; Kirchen, Drake, Lewis, Bastin, Compton, D.

League Cup Winners Championship Match

Arsenal (winners of South Cup) 2 *v.* Blackpool (winners of North Cup) 4. Scorers: Lewis, Compton, D.

1943-4

Football League—South: Fourth

P.30 W.14 D.10 L.6 Goals 72—42 Pts.38 4th

Football League South Cup—Group 4: Third

P.6　W.1　D.2　L.3　Goals 13—15　Pts.4　3rd

1944–5

Football League—South: Eighth

P.30　W.14　D.3　L.13　Goals 77—57　Pts.31　8th

Football League South Cup—Group 1: First.

 v. Reading (h) 3—0; (a) 3—1
 v. Clapton O. (h) 5—0; (a) 3—1
 v. Portsmouth (h) 2—4; (a) 4—2

P.6　W.5　D.0　L.1　Goals 20—8　Pts.10　1st

S.F. *v.* Millwall at Stamford Bridge 0—1

Goal-scorers: Drake 24, Mortensen (Blackpool) 24, Farquhar 10, Wrigglesworth (Man. Utd.) 10, Bastin 8, Steele (Stoke C.) 6, Nelson 3, Horsman 3, Gallimore 2, Briscoe, Paton, Matthews (Stoke C.), Bowden and Holland 1 each. Defenders (o.g.) 2. Total 97 goals.

The above list includes the following scorers in the League South Cup: Drake 7, Mortensen 7, Farquhar 2, Wrigglesworth 2, Bowden and Paton 1 each. Total 20.

1945–6

Football League—South: Eleventh

P.42　W.16　D.11　L.15　Goals 76—73　Pts.43　11th

Goal-scorers: O'Flanagan 10, Drury 9, Bremner 8, Compton, D. 6, Farquhar 6, Bastin 5, Henley 4, Barnard 3, Hodges 3, Morgan 3, Cumner 2, Jones, L. 2, Horsfield 2, Roffi 2, McPherson 2, Lewis, Mercer, Wilson, Bowden, Holland and Nelson one each. Defenders (o.g.) 2. Total 76 goals.

F.A. Challenge Cup—Third Round

 1st Leg *v.* West Ham United (a)　(a)　0—6
 2nd Leg *v.* West Ham United　..　(h)　1—0 (Cumner)
 West Ham won on aggregate of 6—1

Friendly Match: Arsenal 3 *v.* Moscow Dynamo 4
 (Rooke, Mortensen 2)
Team: Griffiths (Cardiff); Scott, Bacuzzi (Fulham); Bastin, B. Joy, Halton (Bury); Matthews (Stoke), Drury, Rooke (Fulham), Mortensen (Blackpool), Cumner. Brown (Q.P.R.) replaced Griffiths in the second half.

Season 1946–7

Football League—Division I

P.42   W.16   D.9   L.17   Goals 72—70   Pts.41   13th

Football Combination—Section A

P.30   W.23   D.3   L.4   Goals 83—29   Pts.49   1st

Championship Match

v. Portsmouth (winners of Section B). Won 3—0

The return to Arsenal Stadium in August, after war-time fare at White Hart Lane, was not a happy homecoming, for it was not until the middle of October that the Gunners first registered a victory there. Lewis, on the other hand, celebrated the return to League football with eleven goals in the first ten matches out of Arsenal's total of fifteen.

From the first eighteen matches Arsenal collected only eleven points and were separated from Huddersfield Town, at the foot of the table, by ·142 of a goal. The turning point came when Mercer (Everton) and Rooke (Fulham) were transferred to Highbury. The half-back line became a settled one, reading: Sloan, Compton and Mercer, while the vigour and enthusiasm of Rooke, who scored twenty-one goals in twenty-four games, infused a new strength into the forward line.

Swindin was peerless in goal, particularly in a classic drawn game against Wolverhampton, and he was well supported at full-back by Scott and Barnes, who made an amazing return after injury. In the problem position of the left-wing no fewer than eleven players were tried; O'Flanagan and Calverly, each with eleven appearances, being the most frequent.

In the first eleven minutes of the second replay against Chelsea, Logie missed an open goal, Rooke hit the crossbar and Lewis shot wide from a penalty. The Pensioners gradually gained the ascendancy, however, and two well-taken goals by Lawton earned them the right to figure in the fourth round.

FOOTBALL LEAGUE RESULTS

Home	Opponents	Away	Home	Opponents	Away
0—2	Aston Villa ..	.. 2—0	1—2	Huddersfield Town ..	0—0
1—3	Blackburn Rovers	.. 2—1	4—2	Leeds United	.. 1—1
1—1	Blackpool ..	.. 1—2	1—2	Liverpool ..	.. 2—4
2—2	Bolton Wanderers	.. 3—1	6—2	Manchester United	.. 2—5
2—2	Brentford ..	.. 1—0	4—0	Middlesbrough ..	0—2
1—0	Charlton Athletic	.. 2—2	2—1	Portsmouth ..	.. 2—0
1—2	Chelsea ..	.. 1—2	4—1	Preston North End	.. 0—2
0—1	Derby County	.. 1—0	2—3	Sheffield United	.. 1—2
2—1	Everton ..	.. 2—3	1—0	Stoke City ..	.. 1—3
5—3	Grimsby Town	.. 0—0	2—2	Sunderland ..	.. 4—1

1—1 Wolverhampton Wanderers .. 1—6

LEAGUE APPEARANCES (31 PLAYERS)

Barnes, W. ..	.. 26	Hodges, C.	.. 2	Platt, E. ..	.. 4
Bastin, C. S.	.. 6	Jones, B.	.. 26	Rooke, R.	.. 24
Calverly, A.	.. 11	Joy, B. ..	.. 13	Rudkin, T.	.. 5
Collett, E. ..	.. 6	Lewis, R.	.. 28	Scott, L. ..	.. 28
Compton, D. C. S.	1	Logie, J.	.. 35	Sloan, P.	.. 30
Compton, L. H.	.. 36	Male, G.	.. 15	Smith, A.	.. 3
Curtis, G. ..	.. 11	McPherson, I. ..	37	Swindin, G.	.. 38
Drury, G. ..	.. 4	Mercer, J.	.. 25	Wade, J. ..	.. 2
Fields, A. ..	.. 8	Morgan, S.	.. 2	Waller, H.	.. 8
Grant, C. ..	.. 2	Nelson, D.	.. 10		
Gudmundsson, A. ..	2	O'Flanagan, K.	14		

LEAGUE GOAL-SCORERS

Lewis, R. ..	.. 29	McPherson, I. ..	6	Compton, D. C. S.	1
Rooke, R. ..	.. 21	O'Flanagan, K.	3	Jones, B. ..	.. 1
Logie, J. ..	.. 8	Rudkin, T. ..	2	Sloan, P. ..	.. 1

Total 72

F.A. CUP COMPETITION

3rd Rd. v. Chelsea .. .. .. (a) 1—1 McPherson
Replay v. Chelsea .. .. (h) 1—1 Rooke
Replay v. Chelsea (at White Hart Lane) 0—2

FOOTBALL COMBINATION CUP

Semi-Final v. Coventry City .. .. (a) 1—0 Morgan (pen.)
Final v. Swansea Town (at White Hart Lane) 1—2 Sherratt.
Team: Platt; Jones, S., Wade; Waller, Smith, L., Horsfield; Holland, Curtis, Sherratt, Morgan, Rudkin.

Jones, B.: Wales *v.* Scotland, Ireland.

Macaulay, A.: Scotland *v.* England; Gt. Britain *v.* Rest of Europe.

Mercer, J.: Football League *v.* Eire.

Scott, L.: England *v.* Scotland, Wales, Ireland, Eire, France, Holland, Switzerland, Portugal; Football League *v.* Scottish League, Irish League.

Sloan, P.: Ireland *v.* Wales.

Dr. K. O'Flanagan: Eire *v.* Spain, Portugal.

J. KELSEY

A. MACAULAY

A. MACKIE

G. MALE

I. McPHERSON

J. MERCER

F. MOSS

T. PARKER

Season 1947-8

Football League—Division I

P.42 W.23 D.13 L.6 Goals 81—32 Pts.59 1st

Football Combination—Section B

P.30 W.20 D.6 L.4 Goals 55—26 Pts.46 1st

Championship Match

v. West Ham Utd. (winners of Section A). Lost 0—2

In equalling the six championship wins of Aston Villa and Sunderland, Arsenal headed the League from start to finish. In addition, the Club enjoyed its best-ever start and its longest run without defeat (seventeen matches from 23rd August to 29th November). By conceding only thirty-two goals, it created a defensive record for Division I and, in calling upon eighteen players to win the championship, equalled the record set up by West Bromwich Albion in 1919–20.

The team, captained by Mercer, was generally: Swindin; Scott, Barnes; Macaulay, Compton, L., Mercer; Roper, Logie, Lewis, Rooke, McPherson.

The first six matches were won with an aggregate of nineteen goals to five, and the unbeaten run was ended at Derby on the last Saturday in November when the County won a thrilling game by an orphan goal. Arsenal ended the glorious campaign on a triumphant note with the biggest win of the season, when goals by Rooke (4), Logie, Compton, D. (2) and Forbes gave them an 8—0 victory over Grimsby Town.

On a day of cup-tie shocks, which included the home defeats of Burnley, Birmingham and Bolton by Swindon, Notts County and Tottenham respectively, Arsenal, too, fell at home at the first hurdle. Second Division Bradford upset all form, and a goal by Elliott, later of England, Burnley and Sunderland fame, was enough to give the Yorkshire team victory.

Home	Opponents	Away	Home	Opponents	Away
1—0	Aston Villa ..	.. 2—4	2—0	Huddersfield Town ..	.. 1—1
2—0	Blackburn Rovers ..	.. 1—0	1—2	Liverpool ..	.. 3—1
2—1	Blackpool ..	.. 0—3	1—1	Manchester City ..	.. 0—0
2—0	Bolton Wanderers ..	.. 1—0	2—1	Manchester United ..	.. 1—1
3—0	Burnley ..	.. 1—0	7—0	Middlesbrough ..	.. 1—1
6—0	Charlton Athletic ..	.. 4—2	0—0	Portsmouth ..	.. 0—0
0—2	Chelsea ..	.. 0—0	3—0	Preston North End ..	.. 0—0
1—2	Derby County ..	.. 0—1	3—2	Sheffield United ..	.. 2—1
1—1	Everton ..	.. 2—0	3—0	Stoke City ..	.. 0—0
8—0	Grimsby Town ..	.. 4—0	3—1	Sunderland ..	.. 1—1
		5—2 Wolverhampton Wanderers .. 1—1			

LEAGUE APPEARANCES (19 PLAYERS)

Barnes, W. ..	.. 35	Logie, J.	.. 39	Scott, L. ..	.. 39			
Compton, D. C. S. ..	14	Macaulay, A. ..	40	Sloan, P. ..	.. 3			
Compton, L. H.	.. 35	McPherson, I. ..	29	Smith, L. ..	.. 1			
Fields, A. ..	.. 6	Male, G.	.. 8	Swindin, G.	.. 42			
Forbes, A. ..	.. 11	Mercer, J.	.. 40	Wade, J. ..	.. 3			
Jones, B. ..	.. 7	Rooke, R.	.. 42					
Lewis, R. ..	.. 28	Roper, D.	.. 40					

LEAGUE GOAL-SCORERS

Rooke, R.	.. 33	Compton, D. C. S.	6	Moss (Aston Villa)	1
Lewis, R. ..	.. 14	McPherson, I.	.. 5	Robinson	
Roper, D.	.. 10	Forbes, A.	.. 2	(Middlesbrough)	1
Logie, J. ..	.. 8	Jones, B. ..	.. 1	Total	81

F.A. CUP COMPETITION

3rd Rd. *v.* Bradford .. .. (h) 0—1

FOOTBALL COMBINATION CUP

Semi-Final *v.* Leicester City .. (h) 0—1

HONOURS

Barnes, W.: Wales *v.* England, Scotland, Ireland.
Compton, L. H.: Football League *v.* League of Ireland.
Jones, B.: Wales *v.* England, Scotland.
Macaulay, A.: Scotland *v.* England, Wales, Ireland,
Belgium, France, Switzerland.
Scott, L.: England *v.* Scotland, Wales, Ireland, Belgium,
Italy, Sweden; Football League *v.* League of Ireland.

Football League—Division I

P.42 W.18 D.13 L.11 Goals 74—44 Pts.49 5th

Football Combination—Section B

P.30 W.20 D.5 L.5 Goals 62—31 Pts.45 1st

Championship Match

v. Chelsea (winners of Section A). Lost 1—3

The brilliance of the previous season was not sustained in this campaign, in which a series of injuries to players was a key factor. Nevertheless, the season was by no means a poor one. Scott was injured on international duty and played in only eleven games, but the switching of Barnes to the right flank and the conversion of Lionel Smith from centre-half to left-back proved to be a very adequate combination.

The outstanding match of the season was the F.A. Charity Shield game *v.* the cup-holders Manchester United at Highbury. It was soccer at its best—seven goals and a wealth of craft. Arsenal scored three times in the first five minutes; clever play by Lewis gave Bryn Jones the chance to open the score, then came a lovely header by Lewis and, a minute later, a low drive from Rooke made the score 3—0. Rowley quickly reduced the arrears but, again, Lewis beat three men to score a grand goal. By half-time Burke had made the score-sheet read 4—2, and after Mitten had pulled Arsenal back to 4—3 early in the second half the result was in doubt until the last kick of the game.

In the League Arsenal rose from the fifteenth position in the second week in September to the fifth place by Christmas. On 19th February, Arsenal put an end to Wolverhampton's fine home record of nine successive victories with flashing non-stop football that well earned a 3—1 success. Two picture-book goals by Lewis early in the game paved the way to victory. Logie, who was the star of the attack, netted the third, while Pye got a consolation goal fifteen minutes from the end when the Wolves were awarded a penalty for hands against Compton. Arsenal's team read: Platt;

Barnes, Smith; Macaulay, Compton, Mercer; McPherson, Logie, Lewis, Lishman, Vallance. Also on that day, at Highbury, Arsenal fielded in their reserves Scott, Rooke, Bryn Jones and Roper. The match—against Southampton Reserves—was drawn, two goals each.

FOOTBALL LEAGUE RESULTS

Home	Opponents	Away	Home	Opponents	Away
3—1	Aston Villa ..	.. 0—1	1—1	Liverpool ..	.. 1—0
2—0	Birmingham ..	.. 1—1	1—1	Manchester City	.. 3—0
2—0	Blackpool ..	.. 1—1	0—1	Manchester United	.. 0—2
5—0	Bolton Wanderers	.. 0—1	1—1	Middlesbrough	.. 1—0
3—1	Burnley ..	.. 1—1	0—1	Newcastle United	.. 2—3
2—0	Charlton Athletic	.. 3—4	3—2	Portsmouth ..	.. 1—4
1—2	Chelsea ..	.. 1—0	0—0	Preston North End	.. 1—1
3—3	Derby County	.. 1—2	5—3	Sheffield United	.. 1—1
5—0	Everton ..	.. 0—0	3—0	Stoke City ..	.. 0—1
3—0	Huddersfield Town	.. 1—1	5—0	Sunderland ..	.. 1—1
		3—1	Wolverhampton Wanderers	.. 3—1	

LEAGUE APPEARANCES (20 PLAYERS)

Barnes, W. ..	.. 40	Lewis, R.	.. 25	Rooke, R.			.. 22	
Compton, D. C. S. ..	6	Lishman, D.	.. 23	Roper, D.			.. 31	
Compton, L. H.	.. 40	Logie, J.	.. 35	Scott, L. ..			.. 12	
Daniel, R. ..	.. 1	Macaulay, A.	.. 39	Smith, L. ..			.. 32	
Fields, A. ..	.. 1	McPherson, I.	.. 33	Swindin, G.			.. 32	
Forbes, A. ..	.. 25	Mercer, J.	.. 33	Vallance, T.			.. 14	
Jones, B. ..	.. 8	Platt, E.	.. 10					

LEAGUE GOAL-SCORERS

Lewis, R. ..	.. 16	McPherson, I.	.. 5	Vallance, T.	.. 2
Rooke, R.	.. 14	Roper, D.	.. 5	Jones, B. ..	.. 1
Lishman, D.	.. 12	Forbes, A.	.. 4	Macaulay, A.	.. 1
Logie, J. ..	.. 11	Compton, D. C. S.	.. 2	o.g. (Sheff. Utd.)..	1

Total 74

F.A. CUP COMPETITION

3rd Rd. v. Tottenham H.	.. (h)	3—0	McPherson, Lishman, Roper
4th Rd. v. Derby County	.. (a)	0—1	

Barnes, W.: Wales *v.* England, Scotland, Ireland.
Jones, B.: Wales *v.* Scotland.
Scott, L.: England *v.* Wales, Ireland, Denmark;
Football League *v.* Scottish League.

Season 1949–50

Football League—Division I

P.42 W.19 D.11 L.12 Goals 79—55 Pts.49 6th

Football Combination—Section A

P.30 W.15 D.4 L.11 Goals 59—33 Pts.34 3rd

Opening the season with four defeats in five matches, there was little to indicate what was in store. The acquisition of Cox from the Spurs and the intelligent play of young Goring at centre-forward helped make such a revival that by Christmas the Club was challenging the leaders, Liverpool.

In the new year the League results, however, paled in the brilliance of a wonderful Cup run, in which Arsenal qualified to appear at Wembley without having to play outside the Metropolis. The two semi-final games against Chelsea at White Hart Lane were particularly memorable. In the first Chelsea led by two goals until Cox reduced the arrears by a goal scored direct from a corner on the stroke of half-time, and then in a pulsating second half Leslie Compton equalized with a terrific header from his brother's well-placed corner.

After ninety minutes in the replay the score-sheet was still blank, and the minutes of extra time were ticking away when Cox set off on a long solo dribble which ended in a fine low shot into the net, to give Arsenal the right to meet Liverpool in the final.

CUP FINAL, WEMBLEY, 1949–50

Arsenal 2 v. Liverpool 0

In winning the trophy for the third time Arsenal in 1950 equalled Bolton Wanderers' record of three victories at Wembley. Newcastle, however, soon claimed the record for themselves, and by 1955 had registered their fifth Cup-final win there.

Arsenal's final against Liverpool was a personal triumph for Reg Lewis, who with typical nonchalant coolness scored two brilliantly taken goals. The first came in the eighteenth minute. Barnes passed upfield to Logie, who brought the ball under control beautifully. Goring moved away from the middle, taking Hughes with him, and Logie slipped the ball into the open space. Lewis, showing superb anticipation, had collected it in a flash. Two strides had taken him clear of the defence and Sidlow, the Liverpool 'keeper, was helpless to deal with a fine low shot to the left-hand corner of the goal.

The second was scored after a similar period of the second half. Goring, out on the left-wing, put over a long diagonal cross, Cox, with his back to the goal, back-heeled the ball inside Spicer and once again Lewis was speeding through with the ball at his toes. A hard and low shot from near the penalty spot and the ball was despatched to the back of the net.

Arsenal's accurate ground passing and their smooth efficiency, in which they made the ball do the work, were too much for Liverpool. Furthermore, the Anfield inside-forwards could do little against the powerful Arsenal half-back line, in which Forbes was often brilliant and always tireless. Nevertheless, Liverpool had their moments, especially in a last dying fling—Swindin saved a shot from Payne at the second attempt on the goal-line and Fagan struck the crossbar with a dangerous header. In addition, Liddell was always very menacing in his raids on the left-wing, but his inside partners were unable to make good use of his passes. In a final brim-full of excellent football, most of the footcraft came from the confident Londoners.

Arsenal saved their peak performance for this game and, whereas so often the team had relied on its mighty defence, against Liverpool it was the forward line that took things into its own hands and had the Anfield defence on the run. Goring, in particular, leading his line with the intelligence and aplomb of a veteran, was a constant source of danger.

CUP FINAL TEAMS

Arsenal: Swindin; Scott, Barnes; Forbes, Compton, L., Mercer; Cox, Logie, Goring, Lewis, Compton, D.

Liverpool: Sidlow; Lambert, Spicer; Taylor, Hughes, Jones; Payne, Baron, Stubbins, Fagan, Liddell.

Home	Opponents	Away	Home	Opponents	Away
1—3	Aston Villa ..	.. 1—1	1—0	Huddersfield Town ..	2—2
4—2	Birmingham ..	.. 1—2	1—2	Liverpool ..	.. 0—2
1—0	Blackpool ..	.. 1—2	4—1	Manchester City ..	2—0
1—1	Bolton Wanderers ..	2—2	0—0	Manchester United ..	0—2
0—1	Burnley ..	.. 0—0	1—1	Middlesbrough ..	1—1
2—3	Charlton Athletic ..	1—1	4—2	Newcastle United ..	3—0
2—3	Chelsea ..	.. 2—1	2—0	Portsmouth ..	.. 1—2
1—0	Derby County ..	2—1	6—0	Stoke City ..	.. 5—2
5—2	Everton ..	.. 1—0	5—0	Sunderland ..	.. 2—4
2—1	Fulham ..	.. 2—2	4—1	West Bromwich Albion	2—1

1—1 Wolverhampton Wanderers .. 0—3

LEAGUE APPEARANCES (22 PLAYERS)

Barnes, W. ..	.. 38	Lewis, R.	.. 31	Scott, L.	.. 15
Compton, D. C. S. ..	11	Lishman, D.	.. 14	Shaw, A. ..	.. 5
Compton, L. H.	.. 35	Logie, J.	.. 34	Smith. L. ..	.. 31
Cox, F. ..	.. 32	Macaulay, A.	.. 24	Swindin, G.	.. 23
Daniel, R. ..	.. 6	McPherson, I. ..	27	Vallance, T.	.. 1
Forbes, A. ..	.. 23	Mercer, J.	.. 35	Wade, J. ..	.. 1
Goring, H. ..	.. 29	Platt, E.	.. 19		
Kelly, N. ..	.. 1	Roper, D.	.. 27		

LEAGUE GOAL-SCORERS

Goring, H. ..	.. 21	Roper, D.	.. 7	Forbes, A.	.. 2
Lewis, R. ..	.. 19	Barnes, W.	.. 5	Compton, D. C. S.	1
Lishman, D.	.. 9	Cox, F.	.. 3	o.g.	.. 2
Logie, J. ..	.. 7	McPherson, I. ..	3	Total	79

F.A. CUP COMPETITION

3rd Rd. v. Sheffield Wednesday	.. (h)	1—0	Lewis
4th Rd. v. Swansea Town ..	.. (h)	2—1	Logie, Barnes
5th Rd. v. Burnley ..	.. (h)	2—0	Lewis, Compton, D.
6th Rd. v. Leeds United ..	.. (h)	1—0	Lewis
S.F. v. Chelsea (at White Hart Lane)		2—2	Cox, Compton, L.
Replay v. Chelsea (at White Hart Lane)		1—0	Cox
Final v. Liverpool ..	.. ..	2—0	Lewis 2

HONOURS

Barnes, W.: Wales v. England, Scotland, Ireland, Belgium.
Forbes, A.: Scotland v. England, France, Portugal.
Scott, L.: Football League v. League of Ireland.

Football League—Division I

P.42   W.19   D.9   L.14   Goals 73—56   Pts.47   5th

Football Combination—Section A

P.30   W.21   D.5   L.4   Goals 73—25   Pts.47   1st

Championship Match

v. Chelsea (winners Section B). Won 5—0

The Arsenal story of this season can be divided into two distinct phases. The period up to the middle of December, when the Club was riding high at the head of the table; and the remainder of the campaign, when less than a point per game was the average reward.

The turning point was the home fixture against Stoke when the leading goal-scorer, Lishman, broke a leg. The inside-left had by then netted sixteen goals, including four against Sunderland and a hat-trick against Fulham. Lewis came into the side for Lishman, but although he scored eight times in fourteen appearances the attack did not blend quite so successfully.

Swindin was also injured on Christmas Day against Stoke, which caused him to miss sixteen games, including the cup-ties. Platt, however, proved an able deputy and, in addition, the young Welsh goalkeeper Kelsey was introduced into the League side for four matches. The full-back partnership was usually Barnes and Smith, L., while it was pleasing to see Scott recover from injuries later in the season. The half-back line of Forbes, Compton, L. and Mercer, with reserves Shaw and Bowen, was well up to the Arsenal standard, and it was particularly satisfying that Compton, L. was at last honoured by the England selectors. Smith and Daniel were also capped for the first time. Among the players who made their League début were Bowen, Holton, Kelsey, Marden and Milton.

FOOTBALL LEAGUE RESULTS

Home	Opponents	Away	Home	Opponents	Away
2—1	Aston Villa ..	.. 1—1	1—1	Bolton Wanderers ..	.. 0—3
4—4	Blackpool ..	.. 1—0	0—1	Burnley ..	.. 1—0

Home	Opponents	Away	Home	Opponents	Away
2—5	Charlton Athletic	.. 3—1	3—1	Middlesbrough	.. 1—2
0—0	Chelsea	.. 1—0	0—0	Newcastle United	.. 1—2
3—1	Derby County	.. 2—4	0—1	Portsmouth ..	.. 1—1
2—1	Everton	.. 1—1	3—0	Sheffield Wednesday	2—0
5—1	Fulham	.. 2—3	0—3	Stoke City ..	.. 0—1
6—2	Huddersfield Town	.. 2—2	5—1	Sunderland ..	.. 2—0
1—2	Liverpool	.. 3—1	2—2	Tottenham Hotspur ..	0—1
3—0	Manchester United	.. 1—3	3—0	West Bromwich Albion	0—2
	2—1 Wolverhampton Wanderers		.. 1—0		

LEAGUE APPEARANCES (23 PLAYERS)

Barnes, W. ..	.. 35	Holton, C. C.	.. 10	Milton, C. A.	.. 1
Bowen, D. L.	.. 7	Kelsey, A. J.	.. 4	Platt, E. ..	.. 17
Compton, L. H.	.. 36	Lewis, R.	.. 14	Roper, D.	.. 34
Cox, F. ..	.. 13	Lishman, D.	.. 26	Scott, L. ..	.. 17
Daniel, R. ..	.. 5	Logie, J.	.. 39	Shaw, A. ..	.. 16
Fields, A. ..	.. 1	Marden, R.	.. 11	Smith, L. ..	.. 32
Forbes, A. ..	.. 32	McPherson, I. ..	.. 26	Swindin, G.	.. 21
Goring, H. ..	.. 34	Mercer, J.	.. 31		

LEAGUE GOAL-SCORERS

Lishman, D.	.. 17	Roper, D.	.. 7	Cox, F. ..	.. 2
Goring, H. ..	.. 15	Holton, C. C. ..	5	Marden, R.	.. 2
Logie, J.	.. 9	Forbes, A.	.. 4	o.g. ..	.. 1
Lewis, R. ..	.. 8	Barnes, W.	.. 3		Total 73

F.A. CUP COMPETITION

3rd Rd. *v.* Carlisle United ..	.. (h)	0—0	
Replay *v.* Carlisle United ..	.. (a)	4—1	Lewis 2, Logie, Goring
4th Rd. *v.* Northampton Town	.. (h)	3—2	Lewis 2, Roper
5th Rd. *v.* Manchester United	.. (a)	0—1	

HONOURS

Barnes, W.: Wales *v.* England, Scotland, Ireland, Portugal.
Compton, L. H.: England *v.* Wales, Yugoslavia.
Daniel, R.: Wales *v.* England, Ireland, Portugal.
Forbes, A.: Scotland *v.* Wales, Ireland, Austria.
Smith, L.: England *v.* Wales.

Season 1951-2

Football League—Division I

P.42 W.21 D.11 L.10 Goals 80—61 Pts.53 3rd

Football Combination—Section B

P.30 W.18 D.7 L.5 Goals 70—32 Pts.43 2nd

So near and yet so far! Arsenal were within an ace of winning the League championship, or the Cup, or both; but, as in 1931, they won neither. The elusive 'double' could have been theirs if they had won their three last games—away to West Bromwich and Manchester United and the Cup final.

Injuries, however, deemed otherwise. Daniel broke his wrist in the Easter games, his deputy Shaw also fractured his arm, while Logie and Lishman had spells in hospital. Several other players, too, were on the injured list during the season.

In the League Arsenal were always hovering near the top, and were actually in the lead during November and December, which speaks in itself of the resources of the reserves. Lishman, who scored four hat-tricks (three in successive home games *v.* Fulham, W.B.A. and Bolton), was the leading goal-scorer, and Holton, converted from right-back, continued as an effective leader of the attack, notching seventeen goals in twenty-eight appearances.

With both Daniel and Shaw injured, Compton, L. was called upon to make his last League appearance for the Gunners in April—twenty years after his début.

CUP FINAL, WEMBLEY, 1951-2

Arsenal 0 v. Newcastle United 1

Arsenal's sixth Cup final can be summed up in five words—'They were glorious in defeat.' It is a fact that the majority of the newspaper headlines indicated that, although Newcastle won the trophy, the honours of the match went to Arsenal.

So cruelly beset by a series of injuries in chasing the 'double', the Gunners were once again unfortunate to lose one of their key men early in this vital game. Barnes twisted a ligament in his knee when

123

tackling Milburn eighteen minutes after the start and went off the field. He returned later with his knee bandaged and pluckily stayed until the thirty-fourth minute, when he went off for good.

Until the moment of Barnes' injury the London side was definitely on top; Swindin had hardly a worthwhile shot to deal with, whereas, at the other end, Lishman, who was playing one of his best games for Arsenal, hooked the ball just the wrong side of the post; then Simpson had to be at his best to save a hard drive from Roper; once Holton lost control when clean through; and so it went on!

When reduced to ten men, Roper moved to right-back and Arsenal operated with four forwards, the versatile Cox being alternately right-winger or centre-forward. Holton, somewhat overawed by the occasion, could do little right and spent most of the second half on the left-wing.

Every Arsenal man fought desperately to keep Newcastle out and to launch attacks of their own. Even Smith, who played a heroic game and once kicked a Milburn header off the line, was taking the ball through to get the forwards going. Roper ran himself to a standstill to counter the tricky moves of Mitchell, Newcastle's best forward; Daniel, with an arm in plaster, kept Milburn in check; Mercer and Forbes were tenacious in both attack and defence, while Swindin was also outstanding. Lishman put in many dangerous dribbles and Logie, out of hospital only three days previously, combined well with Forbes, who often acted as a fifth forward, and Cox repeatedly had Brennan in trouble.

Newcastle had their chances of course; Walker, Mitchell and Foulkes all shot wide when in a good scoring position. But their forwards generally played into the hands of the Gunners by making little headway with their close passing, and Arsenal usually had time to cover up with their splendid defence-in-depth plan.

With eleven minutes to go, and still no score, Arsenal earned a corner. Every Arsenal player, except Swindin, Roper and Daniel, crowded into the Newcastle penalty area. Cox took the kick and the ball sped over to the head of the unmarked Lishman, who headed goalwards. The ball struck the crossbar and bounced over the top. So near!

Five minutes later Mitchell rounded Roper and centred. The ball came across to George Robledo, who headed it against the post. This time it rolled slowly and dramatically to the back of the net.

And so Newcastle became the first team to defend the Cup with success since Blackburn Rovers did so sixty-one years previously.

CUP FINAL TEAMS

Arsenal: Swindin; Barnes, Smith, L.; Forbes, Daniel, Mercer; Cox, Logie, Holton, Lishman, Roper.

Newcastle United: Simpson; Cowell, McMichael; Harvey, Brennan, Robledo (E.); Walker, Foulkes, Milburn, Robledo, G., Mitchell.

FOOTBALL LEAGUE RESULTS

Home	Opponents	Away	Home	Opponents	Away
2—1	Aston Villa ..	.. 0—1	2—2	Manchester City ..	2—0
4—1	Blackpool ..	.. 0—0	1—3	Manchester United ..	1—6
4—2	Bolton Wanderers ..	1—2	3—1	Middlesbrough ..	3—0
1—0	Burnley ..	.. 1—0	1—1	Newcastle United ..	0—2
2—1	Charlton Athletic ..	3—1	4—1	Portsmouth ..	.. 1—1
2—1	Chelsea ..	.. 3—1	3—3	Preston North End ..	0—2
3—1	Derby County ..	2—1	4—1	Stoke City ..	.. 1—2
4—3	Fulham ..	.. 0—0	3—0	Sunderland ..	.. 1—4
2—2	Huddersfield Town ..	3—2	1—1	Tottenham Hotspur ..	2—1
0—0	Liverpool ..	.. 0—0	6—3	West Bromwich Albion	1—3
			2—2	Wolverhampton Wanderers ..	1—2

LEAGUE APPEARANCES (22 PLAYERS)

Barnes, W. ..	.. 41	Holton, C. C. ..	.. 28	Roper, D.	.. 30
Bowen, D. ..	.. 8	Lewis, R.	.. 9	Scott, L. ..	.. 4
Chenhall, J.	.. 3	Lishman, D. ..	.. 38	Shaw, A. ..	.. 8
Compton, L. H.	.. 4	Logie, J.	.. 34	Smith, L. ..	.. 28
Cox, F. ..	.. 25	Marden, R.	.. 7	Swindin, G.	.. 42
Daniel, R. ..	.. 34	Mercer, J.	.. 36	Wade, J. ..	.. 8
Forbes, A. ..	.. 38	Milton, C. A. ..	20		
Goring, H. ..	.. 16	Robertson, J. W.	1		

LEAGUE GOAL-SCORERS

Lishman, D...	.. 23	Milton, C. A. ..	5	Barnes, W.	.. 2
Holton, C. C.	.. 17	Goring, H. ..	4	Forbes, A.	.. 2
Roper, D. ..	.. 9	Logie, J.	.. 4	Marden, R.	.. 2
Lewis, R. ..	.. 8	Cox, F.	.. 3	o.g. ..	.. 1
				Total	80

F.A. CUP COMPETITION

3rd Rd. *v.* Norwich City	..	.. (a)	5—0	Lishman 2, Logie, Roper, Goring
4th Rd. *v.* Barnsley	..	.. (h)	4—0	Lewis 3, Lishman
5th Rd. *v.* Leyton Orient	..	.. (a)	3—0	Lishman 2, Lewis
6th Rd. *v.* Luton Town	..	.. (a)	3—2	Cox 2, Milton
S.F. *v.* Chelsea (at Tottenham)			1—1	Cox
Replay *v.* Chelsea (at Tottenham)			3—0	Cox 2, Lishman
Final *v.* Newcastle United		..	0—1	

HONOURS

Barnes, W.: Wales *v.* England, Scotland, Ireland, Rest of U.K.

Daniel, R.: Wales *v.* England, Scotland, Ireland, Rest of U.K.

Forbes, A.: Scotland *v.* Wales, Denmark, Sweden.

Milton, C. A.: England *v.* Austria.

Smith, L.: England *v.* Wales, Ireland; Football League *v.* League of Ireland.

Season 1952–3

Football League—Division I

P.42 W.21 D.12 L.9 Goals 97—64 Pts.54 1st

Football Combination—Division I

P.30 W.12 D.4 L.14 Goals 47—46 Pts.28 9th

The name of Arsenal was engraved on the League championship trophy for the seventh time at the end of this season, thus exceeding by one the record set up by Aston Villa and Sunderland.

A very spirited challenge from Preston North End threatened the supremacy of the London team and when they defeated Arsenal 2—0 at Deepdale, and so drew level at fifty-two points each with one game to play, it looked serious. The North End played their remaining fixture on the following Wednesday before embarking on a Continental tour and defeated Derby by an orphan penalty goal.

Arsenal, in their turn, took the field against Burnley two days later, knowing that nothing less than a victory would give them the title. On that fateful evening goals by Forbes, Lishman and Logie put them 3—1 in front at half-time, and then Burnley scored again, and it was a thankful Arsenal team that managed to keep its goal intact for the remaining hectic minutes of the game.

Following his 1952 Cup-final injury, Barnes did not play at all during the season, but Wade and Chenhall filled the breach admirably. The brilliance of Logie's play was recognized by the Scottish selectors for the international against Ireland—an honour long overdue and richly deserved by Soccer's 'post-war Alex James'.

FOOTBALL LEAGUE RESULTS

Home	Opponents	Away	Home	Opponents	Away
3—1	Aston Villa	2—1	2—1	Manchester United	0—0
3—1	Blackpool	2—3	2—1	Middlesbrough	0—2
4—1	Bolton Wanderers	6—4	3—0	Newcastle United	2—2
3—2	Burnley	1—1	3—1	Portsmouth	2—2
0—1	Cardiff City	0—0	1—1	Preston North End	0—2
3—4	Charlton Athletic	2—2	2—2	Sheffield Wednesday	4—1
2—0	Chelsea	1—1	3—1	Stoke City	1—1
6—2	Derby County	0—2	1—2	Sunderland	1—3
5—3	Liverpool	5—1	4—0	Tottenham Hotspur	3—1
3—1	Manchester City	4—2	2—2	West Bromwich Albion	0—2
		5—3	Wolverhampton Wanderers	1—1	

LEAGUE APPEARANCES (21 PLAYERS)

Bowen, D. ..	.. 2	Holton, C. C.	.. 21	Oakes, D.	.. 2
Chenhall, J. ..	.. 13	Kelsey, A. J.	.. 25	Platt, E. ..	.. 3
Cox, F. ..	.. 9	Lishman, D.	.. 39	Roper, D.	.. 41
Daniel, R. ..	.. 41	Logie, J.	.. 32	Shaw, A. ..	.. 25
Dodgin, W. ..	.. 1	Marden, R.	.. 8	Smith, L. ..	.. 31
Forbes, A. ..	.. 33	Mercer, J.	.. 28	Swindin, G.	.. 14
Goring, H. ..	.. 29	Milton, C. A.	.. 25	Wade, J. ..	.. 40

LEAGUE GOAL-SCORERS

Lishman, D.	.. 22	Milton, C. A.	.. 7	Forbes, A.	.. 1
Holton, C. C.	.. 19	Daniel, R.	.. 5	Oakes, D.	.. 1
Roper, D. ..	.. 14	Marden, R.	.. 4	o.g.	.. 1
Goring, H. ..	.. 10	Mercer, J.	.. 2	Total	97
Logie, J. ..	.. 10	Cox, F.	.. 1		

F.A. CUP COMPETITION

3rd Rd. *v.* Doncaster Rovers .. (h) 4—0 Lishman, Holton, Logie
Roper

4th Rd. *v.* Bury .. .. (h) 6—2 Holton, Lishman, Logie,
Milton, Roper, o.g.

5th Rd. *v.* Burnley .. .. (a) 2—0 Holton, Lishman

6th Rd. *v.* Blackpool .. .. (h) 1—2 Logie

HONOURS

Daniel, R.: Wales *v.* England, Scotland, Ireland, France, Yugoslavia.
Lishman, D.: Football League *v.* Denmark.
Logie, J.: Scotland *v.* Ireland.
Roper, D.: Football League *v.* Denmark.
Smith, L.: England *v.* Scotland, Wales, Belgium; Football League
v. Scottish League.
Wade, J.: Football League *v.* League of Ireland.

H. ROBERTS

R. ROOKE

D. ROPER

L. SCOTT

J. SHAW

L. SMITH

D. TAPSCOTT

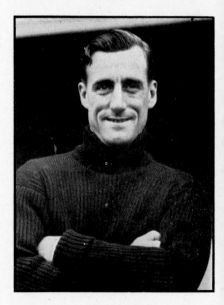

G. SWINDIN

Football League—Division I

P.42   W.15   D.13   L.14   Goals 75—73   Pts.43   12th

Football Combination—Division I

P.30   W.13   D.8   L.9   Goals 56—36   Pts.34   6th

Eight games without a win (and a 7—1 defeat at Roker Park into the bargain!). Such was the staggering start to 1953-4. Arsenal, with a record of P.8 W.0 D.2 L.6 Goals 6—18 Pts.2, were at the foot of the table. A win at Chelsea on 15th September was the turning point, and of the next eighteen games ten were won and six drawn, which pulled the team up to seventh place. A surprise defeat by Norwich in the Cup set the team back again and the season finished with Arsenal occupying twelfth place.

Barnes, with characteristic determination, came back after a blank season and new recruits included Lawton and Dickson. The home encounter against Liverpool saw a sparkling League début by Tapscott, a youngster from Barry Town, who earned a Welsh cap *v.* Austria in the close season. In the same match Mercer had the misfortune to break a leg, which ended his fine playing career.

At Sunderland, earlier in the season, Swindin played his last League game for Arsenal, who were losing only 2—1 at half-time. After the interval, however, Shackleton and Co. hit peak form and slammed in another five goals.

In June 1953 there came the sad announcement of Alex James' death. This brilliant Scot, with the dazzling footwork, will always be remembered wherever football is played.

FOOTBALL LEAGUE RESULTS

Home	Opponents	Away	Home	Opponents	Away
1—1	Aston Villa ..	.. 1—2	0—0	Huddersfield Town ..	2—2
1—1	Blackpool ..	.. 2—2	3—0	Liverpool ..	.. 2—1
4—3	Bolton Wanderers	.. 1—3	2—2	Manchester City	.. 0—0
2—5	Burnley ..	.. 1—2	3—1	Manchester United	.. 2—2
1—1	Cardiff City ..	.. 3—0	3—1	Middlesbrough	.. 0—2
3—3	Charlton Athletic	.. 5—1	2—1	Newcastle United ..	2—5
1—2	Chelsea ..	.. 2—0	3—0	Portsmouth ..	.. 1—1

Home	Opponents	Away	Home	Opponents	Away
3—2	Preston North End ..	1—0	1—4	Sunderland ..	.. 1—7
1—1	Sheffield United ..	0—1	0—3	Tottenham Hotspur ..	4—1
4—1	Sheffield Wednesday	1—2	2—2	West Bromwich Albion	0—2
	2—3 Wolverhampton Wanderers	.. 2—0			

LEAGUE APPEARANCES (26 PLAYERS)

Barnes, W. ..	.. 19	Lawton, T.	.. 9	Sullivan, C.	.. 1
Bowen, D. ..	.. 10	Lishman, D.	.. 39	Swindin, G.	.. 2
Dickson, W.	.. 24	Logie, J.	.. 35	Tapscott, D.	.. 5
Dodgin, W. ..	.. 39	Marden, R.	.. 9	Tilley, P. ..	.. 1
Evans, D. ..	.. 10	Mercer, J.	.. 19	Wade, J. ..	.. 18
Forbes, A. ..	.. 30	Milton, C. A.	.. 21	Walsh, B.	.. 10
Goring, H. ..	.. 9	Roper, D.	.. 39	Ward, G. ..	.. 3
Holton, C. C.	.. 32	Shaw, A.	.. 2	Wills, L.	.. 30
Kelsey, A. J.	.. 39	Smith, L.	.. 7		

LEAGUE GOAL-SCORERS

Lishman, D.	.. 18	Tapscott, D.	.. 5	Barnes, W.	.. 1
Holton, C. C.	.. 17	Forbes, A.	.. 4	Dickson, W.	.. 1
Roper, D. ..	.. 12	Marden, R.	.. 3	Lawton, T.	.. 1
Logie, J. ..	.. 8	Milton, C. A.	.. 3	o.g.	.. 2

Total 75

F.A. CUP COMPETITION

3rd Rd. *v.* Aston Villa .. (h) 5—1 Roper 2, Holton, Logie, Milton

4th Rd. *v.* Norwich City .. (h) 1—2 Logie

LONDON F.A. CHALLENGE CUP

Final *v.* Chelsea .. .. .. (a) 1—1 Ward

Replay *v.* Chelsea .. .. .. (h) 3—2 Oakes 2, Ward

HONOURS

Barnes, W.: Wales *v.* England, Scotland.
Dickson, W.: Ireland *v.* Wales.
Kelsey, A. J.: Wales *v.* Ireland, Austria.
Lawton, T.: England trial
Smith, L.: England trial.
Tapscott, D.: Wales *v.* Austria.

Season 1954–5

Football League—Division I

P.42 W.17 D.9 L.16 Goals 69—63 Pts.43 9th

Football Combination—Division I

P.30 W.15 D.6 L.9. Goals 73—43 Pts.36 4th

Another wretchedly poor start put Arsenal at an immediate disadvantage, and near the half-way stage they, coupled with Leicester and Sheffield United, were in the second-last position in Division I with the following record: P.20 W.5 D.4 L.11 Goals 34—37 Pts.14.

Two individual displays shone through the gloomy autumn, which included a 5—0 defeat in Moscow v. the Dynamos. They were the promising League débuts of Bloomfield at Hillsborough early in October and of Fotheringham a month later when he faced England centre-forward Lofthouse at Bolton. The 6 ft. 4 in. ex-Corby man retained the centre-half berth for the remainder of the season.

The tide turned at Christmas with three points v. Chelsea. Easter, too, was a happy holiday for Arsenal who obtained the maximum six points. Sandwiched in between were eleven League games of which only one was lost (at Burnley). This included seven successive victories, which failed by one to equal the Club's best. Arsenal had, by then, climbed to fifth place, but three defeats in the last four games put them out of the running for talent money.

Goring, converted to right-half, had a splendid season, but Dickson, on the other hand, had a most unhappy time with a continual crop of injuries. Two internationals left Highbury in February, Logie moving to Gravesend and Milton joining Bristol City in their successful promotion bid from Division III (S.).

FOOTBALL LEAGUE RESULTS

Home	Opponents	Away	Home	Opponents	Away
2—0	Aston Villa ..	.. 1—2	1—0	Chelsea ..	.. 1—1
3—0	Blackpool ..	.. 2—2	2—0	Everton ..	.. 0—1
3—0	Bolton Wanderers	.. 2—2	3—5	Huddersfield Town	.. 1—0
4—0	Burnley ..	.. 0—3	1—1	Leicester City..	.. 3—3
2—0	Cardiff City ..	.. 2—1	2—3	Manchester City	.. 1—2
3—1	Charlton Athletic	.. 1—1	2—3	Manchester United	.. 1—2

Home	Opponents	Away	Home	Opponents	Away
1—3	Newcastle United ..	1—5	3—2	Sheffield Wednesday	2—1
0—1	Portsmouth	1—2	1—3	Sunderland	1—0
2—0	Preston North End ..	1—3	2—0	Tottenham Hotspur ..	1—0
4—0	Sheffield United ..	1—1	2—2	West Bromwich Albion	1—3
	1—1 Wolverhampton Wanderers .. 1—3				

LEAGUE APPEARANCES (30 PLAYERS)

Barnes, W. ..	.. 25	Guthrie, R.	.. 2	Oakes, D.		.. 9
Bloomfield, J.	.. 19	Haverty, J.	.. 6	Roper, D.		.. 35
Bowen, D. ..	.. 21	Herd, D.	.. 3	Shaw, A. ..		.. 1
Clapton, D. ..	.. 16	Holton, C. C.	.. 8	Sullivan, C.		.. 2
Dickson, W.	.. 4	Kelsey, A. J.	.. 38	Swallow, R.		.. 1
Dodgin, W. ..	.. 3	Lawton, T.	.. 18	Tapscott, D.		.. 37
Evans, D. ..	.. 21	Lishman, D.	.. 32	Wade, J. ..		.. 14
Forbes, A. ..	.. 20	Logie, J.	.. 13	Walsh, B.		.. 6
Fotheringham, J.	.. 27	Marden, R.	.. 7	Wilkinson, J.		.. 1
Goring, H. ..	.. 41	Milton, C. A.	.. 8	Wills, L.		.. 24

LEAGUE GOAL-SCORERS

Lishman, D.	.. 19	Bloomfield, J.	.. 4	Goring, H.	.. 1
Roper, D. ..	.. 17	Logie, J. ..	.. 3	Herd, D. ..	.. 1
Tapscott, D.	.. 13	Milton, C. A. ..	.. 3	Wills, L. ..	.. 1
Lawton, T. ..	.. 6	Forbes, A. ..	.. 1	Total	69

F.A. CUP COMPETITION

3rd Rd. *v.* Cardiff City .. .. (h) 1—0 Lawton
4th Rd. *v.* Wolverhampton Wanderers (a) 0—1

LONDON F.A. CHALLENGE CUP

Final *v.* West Ham United .. (h) 1—1 Wilkinson
Replay *v.* West Ham United .. (a) 2—1 Haverty, Herd

HONOURS

Barnes, W., Bowen, D., Kelsey, A. J. and *Tapscott, D.:*
Wales *v.* Scotland, Yugoslavia.
Kelsey, A. J.: Wales *v.* Ireland.
Tapscott, D.: Wales *v.* England, Ireland.
Dickson, W.: Ireland *v.* England.

Football League—Division I

P.42 W.18 D.10 L.14 Goals 60—61 Pts.46 5th

Football Combination

P.42 W.19 D.8 L.15 Goals 96—76 Pts.46 9th

The team-sheet for much of this season had an unfamiliar look about it. With the departure from Highbury of Barnes, Marden, Lawton, Lishman, Wade and Walsh, youth was given its chance. Nutt and Tiddy, wingers from Cardiff, and Charlton and Groves from Leyton Orient were drafted into the team, whose average age was often no more than twenty-four years—the youngest in the Club's history.

With the change of players there naturally came a change in the style of play. Gone was some of the cool calculated football of a few years earlier, to be replaced by greater energy and enthusiasm. When Arsenal rather unexpectedly beat Charlton 2—0 at the Valley in the Cup, with four twenty-two-year-olds in the forward line (i.e. Clapton, Tapscott, Groves and Bloomfield), it was said that here was the liveliest and fastest combination since the 'Buckley Babes' of pre-war days.

Nevertheless, Arsenal hovered (albeit never dangerously) just above the relegation zone until the middle of March. But as there was a margin of only ten points between 17th (Arsenal) and 2nd (Blackpool) positions, a run of six successive victories, producing an aggregate of ten goals to nil and including an Easter maximum, shot the Club up the table to fourth place in four weeks. At the final reckoning Arsenal were edged out of the talent money by a fraction of a goal.

FOOTBALL LEAGUE RESULTS

Home	Opponents	Away	Home	Opponents	Away
1—0	Aston Villa ..	.. 1—1	2—4	Charlton Athletic	.. 0—2
1—0	Birmingham City	.. 0—4	1—1	Chelsea ..	.. 0—2
4—1	Blackpool ..	.. 1—3	3—2	Everton ..	.. 1—1
3—1	Bolton Wanderers	.. 1—4	2—0	Huddersfield Town	.. 1—0
0—1	Burnley ..	.. 1—0	3—0	Luton Town ..	.. 0—0
3—1	Cardiff City ..	.. 2—1	0—0	Manchester City	.. 2—2

Home	Opponents	Away	Home	Opponents	Away
1—1	Manchester United ..	1—1	2—1	Sheffield United ..	2—0
1—0	Newcastle United ..	0—2	3—1	Sunderland ..	1—3
1—3	Portsmouth ..	2—5	0—1	Tottenham Hotspur ..	1—3
3—2	Preston North End ..	1—0	2—0	West Bromwich Albion	1—2
	2—2 Wolverhampton Wanderers ..			3—3	

LEAGUE APPEARANCES (26 PLAYERS)

Barnes, W. ..	.. 8	Fotheringham, J.	25	Nutt, G.		.. 8
Bowen, D. ..	.. 22	Goring, H.	.. 37	Roper, D.		.. 16
Bloomfield, J.	.. 32	Groves, V.	.. 15	Sullivan, C.		.. 10
Charlton, S.	.. 19	Haverty, J.	.. 8	Swallow, R.		.. 1
Clapton, D. ..	.. 39	Herd, D.	.. 5	Tapscott, D.		.. 31
Dickson, W.	.. 1	Holton, C. C. ..	31	Tiddy, M.		.. 21
Dodgin, W. ..	.. 15	Kelsey, A. J. ..	32	Walsh, B.		.. 1
Evans, D. ..	.. 42	Lawton, T. ..	8	Wills, L. ..		.. 15
Forbes, A. ..	.. 5	Lishman, D. ..	15			

LEAGUE GOAL-SCORERS

Tapscott, D.	.. 17	Roper, D.	.. 4	Nutt, G.		.. 1
Groves, V. ..	.. 8	Bloomfield, J.	3	Swallow, R.		.. 1
Holton, C. C.	.. 8	Clapton, D. ..	2	o.g.	..	.. 1
Lawton, T. ..	.. 6	Haverty, J. ..	2		Total	60
Lishman, D.	.. 5	Herd, D. ..	2			

F.A. CUP COMPETITION

3rd Rd. *v.* Bedford Town	.. (h)	2—2	Tapscott, Groves
Replay *v.* Bedford Town	.. (a)	2—1	Groves, Tapscott
4th Rd. *v.* Aston Villa ..	.. (h)	4—1	Tapscott 2, Groves, Charlton
5th Rd. *v.* Charlton Athletic	.. (a)	2—0	Groves, Bloomfield
6th Rd. *v.* Birmingham City	.. (h)	1—3	Charlton

HONOURS

Haverty, J.: Eire *v.* Holland.
Kelsey, A. J.: Wales *v.* England, Scotland, Ireland, Austria.
Tapscott, D.: Wales *v.* England, Scotland, Ireland, Austria.

Season 1956-7

Football League—Division I

P.42 W.21 D.8 L.13 Goals 85—69 Pts.50 5th

Football Combination

P.42 W.22 D.9 L.11 Goals 105—65 Pts.53 7th

The events of the season were overshadowed by the sudden death in October of Tom Whittaker. Joining Arsenal in 1919, he gave thirty-seven years of loyal service as player, trainer, assistant manager and secretary-manager, and his untimely passing was a sad loss to the football world. Arsenal appointed Jack Crayston as manager and Bob Wall took over the duties of secretary.

On the playing field, one remembers of this season: Arsenal leading at Birmingham 2—0 until nineteen minutes from the end and then conceding four goals; bad luck in the 3—1 defeat at Burnley when they hit the goalposts four times; being 2—0 up in three minutes at Portsmouth who eventually equalized and Herd netting the winner in the eighty-eighth minute; leading twice at Wolverhampton, only to lose 5—2; drawing at Leeds 3—3 after being three-nil up at the interval; and winning 3—2 at Cardiff after trailing 2—0 for three-quarters of the game.

But the matches which stood out most of all were the four cup-ties *v.* Preston and West Bromwich. Of the performances in these it was said: 'It would take very little to make this Arsenal into a great side.' In the replay against Preston, Dodgin scored his first goal in professional football, while at West Bromwich first Wills put through his own goal and then his full-back partner Charlton scored the equalizer with a shot from fully forty yards.

FOOTBALL LEAGUE RESULTS

Home	Opponents	Away	Home	Opponents	Away
2—1	Aston Villa ..	.. 0—0	3—1	Charlton Athletic	.. 3—1
4—0	Birmingham City	.. 2—4	2—0	Chelsea ..	.. 1—1
1—1	Blackpool ..	.. 4—2	2—0	Everton ..	.. 0—4
3—0	Bolton Wanderers	.. 1—2	1—0	Leeds United	.. 3—3
2—0	Burnley ..	.. 1—3	1—3	Luton Town ..	.. 2—1
0—0	Cardiff City ..	.. 3—2	7—3	Manchester City	.. 3—2

Home	Opponents	Away	Home	Opponents	Away
1—2	Manchester United ..	2—6	6—3	Sheffield Wednesday	4—2
0—1	Newcastle United ..	1—3	1—1	Sunderland	0—1
1—1	Portsmouth	3—2	3—1	Tottenham Hotspur ..	3—1
1—2	Preston North End ..	0—3	4—1	West Bromwich Albion	2—0
	0—0 Wolverhampton Wanderers .. 2—5				

LEAGUE APPEARANCES (20 PLAYERS)

Barnwell, J. ..	.. 1	Goring, H.	.. 13	Roper, D.	.. 4
Bowen, D. ..	.. 30	Groves, V.	.. 5	Sullivan, C.	.. 12
Bloomfield, J.	.. 42	Haverty, J.	.. 28	Swallow, R.	.. 4
Charlton, S.	.. 40	Herd, D.	.. 22	Tapscott, D.	.. 38
Clapton, D. ..	.. 39	Holton, C. C.	.. 39	Tiddy, M.	.. 15
Dodgin, W. ..	.. 41	Kelsey, A. J.	.. 30	Wills, L. ..	.. 18
Evans, D. ..	.. 40	Nutt, G.	.. 1		

LEAGUE GOAL-SCORERS

Tapscott, D.	.. 25	Haverty, J.	.. 8	Bowen, D.	.. 2
Holton, C. C.	.. 12	Tiddy, M.	.. 6	Clapton, D.	.. 2
Bloomfield, J.	.. 10	Evans, D.	.. 4	Groves, V.	.. 2
Herd, D. ..	.. 10	Roper, D.	.. 3	Watts (Birm'ham)	1
					Total 85

F.A. CUP COMPETITION

3rd Rd. *v.* Stoke City	..	.. (h)	4—2 Herd 2, Haverty, Tapscott
4th Rd. *v.* Newport County	..	(a)	2—0 Tapscott, Herd
5th Rd. *v.* Preston North End	..	(a)	3—3 Dunn (o.g.), Clapton, Herd
Replay *v.* Preston North End	..	(h)	2—1 Dodgin, Herd
6th Rd. *v.* West Bromwich Albion		(a)	2—2 Herd, Charlton
Replay *v.* West Bromwich Albion		(h)	1—2 Holton

HONOURS

Bowen, D.: Wales *v.* Ireland, Czechoslovakia, Eastern Germany.

Haverty, J.: Eire *v.* Denmark, Germany, England (twice).

Kelsey, A. J.: Wales *v.* England, Scotland, Ireland, Czechosolvakia, Eastern Germany.

Tapscott, D.: Wales *v.* Ireland, Czechoslovakia, Eastern Germany.

Football League—Division I

P.42   W.16   D.7   L.19   Goals 73—85   Pts.39   12th

Football Combination

P.42   W.22   D.7   L.13   Goals 103—64   Pts.51   6th

Finishing just below the half-way position in the table, Arsenal's collection of thirty-nine points was the Club's lowest total for twenty-one seasons. There was, all through the season, an irritating uncertainty about the team; at times the brand of football was a joy to watch while, at others, it sank to the depths of despair.

One remembers, for instance, a feast of football in the rain one Tuesday evening in September when Everton won 3—2 at Highbury; the thrill-packed game at Old Trafford when Clapton jinked round Byrne with bewildering ball control at speed; both the encounters against Portsmouth, particularly at Fratton Park, where Arsenal fought back after being four goals down; a 5—4 epic in the London 'derby' *v.* Chelsea and the beautifully controlled football at Maine Road to beat Manchester City 4—2.

But on the debit side there was the tepid stuff in the 2—1 victory over Leeds and the goalless draw *v.* Chelsea; the débâcle at Notts Forest with the whole team, apart from Kelsey, well below par and the all-time low in the cup-tie at Northampton. This was a lethargic Arsenal side which, even when the situation became desperate, showed little ability to fight back. The manner of this defeat made it a sorry day for the Club.

Almost immediately afterwards, Bowen, already captain of his country, was appointed captain, and his leadership and example on the field in subsequent matches instilled a new enthusiasm into the team.

During December, Ron Greenwood, the former Chelsea and Brentford half-back, was appointed coach—a new departure for the Club. At the end of the season Jack Crayston resigned from the managerial chair and so ended a long association at Highbury as player, assistant manager and manager.

FOOTBALL LEAGUE RESULTS

Home	Opponents	Away	Home	Opponents	Away
4—0	Aston Villa ..	.. 0—3	2—1	Manchester City	.. 4—2
1—3	Birmingham City	.. 1—4	4—5	Manchester United ..	.. 2—4
2—3	Blackpool ..	.. 0—1	2—3	Newcastle United	.. 3—3
1—2	Bolton Wanderers	.. 1—0	1—1	Notts Forest	.. 0—4
0—0	Burnley ..	.. 1—2	3—2	Portsmouth ..	.. 4—5
5—4	Chelsea ..	.. 0—0	4—2	Preston North End ..	.. 0—3
2—3	Everton ..	.. 2—2	1—0	Sheffield Wednesday	0—2
2—1	Leeds United	.. 0—2	3—0	Sunderland ..	.. 1—0
3—1	Leicester City..	.. 1—0	4—4	Tottenham Hotspur ..	1—3
2—0	Luton Town ..	.. 0—4	2—2	West Bromwich Albion	2—1
		0—2	Wolverhampton Wanderers .. 2—1		

LEAGUE APPEARANCES (24 PLAYERS)

Biggs, A. ..	..	2	Goring, H.	..	10	Petts, J. ..	..	9
Bloomfield, J.	..	40	Groves, V.	..	30	Standen, J.	..	1
Bowen, D. ..	..	30	Haverty, J.	..	15	Sullivan, C.	..	3
Charlton, S.	..	36	Herd, D.	..	39	Swallow, R.	..	7
Clapton, D. ..	..	28	Holton, C. C.	..	26	Tapscott, D.	..	8
Dodgin, W. ..	..	23	Kelsey, A. J.	..	38	Tiddy, M.	..	12
Evans, D. ..	..	32	Le Roux, D.	..	5	Ward, G. ..	..	10
Fotheringham, J.	..	19	Nutt, G.	..	21	Wills, L. ..	..	18

LEAGUE GOAL-SCORERS

Herd, D. ..	..	24	Nutt, G.	..	3	Dunn (Preston N. E.)		1
Bloomfield, J.	..	16	Swallow, R.	..	3	Gunter (Ports'mth)		1
Groves, V. ..	..	10	Tapscott, D.	..	2	Henry (Spurs.) ..		1
Clapton, D. ..	..	5	Tiddy, M.	..	2		Total	73
Holton, C. C.	..	4	Wills, L.	..	1			

F.A. CUP COMPETITION

3rd Rd. *v.* Northampton Town .. (a) 1—3 Clapton

HONOURS

Bowen, D.: Wales *v.* England, Scotland, Ireland, Israel (2), Hungary (2), Mexico, Sweden, Brazil.

Kelsey, A. J.: Wales *v.* England, Scotland, Ireland, Israel (2), Hungary (2), Mexico, Sweden, Brazil.

Haverty, J.: Eire *v.* Poland.

Season 1958–9

Football League—Division I

P.42 W.21 D.8 L.13 Goals 88—68 Pts.50 3rd

Football Combination—Division I

P.34 W.15 D.10 L.9 Goals 86—60 Pts.40 4th

Goalkeepers! The Club's former goalkeeper, George Swindin, takes over the managerial chair; Welsh-international-goalkeeper Kelsey breaks an arm in the cup-tie replay at Sheffield; goalkeeper Standen proves a very capable deputy, as does third-team 'keeper Goy when Standen was also injured.

Changes in the playing personnel occurred with the signing of Scottish internationals Docherty from Preston and Henderson from Wolverhampton, and Julians in mid-season too; and with the departure of Tapscott, Holton, Charlton and Fotheringham.

In the international field Herd and Clapton deservedly won recognition for the first time, and five players appeared in the Scotland *v.* Wales match—Herd, Docherty, Henderson, Kelsey and Bowen—on which day Arsenal held the champions Wolves to a 1—1 draw. On another occasion, with Kelsey, Bowen and Clapton in the Wales *v.* England match, Arsenal, whose line-up included reserves Petts, Barnwell and Goulden, beat the Italian champions Juventus 3—1.

Arsenal, after six games the heaviest scorers in Division I, topped the table at the half-way stage, but three successive and inexplicable home defeats in December and a series of injuries to key players caused the hopes of a championship triumph to recede. Nevertheless, the obstacles were overcome to such an extent that third place was reached at the final reckoning and a standard of constructive play was achieved to augur well for the future.

Bloomfield (cartilage operation), Herd (hair-line fracture in shinbone), Kelsey (broken arm), Bowen, Henderson, Ward, Wills and Groves were all on the injured list for lengthy periods. After Kelsey broke his arm in the cup-tie replay at Sheffield, Standen proved a very capable deputy; as did third-string goalkeeper Goy when Standen, too, was injured on two occasions.

139

FOOTBALL LEAGUE RESULTS

Home	Opponents	Away	Home	Opponents	Away
1—2	Aston Villa ..	.. 2—1	1—0	Luton Town ..	.. 3—6
2—1	Birmingham City	.. 1—4	4—1	Manchester City	.. 0—0
1—1	Blackburn Rovers	.. 2—4	3—2	Manchester United	.. 1—1
1—4	Blackpool ..	.. 2—1	3—2	Newcastle United	.. 0—1
6—1	Bolton Wanderers	.. 1—2	3—1	Nottingham Forest	.. 1—1
3—0	Burnley ..	.. 1—3	5—2	Portsmouth ..	.. 1—0
1—1	Chelsea ..	.. 3—0	1—2	Preston North End	.. 1—2
3—1	Everton ..	.. 6—1	3—1	Tottenham Hotspur	.. 4—1
1—0	Leeds United ..	.. 1—2	4—3	West Bromwich Albion	1—1
5—1	Leicester City..	.. 3—2	1—2	West Ham United	.. 0—0
		1—1 Wolverhampton Wanderers .. 1—6			

LEAGUE APPEARANCES (26 PLAYERS)

Barnwell, J. ..	.. 16	Fotheringham, J.	1	Julians, L.		.. 10
Biggs, A. ..	.. 2	Goring, H. ..	2	Kelsey, A. J.		.. 27
Bloomfield, J.	.. 29	Goulden, R. ..	1	McCullough, W.		10
Bowen, D. ..	.. 16	Goy, P. ..	2	Nutt, G. ..		.. 16
Charlton, S. ..	.. 4	Groves, V. ..	33	Petts, J. ..		.. 3
Clapton, D. ..	.. 39	Haverty, J. ..	10	Standen, J.		.. 13
Docherty, T. ..	.. 38	Henderson, J. ..	21	Ward, G. ..		.. 31
Dodgin, W. ..	.. 39	Herd, D. ..	26	Wills, L. ..		.. 33
Evans, D. ..	.. 37	Holton, C. C. ..	3			

LEAGUE GOAL-SCORERS

Herd, D. ..	.. 15	Evans, D. ..	.. 5	Biggs, A. ..	.. 1
Henderson, J.	.. 12	Julians, L. ..	.. 5	Docherty, T. ..	.. 1
Bloomfield, J.	.. 10	Ward, G. ..	.. 4	Wills, L. ..	.. 1
Groves, V. ..	.. 10	Barnwell, J. ..	.. 3	Barlow (W.B.A.)	1
Clapton, D. ..	.. 6	Haverty, J. ..	.. 3	Gunter (Portsm'th)	1
Nutt, G. ..	.. 6	Holton, C. C. ..	.. 3	McKinlay (Forest)	1
				Total	88

F.A. CUP COMPETITION

3rd Rd. *v.* Bury ..	..	(a)	1—0	Herd
4th Rd. *v.* Colchester United	..	(a)	2—2	Groves 2
Replay *v.* Colchester United	..	(h)	4—0	Julians, Groves, Herd, Henderson
5th Rd. *v.* Sheffield United	..	(h)	2—2	Evans, Julians
Replay *v.* Sheffield United	..	(a)	0—3	

Bowen, D.: Wales *v.* England, Scotland, Ireland.
Clapton, D.: England *v.* Wales.
Docherty, T.: Scotland *v.* England, Wales, Ireland.
Haverty, J.: Eire *v.* Sweden, Chile.
Henderson, J.: Scotland *v.* Wales, Ireland.
Herd, D.: Scotland *v.* England, Wales, Ireland.
Kelsey, A. J.: Wales *v.* England, Scotland.

Season 1959–60

Football League—Division I
P.42 W.15 D.9 L.18 Goals 68—80 Pts.39 13th

Football Combination—Division I
P.34 W.15 D.6 L.13 Goals 62—45 Pts.36 7th

After a quarter of the programme had been completed, Arsenal were in fourth position, lying handy behind Spurs, Wolves and Burnley. With only two defeats in the first eleven games, Clapton and Herd had scored six goals apiece and, notwithstanding Evans' chipped ankle-bone and Charles' cartilage trouble, the promise of a good season seemed to be prominent.

It was not to be, however! Docherty broke an ankle in October *v.* his old club and by the time he returned in January the Gunners had slumped to sixteenth place. A superb display at Stamford Bridge, reminiscent of the old Arsenal's marshalled magic, was followed by a series of five defeats *v.* W.B.A. (h), Newcastle (a), Burnley (h), Sheffield Wednesday (a) and Luton (h)—the latter was the fourth successive home defeat—and in this spell twenty goals were conceded.

On the brighter side, Charles netted eight goals in nine games at centre-forward, including a hat-trick *v.* Blackburn on 6th February —this, incidentally, was the first home win since 31st October. Hat-tricks were also scored by Bloomfield *v.* Manchester United and Clapton at Notts Forest, the latter being the first by an Arsenal winger since Marden's trio *v.* Charlton in 1953–4.

Evans came back for three games and then had the misfortune to break his other ankle, while Clapton also had a cartilage operation. These and other too-numerous injuries gave opportunities to young players like Magill, Everitt, Sneddon and Dennis Clapton, whose displays showed promise for the future.

In the F.A. Cup the Gunners ran up against a Second Division club which was riding on the crest of success. An own goal saved Arsenal in the first tie, and the survival of Rotherham at Highbury was nothing of a fluke, as was proved in the second replay at Hillsborough where the Yorkshiremen were clear-cut winners.

At the end of the season, trainer Billy Milne retired after thirty-nine years at Highbury. He first appeared in the League team in 1921–2, and had made 114 appearances before a broken leg curtailed his playing career in 1927.

FOOTBALL LEAGUE RESULTS

Home	Opponents	Away	Home	Opponents	Away
5—2	Blackburn Rovers ..	1—1	0—3	Luton Town ..	1—0
2—1	Blackpool ..	1—2	3—1	Manchester City ..	2—1
3—0	Birmingham ..	0—3	5—2	Manchester United ..	2—4
2—1	Bolton Wanderers ..	1—0	1—0	Newcastle United ..	1—4
2—4	Burnley ..	2—3	1—1	Nottingham Forest ..	3—0
1—4	Chelsea ..	3—1	0—3	Preston North End ..	3—0
2—1	Everton ..	1—3	0—1	Sheffield Wednesday	1—5
2—0	Fulham ..	0—3	1—1	Tottenham Hotspur ..	0—3
1—1	Leeds United ..	2—3	2—4	West Bromwich Albion	0—1
1—1	Leicester City..	2—2	1—3	West Ham United ..	0—0
	4—4 Wolverhampton Wanderers .. 3—3				

LEAGUE APPEARANCES (23 PLAYERS)

Barnwell, J. ..	28	Everitt, M. ..	5	Magill, E. ..	17
Bloomfield, J.	36	Groves, V. ..	30	Nutt, G. ..	3
Charles, M. ..	20	Haverty, J. ..	35	Petts, J. ..	7
Clapton, D. ..	23	Henderson, J. ..	31	Sneddon, J. ..	1
Clapton, D. P.	3	Herd, D. ..	31	Standen, J. ..	20
Docherty, T.	24	Julians, L. ..	8	Ward, G. ..	15
Dodgin, W. ..	30	Kelsey, A. J. ..	22	Wills, L. ..	33
Evans, D. ..	7	McCullough, W. 33			

LEAGUE GOAL-SCORERS

Herd, D. ..	14	Henderson, J.	7	Ward, G. ..	1
Bloomfield, J.	10	Clapton, D. ..	7	Wills, L. ..	1
Charles, M. ..	8	Julians, L. ..	2	o.g. ..	1
Haverty, J. ..	8	Evans, D. ..	1	Total	68
Barnwell, J. ..	7	Groves, V. ..	1		

F.A. CUP COMPETITION

3rd Rd. v. Rotherham .. .. (a) 2—2 Julians, o.g.
Replay v. Rotherham .. .. (h) 1—1 Bloomfield
Replay v. Rotherham (at Hillsborough) 0—2

HONOURS

Kelsey A. J.: Wales v. England, Scotland, Ireland.

Season 1960-1

Football League—Division I

P.42   W.15   D.11   L.16   Goals 77—85   Pts.41   11th

Football Combination—Division I

P.34   W.12   D.11   L.11   Goals 76—62   Pts.35

A season in which transfers, rumours of transfers and player exchanges hit the Press headlines more often than the feats of Arsenal on the football field. Standen (Luton), Everitt Northampton), Dodgin (Fulham), Docherty (Chelsea), Bloomfield (Birmingham), Nutt (Southend) and coach Greenwood (West Ham) all left Highbury, while Arsenal signed McClelland (goal) from Glentoran, and three inside-forwards, Kane from Northampton, Eastham from Newcastle and Griffiths from Wrexham—an Irishman, a Scotsman, an Englishman and a Welshman!

The Gunners' thirty-year-old record of 66 points from 42 Division I matches (and 33 points from away games) looked as if it would be expunged from the record books by the all-conquering Spurs but, at the final reckoning, it still stood firm, although now shared with the fellow North Londoners. Tottenham bettered Arsenal's record of 28 victories by three but, on the other hand, lost seven matches whereas the Gunners suffered only four defeats.

After jockeying around the seventh position for a long time Arsenal slumped towards the end, with only two victories in the last twelve encounters, to finish in the eleventh place. Although football skill was evident, defensive slips and approach work which lacked final penetration was often the pattern of Arsenal's play. Four or more goals were conceded in a match on no less than eight occasions, while in more than half of the programme the forwards could not better a goal in a match.

Herd's deadly shooting and opportunism earned twenty-nine League goals, which included four hat-tricks—the best individual total by an Arsenal player since Rooke's thirty-three in 1947-8—and regained him a place in the Scottish team. It was also pleasing that Charles was re-instated in the Welsh team for the first time since he joined the Gunners.

Among the young players drafted into the League side and who established a regular place were Strong, Skirton, Neill and Bacuzzi. Eastham, the £47,500 buy from Newcastle United, made his first-team début for Arsenal on December 10th at Highbury against his father's old club Bolton Wanderers. Arsenal won 5—1, Eastham getting the last two goals, and the artistry and the deft touches of the young inside-forward augur well for the future.

FOOTBALL LEAGUE RESULTS

Home	Opponents	Away	Home	Opponents	Away
2—1	Aston Villa ..	.. 2—2	1—3	Leicester City..	.. 1—2
2—0	Birmingham City	.. 0—2	5—4	Manchester City	.. 0—0
0—0	Blackburn Rovers	.. 4—2	2—1	Manchester United	.. 1—1
1—0	Blackpool ..	.. 1—1	5—0	Newcastle United	.. 3—3
5—1	Bolton Wanderers	.. 1—1	3—0	Nottingham Forest	.. 5—3
2—5	Burnley ..	.. 2—3	1—0	Preston North End	.. 0—2
2—3	Cardiff City ..	.. 0—1	1—1	Sheffield Wednesday..	.. 1—1
1—4	Chelsea ..	.. 1—3	2—3	Tottenham Hotspur ..	.. 2—4
3—2	Everton ..	.. 1—4	1—0	West Bromwich Albion	3—2
4—2	Fulham ..	.. 2—2	0—0	West Ham United ..	.. 0—6
	1—5 Wolverhampton Wanderers .. 3—5				

LEAGUE APPEARANCES (29 PLAYERS)

Bacuzzi, D. R.	.. 13	Groves, V.	.. 32	O'Neill, F. S.	.. 2
Barnwell, J. ..	.. 26	Haverty, J.	.. 12	Petts, J. ..	.. 1
Bloomfield, J.	.. 12	Henderson, J.	.. 39	Skirton, A.	.. 16
Charles, M. ..	.. 19	Herd, D.	.. 40	Sneddon, J.	.. 23
Clapton, D. ..	.. 18	Kane, P.	.. 4	Standen, J.	.. 1
Clapton, D. P.	.. 1	Kelsey, J.	.. 37	Strong, G.	.. 19
Docherty, T.	.. 21	Magill, E.	.. 6	Ward, G. ..	.. 9
Eastham, G.	.. 19	McClelland, J.	4	Wills, L. ..	.. 24
Everitt, M. ..	.. 4	McCulloch, W.	41	Young, A.	.. 4
Griffiths, A. ..	.. 1	Neill, W. J. T. ..	14		

LEAGUE GOAL-SCORERS

Herd, D. ..	.. 29	Haverty, J.	.. 4	Everitt, M.	.. 1
Henderson, J.	.. 10	Charles, M.	.. 3	Kane, P. ..	.. 1
Strong, G. ..	.. 10	Skirton, A.	.. 3	Neill, W. J. T.	.. 1
Barnwell, J. ..	.. 6	Clapton, D.	.. 2	Ward, G. ..	.. 1
Eastham, G.	.. 5	Bloomfield, J.	1	Total 77	

3rd Rd. *v.* Sunderland .. .. .. (a) 1—2 Herd

HONOURS

Barnwell, J.: Young England *v.* West Germany.

Charles, M.: Wales *v.* Ireland, Spain.

Eastham, G.: England XI *v.* Young England.

Haverty, J.: Eire *v.* Wales, Scotland.

Herd, D.: Scotland *v.* Scottish League, Eire.

Kelsey, J.: Wales *v.* Scotland, England, Ireland, Spain.

McClelland, J.: Ireland *v.* Wales, West Germany, Italy, Greece.

McCulloch, W.: Ireland *v.* Italy.

Neill, W. J. T.: Ireland *v.* Italy.

PART TWO

Career records of some of the leading Arsenal players

Some of the leading
Arsenal players since 1906

Appearances and goals are the totals up to the
end of season 1959–60
Appearances and goals marked * do not include
any prior to 1906–7
Dates given are for the second half of the season.
Thus 1921 refers to season 1920–1

			League Apps.	Goals	From	To
Ashcroft, J.	G.	–1908	71	—	Sheppey	Blackburn R.
Blyth, W.	I.F.	1915–29	313	47	Man. City	Birmingham
Bradshaw, F.		1915–23	132	4	Northampton	
Buckley, C. S.	C.H.	1915–21	56	2	Aston Villa	Wolves
Baker, A.	W.H.	1920–31	311	21	Huddersfield	
Butler, J. D.	C.H.	1920–30	266	7	Dartford	Torquay
Brain, J.	I.R.	1925–31	204	123	Ton Pentre	Tottenham
Buchan, C. M.	I.R.	1926–8	102	49	Sunderland	Rtd.
Bastin, C. S.	O.L.	1930–47	350	150	Exeter	Rtd.
Beasley, A.	O.L.	1932–7	79	17	Stourbridge	Huddersfield
Bowden, E. R.	I.R.	1933–7	123	43	Plymouth	Newcastle
Birkett, R.	O.R.	1934–5	19	6	Torquay	Middlesbro'
Boulton, F.	G.	1937–8	36	—	Bath City	Derby Co.
Bremner, G.	O.L.	1938–9	15	4	Glasgow jun.	Motherwell
Barnes, W.	F.B.	1947–56	267	11	Army football	Rtd.
Bowen, D.	W.H.	1951–9	146	2	Northampton	Northampton
Bloomfield, J.	I.L.	1955–61	198	53	Brentford	Birmingham
Barnwell, J.	I.F.	1957–	45	10	Bishop Auckland	
Coleman, J.	I.F.	–1908	60	23*		Everton
Cross, A. G.	R.B.	–1910	49	—*	Dartford	
Chalmers, J.	C.F.	1911–12	48	21		Greenock
Common, A.	I.F.	1911–13	77	23	Middlesbro'	
Cope, A.	R.B.	1927–33	65	—	Notts Co.	Bristol R.
Coleman, E.	C.F.	1932–4	45	26	Grimsby T.	Middlesbro'
Compton, L. H.	C.H.	1932–52	253	5	Hendon	Rtd.
Copping, W.	L.H.	1935–9	166	—	Leeds Utd.	Leeds Utd.
Crayston, W. J.	R.H.	1935–9	168	16	Bradford	Rtd.
Compton, D. C. S.	O.L.	1937–50	54	15	Hendon	Rtd.
Carr, E.	C.F.	1938–9	15	7	Margate	Newport Co.
Collett, E.	H.B.	1938–47	20	—	Oughtybridge	Rtd.
Cumner, H.	O.L.	1939	12	2	Hull City	Notts Co.
Curtis, G.	I.F.	1939–47	13	—	Purfleet	Southampton
Calverly, A.	O.L.	1947	11	—	Peterborough	Doncaster R.
Cox, F.	O.R.	1950–3	79	9	Tottenham	West Brom. A.

149

		League			
		Apps.	Goals	*From*	*To*
Chenhall, J. C.	F.B.	1952–3	16	—	Bristol jun.	Fulham
Clapton, D.	O.R.	1955–	184	22	Leytonstone	
Charlton, S.	R.B.	1956–9	99	—	Leyton O.	Leyton O.
Charles, M.	H.B.	1960–	20	8	Swansea T.	
Ducat, A.	R.H.	–1912	150	14*	Southend U.	Aston V.
Dunn, S.	G.	1920–3	42	—		
Dougall, J.	I.F.	1934–6	21	4	Burnley	
Drake, E.	C.F.	1934–9	168	123	Southampton	Rtd.
Dunne, J.	C.F.	1934–6	28	10	Sheff. Utd.	Southampton
Davidson, R.	I.R.	1935–8	57	13	St. Johnstone	Coventry
Drury, G. B.	I.F.	1938–47	38	3	Sheff. Wed.	West Brom. A.
Daniel, R.	C.H.	1948–53	87	5	Swansea	Sunderland
Dodgin, W.	C.H.	1953–61	191	—	Fulham	Fulham
Dickson, W.	W.H.	1954–6	29	1	Chelsea	Mansfield
Docherty, T.	L.H.	1959–61	62	1	Preston N.E.	Chelsea
Evans, D. J.	L.B.	1954–	189	10	Ellesmere P.	
Freeman, B. C.	C.F.	–1908	27	11*		Everton
Fitchie, T. T.		1909	21	8	Queen's Park	
Fields, A.	C.H.	1939–51	19	—	Margate	Rtd.
Forbes, A.	W.H.	1948–56	217	20	Sheff. Utd.	Leyton O.
Fotheringham, J.	C.H.	1955–9	72	—	Corby Town	Hearts
Greenaway, D.	O.R.	1909–21	162	11		
Graham, A.		1913–24	166	16		Brentford
Groves, F. W.		1913–21	50	5		Brighton
Goring, H.	C.F/W.H.	1950–9	220	51	Cheltenham	
Groves, V.	I.F/W.H.	1956–	113	31	Leyton O.	
Hardinge, H. W.		–1920	54	14		
Hutchins, A. V.	F.B.	1920–3	104	1	Croydon Com.	Charlton
Hopkins, J.	I.L.	1921–3	21	7		Brighton
Haden, S.	O.R.	1924–7	88	10		Notts Co.
Hoar, S.	O.L.	1925–9	99	18	Luton Town	Clapton O.
Harper, W.	G.	1926–32	63	—	Hibernian	Plymouth A.
Hulme, J. H. A.	O.R.	1926–38	333	108	Blackburn R.	Huddersfield
Hapgood, E. A.	L.B.	1928–39	393	2	Kettering	Rtd.
Halliday, D.	C.F.	1930	15	8	Sunderland	Man. City
Haynes, A. E.	H.B.	1930–4	29	—	Oxford City	Crystal P.
Hill, F.	W.H.	1933–5	76	4	Aberdeen	Blackpool
Hunt, G.	C.F.	1938	18	3	Tottenham	Bolton W.
Holton, C.	C.F/W.H.	1951–9	198	83	Oxford City	Watford
Haverty, J.	O.L.	1955–	112	21	Dublin	
Herd, D.	I.F.	1955–	126	68	Stockport Co.	
Henderson, J.	O.L.	1959–	52	19	Wolves	
Jobey, G.	W.H.	1914–	28	3		
John, R. F.	L.H.	1923–37	421	12	Barry Town	Rtd.

		League Apps.	Goals	From	To
Jack, D. B. N.	I.R.	1929–34	181	112	Bolton Wand.	Rtd.
Jones, C.	R.H.	1929–34	176	8	Notts Forest	
James, A.	I.L.	1930–7	231	26	Preston N. E.	Rtd.
Joy, B.	C.H.	1936–47	86	—	Casuals	Rtd.
Jones, L. J.	I.R.	1938–9	46	3	Coventry City	Scunthorpe
Jones, B.	I.L.	1939–49	71	7	Wolves	Norwich City
Kyle, P.	C.F.	–1908	52*	—	Rutherglen	
Kennedy, A. L.	L.B.	1923–8	122	—	Ireland	
Keyser, P. G.	G.	1931	12	—	Margate	Charlton A.
Kirchen, A. J.	O.R.	1935–9	92	38	Norwich City	Rtd.
Kelsey, J.	G.	1951–	255	—	Winch Wen	
Lee, H. G.		1908–10	41	16		
Lewis, C.	C.F.	1908–20	206	30		
Lievesley, J.	G.	1914–15	73	—	Sheff. Utd.	
Lewis, D.	G.	1925–30	142	—	Clapton O.	
Lawson, H.	O.R.	1926	13	2	Luton Town	
Lambert, J.	C.F.	1927–34	143	98	Doncaster R.	Rtd.
Lewis, R.	C.F.	1938–52	154	103	Nunhead	Rtd.
Logie, J.	I.R.	1947–55	296	68	Lochore	Gravesend
Lishman, D.	I.L.	1949–56	226	125	Walsall	Notts Forest
Lawton, T.	C.F.	1954–6	35	13	Brentford	Kettering
M'Eachrane, R. J.	L.H.	–1914	197*			
Mordue, J.	O.R.	1908	26*	I		Sunderland
McDonald, W.		1909–13	92	—		
McKinnon, A.	L.H.	1909–22	211	4		Charlton A.
Milne, W.	R.H.	1922–7	114	I	Buckie	Rtd.
Mackie, J. A.	R.B.	1923–6	108	—	Forth River	Portsmouth
Male, G.	R.B.	1931–48	285	—	Clapton	Rtd.
Moss, F.	G.	1932–6	143	I	Oldham A.	Rtd.
Milne, J. V.	O.R.	1936–8	49	19	Blackburn	Middlesbro'
McPherson, I.	O.R.	1947–51	152	19	Notts County	Notts County
Mercer, J.	L.H.	1947–54	247	2	Everton	Rtd.
Macaulay, A.	R.H.	1948–50	103	I	Brentford	Fulham
Marden, R.	O.L.	1951–5	42	11	Chelmsford	Watford
Milton, A.	O.R.	1951–5	75	18	Bristol	Bristol C.
McCullough, W.	L.B.	1958–	43	—	Portadown	
Neave, D.	O.L.	–1912	133*	23*		
North, F. J.		1920–2	23	6		Gillingham
Neil, A.	I.R.	1924–6	54	9	Brighton	
Nelson, D.	I.F.	1937–47	19	—	St. Bernards	Fulham
Nutt, G.	W.F.	1956–60	49	10	Cardiff City	Southend
Peart, J. C.		1911–21	64	—		
Pagnam, F.	C.F.	1920–21	50	26		Watford
Paterson, J. A.		1921–6	71	2	Glasgow R.	
Parker, T. R.	R.B.	1926–35	258	17	Southampton	Norwich City

			League Apps.	Goals	From	To
Peel, H.	I.L.	1927–30	47	5	Bradford	Bradford C.
Patterson, W.	G.	1928–9	15	—		
Parkin, R.	I.F.	1929–34	29	11	Crook Town	Middlesbro'
Preedy, C. J.	G.	1930–33	37	–	Wigan	Bristol R.
Platt, E.	G.	1947–53	53	—	Bath City	Portsmouth
Randle, C. E.		1912–14	43	12		
Roose, L. R.	G.	1912	13	—		
Rutherford, J.	O.R.	1914–26	223	25	Newcastle U.	
Robson, J. H.	G.	1923–6	97	—		Bournemouth
Ramsay, J. H.	I.L.	1924–7	69	11		Kilmarnock
Roberts, H.	C.H.	1927–38	297	4	Oswestry	Rtd.
Rogers, E.	O.R.	1935–6	16	5	Wrexham	Newcastle U.
Rooke, R.	C.F.	1947–9	88	68	Fulham	Crystal P.
Roper, D.	W.F.	1948–57	297	88	Southampton	Southampton
Sands, P.	C.H.	–1915	238*	7*		
Satterthwaite, C.	I.L.	–1908	61*	21*		
Sharp, Jas.	L.B.	–1908	68*	2*	Fulham	Glasgow R.
Satterthwaite, J.		1907–10	25	5		
Shaw, J.	F.B.	1908–22	308	4	Accrington	Rtd.
Stonley, S.		1912–13	38	14		
Seddon, W. C.	H.B.	1926–32	69	—	Local	Grimsby T.
Stockhill, R.	C.F.	1932–3	7	4	York C.	Derby Co.
Sidey, N.	C.H.	1933–8	40	—	Nunhead	Rtd.
Swindin, G.	G.	1937–54	272	—	Bradford C.	Peterborough
Sloan, J.	I.F.	1947–8	33	1	Tranmere R.	Sheffield U.
Scott, L.	R.B.	1947–52	115	—	Bradford C.	Crystal P.
Smith, L.	L.B.	1948–55	162	—	Mexborough	Watford
Shaw, A.	W.H.	1950–5	41	—	Brentford	Watford
Sullivan, C.	G.	1954–8	28	—	Bristol C.	Rtd.
Standen, J.	G.	1958–61	34	—	Rickmansworth	Luton Town
Snedden, J.	C.H.	1960–			Bonnyvale Star	
Strong, G. H.	C.F.	1961–			Stanley Utd.	
Thomson, M.		1909–14	60	1		
Toner, J.	O.L.	1920–6	87	6	Ireland	Burnley
Turnbull, R.	C.F.	1922–5	59	26		Chelsea
Thompson, L.	I.F.	1928–32	26	6	Swansea Town	Crystal P.
Tapscott, D.	I.R.	1954–8	119	62	Barry Town	Cardiff City
Tiddy, M.	W.F.	1956–9	48	8	Cardiff City	Brighton
Voysey, C. R.		1920–6	35	6		
Vallance, T.	O.L.	1949–50	15	2		
Winship, T.	O.L.	1911–15	55	7		
White, H. A.	C.F.	1920–3	102	40	Brentford	Blackpool
Whittaker, T. J.	W.H.	1920–5	64	2		
Williamson, E. C.	G.	1920–3	105	—	Croydon Com.	Norwich City
Woods, H.	C.F.	1924–6	70	21	Newcastle U.	Luton Town

		League Apps.	Goals	From	To
Williams, J. J.	O.R.	1930–2	22	5	Stoke City	Middlesbro'
Wilson, A.	G.	1934–9	82	—	Greenock M.	
Wade, J.	F.B.	1947–55	86	—	Local	Hereford
Walsh, J. B.	O.R.	1954–6	17	—	Local	Cardiff City
Ward, G.	W.H/O.L.	1954–	59	5	Local	
Wills, L.	R.B.	1954–	171	4	Eton Manor	
Young, A.	C.F.	1922–7	68	9	Aston Villa	Bournemouth

Baker, A. (1920–31). *Wing-half.* A former miner from Ilkeston and a fine utility player who commanded a place in the League side for eleven years. Was originally a left-winger but was chosen for every position for Arsenal except goal—he even played there in emergencies on occasion! His favourite and most frequent position, however, was at right-half.

Baker, naturally known as 'Doughy', captained Arsenal in the 1924 season, during which he represented the Professionals *v.* the Amateurs in the F.A. Charity Shield. Although chosen to appear in England trial games in 1921, 1925 and 1926, he did not win an England cap until 1928. It has been said that Baker would have earned more honours if he had stuck to one position, but he was the valuable type of club-man who was happy to play anywhere he was needed. He played for the Football League twice against the Irish League (1925 and 1926).

His consistent appearances from 1921 to 1929 are shown by the following season-by-season figures: 37, 32, 29, 21, 32, 31, 24, 37 and 31. Baker had in all 311 League outings with the Gunners—his only League club—although he did gain experience on the wing with Huddersfield Town during World War I. Retired in 1931 and became a talent scout for the Arsenal.

Barnes, W. (1943–55). *Full-back.* Although his parents came from Islington, Walley was born in Brecon where his father was stationed in the Army. Spotted as an amateur inside-left with Southampton, when Arsenal decided to sign him in 1943, and during wartime games turned out for the Gunners in every position except centre-half and centre-forward, including one match in goal against

Brighton and Hove Albion. Toured the Continent with an F.A. XI in 1945 and scored a goal when playing at outside-left against Belgium.

Damaged a knee in an Army P.T. display in 1945 and it was thought that his playing days were over, but Barnes, determined to fight his way back, returned to first-team duty at Preston in November 1946 after one outing in the Combination side. Immediately gained a regular place in the League team at left-back and won a championship medal and Welsh team honours during 1947–8. Switched to right-back in the following season after Scott was injured and also appeared for Wales in this position.

Became Arsenal's penalty expert and netted five from the spot in 1949–50 and captained Wales and won a Cup medal during the same season. Missed only one League game in 1951–2 but was unlucky enough to suffer a severe leg injury in the 1952 Cup final, putting him out of the game throughout 1952–3. Barnes, who both on and off the field never knew when he was beaten, emulated his former partner Scott, in that he fought his way back not only to the League side but also to international-team duty.

His first senior game after the 1952 Cup final was the public trial in August 1953 and in October he led Wales against England. Was appointed team manager of the Welsh touring side in Austria in the summer of 1954. Retired from the game in September 1955 to become soccer adviser to the B.B.C. Television Service. Played 267 League games for Arsenal (144 at right-back) made up as follows: 1946–7 (26); 1947–8 (35); 1948–9 (40); 1949–50 (38); 1950–1 (35); 1951–2 (41); 1953–4 (19); 1954–5 (25); 1955–6 (8). Capped for Wales v. E., S. and I. 1948–9–50–1–2; v. E. 1954; v. S. 1954–5; v. Belgium 1950; v. Portugal 1951; v. Rest of U.K. 1952; v. Yugoslavia 1955. Medals: League championship 1948; cup-winner's 1950; cup-loser's 1952.

Bastin, C. S. (1929–46). *Outside-left.* One of the most brilliant players of modern times. Of him 'Arbiter' (the late Frank Carruthers) of the *Daily Mail* once wrote: 'I would never leave Bastin out of any team.' A schoolboy international (E. v. W. 1926) who played his first League game with Exeter City at the age of fifteen. Joined Arsenal in 1929 (when seventeen years old) and, as is well known, became the talk of football. 'Boy' Bastin had won every major football honour at nineteen. Gained twenty-one caps (twelve at inside-left) for England; championship medals 1931-3-4-5-8; cup-winner's medals 1930-6; cup-finalist's medal 1932. His thirty-three goals from the wing in season 1933 is still a record in the Football League. Made 350 League appearances for Arsenal and scored 150 goals.

Played for England v. S. 1934-5-6-8; v. W. 1932-4-6-7; v. I. 1934-5-7; v. G. 1936-8; v. It. 1933-5; v. A. 1936; v. Cz. 1934; v. F. 1938; v. Hungary 1934; v. Swit. 1933-8. Represented the Football League v. S.L. 1932-4-7; v. I.L. 1934. Bastin's season-by-season appearances and goals were as follows: 1929-30 (21 apps. 7 goals); 1930-1 (42—28); 1931-2 (40—15); 1932-3 (42—33); 1933-4 (38—13); 1934-5 (36—20); 1935-6 (31—11); 1936-7 (33—5); 1937-8 (38—15); 1938-9 (23—3); 1946-7 (6—0). Retired in November 1946 at the age of thirty-four.

Beasley, A. (1931-6). *Wing-forward.* A forceful winger who was capable of playing in either outside position. Pat, as he was known, was born in Stourbridge, and after playing for his home town in the Birmingham League for only a few weeks Arsenal paid £550 for his transfer in May 1931. Made three appearances in the first team in 1931-2 and narrowly missed a place in the Cup-final team of that season. Gained championship medals in 1934 and 1935 with twenty-three and twenty outings respectively. Was again unlucky in missing a place in the cup-winning team of 1936 when he had played in twenty-six League games during the season. A further seven games in 1936-7 brought his total to seventy-nine League appearances (19 goals) before moving to Huddersfield in October 1936.

Won a cup-finalist's medal with the Town in 1938 and earned an English cap v. Scotland in 1939, scoring the winning goal. Toured South Africa in the close season and played in two internationals. Became captain of Fulham after the war, gaining a Division II championship medal in 1949 with thirty-nine appearances. Left Craven Cottage summer 1950 to take over the post of player-manager with Bristol City. Eight years later was appointed joint-manager of Birmingham City.

Bloomfield, J. (1954-60). *Inside-left.* A Londoner from North Kensington who was on Brentford's books when signed by Arsenal in July 1954. Had made forty-two appearances in the previous two seasons in Brentford's League team.

Came into Arsenal's senior side on 9th October 1954 at Hillsborough and scored the winning goal with a brilliant shot from the edge of the penalty area. During the season he totalled nineteen appearances (nine of them being on the left-wing) and scored four goals. Was a lively left-winger in the first two matches of 1955-6, but was then injured. Back in the side *v.* Newcastle, Bloomfield, clever in approach work, three times outstripped the defence, only to fail with his shooting. Aggregate for 1955-6 was thirty-two League games and three goals.

Was Arsenal's only ever-present in 1956-7 and was, by his intelligent play and often brilliant scheming, the key to the smooth working of a young and enthusiastic forward line. At the end of the season took part in the England (Under-23) tour and played against Bulgaria. Total League appearances at the end of season 1959-60 stood at 198 with fifty-three goals to his credit. Was transferred to Birmingham City in November 1960.

Blyth, W. N. (1915-29). *Inside-forward.* A happy-go-lucky player from Dalkeith in Midlothian. Playing football was the greatest happiness in his life and he was determined to make good at the game in spite of his parents' plans for him to follow another career. Came south to Manchester and signed professional forms for the City.

Was transferred to Arsenal in 1914-15 and won a regular place in the League team immediately after the war. Played most of his games at inside-left, as in the 1927 Cup final, or at left-half, but was equally successful almost anywhere. Missed only two League games in 1925-6 and three in each of the seasons 1920-1 and 1927-8.

In a span of eleven campaigns he made 313 League appearances for Arsenal and scored forty-seven goals. Although only slightly built, Blyth is remembered for his courage and his lack of fear of injury. Afterwards moved to Birmingham, for whom he scored four goals in twenty-one games. Was also an expert golfer.

Bowden, E. R. (1933-8). *Inside-right.* A native of the Cornish resort Looe, who first came to the notice of the League clubs when he scored ten goals for the local team against Tavistock. As a result, he became a professional player with Plymouth Argyle in 1926. Gained a Division III (S.) championship medal in 1930 and took part in the F.A. tour of Canada in 1931. Netted eighty-three goals for the Argyle before leaving to join Arsenal early in 1933.

At Highbury, Bowden filled all three inside-forward berths and helped Arsenal to many of the Club's successes. Won championship medals 1934-5 and a cup-winner's medal 1936. In addition, was capped for England on six occasions: *v*. W. 1935-6, *v*. I. 1936, *v*. Italy 1935, *v*. Austria 1936, *v*. Hungary 1937. Represented the Football League *v*. Scottish League 1935 and 1936. League appearances for Arsenal: 1932-3 (7), 1933-4 (32), 1934-5 (24), 1935-6 (22), 1936-7 (28), 1937-8 (10). Total 123, in which he scored forty-three goals.

Moved to Newcastle United in 1938 for whom he added another six goals to his individual total of 132. Was formerly an auctioneer's clerk, but after retiring from the game became a sports outfitter in Plymouth.

Bowen, D. (1950-9). *Wing-half.* Born Nantyffyllon, near Maesteg, Wales, and was an underground surveyor in a pit at Cwmdu. His family moved to Northampton and the Cobblers signed him as an amateur. After playing in the English Boys *v*. Scottish Boys match in 1948 (won, incidentally by the English Boys 9—1) he became a professional on Northampton's books.

First League game for the Cobblers was against Notts County who had Lawton in their line-up for the first time. Arsenal signed him as a left-winger in July 1950, and in his first game in their colours Bowen scored twice in a 3—0 victory over Bristol City in the London Combination.

Was soon switched, however, to wing-half on arrival at Highbury and made his League début for Arsenal in an Easter game against the Wolves in 1951. Was chosen as reserve for Wales 1952 and gained his first cap *v*. Yugoslavia in September 1954, which was before he had commanded a regular place in the Gunners' League side.

Made the left-half position his own when Mercer broke a leg and retired from the game in April 1954. Was captain of Wales in the World Cup series in 1958. In nine seasons made 146 League appearances for Arsenal. Won eighteen Welsh caps. Left Highbury in 1959 to become player-manager of Northampton Town.

Brain, J. (1924-31). *Centre-forward.* A Bristol-born centre-forward who made the most of opportunism and positional play. Was once on Cardiff City's books as an amateur, but turned pro with Ton Pentre. Signed for Arsenal in 1924 and had the satisfaction of scoring the only goal in his début match *v.* Tottenham—at inside-right that day. Went on to score twelve goals in twenty-eight League appearances during the remainder of the season. In the next (1925-6) he appeared in an England trial and also set up an individual goal-scoring record for the Club in netting thirty-four League goals. Was Arsenal's centre-forward in the Cup final of 1927 against his old club Cardiff City.

Gained a Charity Shield medal in 1930 when Arsenal, the cup-holders, beat the champions, Sheffield Wednesday, 2—1 at Chelsea, and earned a championship medal in 1931. Scored 123 goals in 204 League appearances for Arsenal, made up as follows: 1924-5 (28 apps. 12 goals); 1925-6 (41—34); 1926-7 (37—30); 1927-8 (39—22); 1928-9 (37—21); 1929-30 (6—0); 1930-1 (16—4). Moved on to Spurs (45 games 10 goals), Swansea (51—25) and then to Bristol City (32—9), making a grand total of 332 League games and 167 goals. On retiring from the football field he became manager of Cheltenham.

Buchan, C. M. (1925-8). *Inside-right.* One of the most prolific goal-scoring inside-rights ever to appear in the Football League. Although tall and somewhat awkward-looking in his gait, once he had the ball at his feet his deft touches had it in his complete command. Born at Plumstead, quite close to Arsenal's old home at Manor Ground, Buchan was an amateur with Arsenal and North-fleet but turned professional with Leyton in 1910. Scored seventeen goals for them before joining Sunderland a year later for £1,000 transfer fee.

Was their leading scorer with twenty-seven goals in thirty-six appearances in the championship season of 1912-13 and just missed a unique double when Sunderland lost by one goal to nil to Aston Villa in the Cup final of that campaign. Capped for England *v.* I. 1913; *v.* W. 1920-1; *v.* S. 1924; *v.* Bel. 1921; *v.* France 1923. Represented the Football League *v.* S.L. 1912-13-15-21-3; *v.* I.L. 1913-15-22. His 212 goals for Sunderland is still the highest individual aggregate for the club.

Came to Arsenal in 1925 on the basis of £2,000 and £100 for each goal he scored in his first season—he bagged twenty-one! League appearances for Arsenal: 1925-6 (39), 1926-7 (33), 1927-8 (30). Total 102 and forty-nine goals, which brought his personal total of League goals to 261. Captained the Gunners in their first Cup final in 1927. Became a well-known journalist and broadcaster. Died while on holiday on the Continent during the summer of 1960.

Butler, J. D. (1920–30). *Centre-half.* The keystone of the famous half-back line of the 'twenties—Baker, Butler and Blyth. This Colombo-born centre-half was developed by Dartford and went into the Arsenal team immediately after the war. Was a regular during the following ten seasons. An old type of centre-half who enjoyed the occasional sortie into the opponents' territory; scored a vital and winning goal that way in the sixth round of the F.A. Cup in 1927, to beat the Wolves 2—1. He pressed home an attack by heading a spectacular goal from a centre by Hulme.

Butler played for England *v.* Belgium in 1925 and appeared in an England trial in the following year. Took part in the 1927 Cup final against Cardiff and had made 266 League appearances for Arsenal when he moved to Torquay in 1930. Retired two years later after fifty-six games for the United and has since taken a prominent part in football management. Was manager-coach to a Belgium club and manager of Torquay for several seasons. Also managed Crystal Palace and took over from Jimmy Allen at Colchester in June 1953.

Charlton, S. (1956–8). *Right-back.* A former amateur international full-back who won four England caps while with Bromley. Born Exeter. Was a regular in Leyton Orient's team, missing only three games in three seasons. Ever-present 1952-3 (46) and 1954-5 (46) while he made forty-three appearances in 1953-4. Had played a further sixteen League games for the Orient when he moved to Arsenal with his centre-forward colleague Groves in November 1955.

Made his First Division début for the Gunners 24th December 1955 at Chelsea in a 2—0 defeat. Apart from missing two games, *v.* Spurs and Portsmouth, kept his place for the rest of the season, making nineteen appearances. Continued to be first choice at right-back in the following two seasons, with forty and thirty-six League outings, but lost his place to Wills after the first four matches of 1958–9.

Charlton's solitary goal for Arsenal's senior side was an opportune and a valuable one. It was an equalizer in the sixth-round F.A. cup-tie at the Hawthorns in 1957. With a half-time score of 1—1, four minutes after the interval Wills diverted a Kevan shot into his own net, but in the fifty-fifth minute a tremendous forty-yard shot by Charlton crashed through a mass of players past goalkeeper Sanders into the net.

Charlton was one short of a century of League appearances for Arsenal when he returned to his former club Leyton Orient in 1958.

Chenhall, J. (1944–53). *Right-back.* A product of Navy football and a native of Bristol who signed for Arsenal as an amateur in October 1944. Became a professional a year later. Made eight appearances in the Combination side in 1946–7 and nine in the following campaign. Then developed into a very useful reserve for five seasons, having a regular place in the side with the following totals: 1948–9 (29); 1949–50 (26); 1950–1 (41); 1951–2 (38); 1952–3 (21). During this period Chenhall won a Combination championship medal.

Had few opportunities in the League team, with only three outings in 1951–2 and thirteen in 1952–3, making his début at Charlton in a 3—1 victory, 20th October 1951. During his total of sixteen League matches Chenhall was rarely on the losing side; in fact, an analysis shows that eight were won, four drawn and four lost. His last four appearances were actually on the left flank.

Transferred to Fulham in 1953, Chenhall established his place in the League side at Craven Cottage and was ever-present during 1953–4. Made twenty-three appearances in 1954–5 and twenty-one in 1955–6. A useful cricketer and was an England Schools Boxing Champion at the age of thirteen.

Clapton, D. (1953–). *Right-winger.* A Londoner who had experience with Leytonstone before requesting a trial in August 1953. Was immediately signed on and played in his first Combination game in the second match of the season, in a home fixture against Chelsea. Took part in thirty-eight matches for Arsenal during that season (1953–4) of which fourteen were in the reserves and one, his début in the senior team, in a friendly against the South Africans in September 1953.

In the following season Clapton made his first appearance in the League (as in his Combination début, it was a home game against Chelsea) and had fifteen further League outings. In 1954–5 he totalled fifty-three games for Arsenal, scoring twelve goals. Made the first-team right-wing berth his own during 1955–6 and missed only three League matches.

A very clever ball-player, with a deceptive swerve, Clapton can often create havoc among the opposing defenders. When chosen to play for England *v*. Wales in 1959 he was the first Arsenal player to be capped by England for six years. Scored a hat-trick at Nottingham when Arsenal beat the Forest in the second match of season 1959–60. In the six seasons 1954–5 to 1959–60 Clapton made 184 League appearances and scored twenty-two goals.

Coleman, E. (1932–4). *Centre-forward.* Had early experience in Hucknall (Notts) junior football, but after being turned down by the Forest was secured by Halifax Town in 1927. Made forty-seven League appearances for fifteen goals before joining Grimsby in 1929, when he helped the Lincolnshire club to promotion from Division II. His thirty-five goals in 1930–1 is the highest score by a Grimsby player in First Division football. A year later the club was back in the lower division and Coleman came to Highbury to try to solve the Londoners' centre-forward problem. While at Blundell Park he had eighty-five League outings and scored fifty-seven goals. He stayed three seasons with Arsenal and collected a championship medal and also a Charity Shield medal in 1933. Made forty-five League appearances for twenty-six goals, with the following season-by-season figures: 1931–2 (6 apps. 1 goal); 1932–3 (27—24); 1933–4 (12—1).

In 1934 he moved to Middlesbrough, where he also stayed three seasons (85 apps. 20 goals) before joining Norwich City. By this time he was mainly appearing at inside-right, and when the war intervened he had scored twenty-four goals in sixty-three appearances for the Canaries. After the war one found him as player-manager of Linby Colliery where he was the inspiration behind their successful Cup run in 1950.

Compton, D. (1935–50) *Left-winger.* Signed for Arsenal 1935 and made his début in the League *v.* Derby County at Highbury in September 1936. In pre-war soccer, Compton appeared in twenty-two League games, scoring five goals, while in the Combination side his total was 128 for eighty-seven goals, which earned him a London F.A. Cup and three Combination medals. Compton twice scored five goals in a London Combination match.

Played in twelve war-time internationals (including the 8—0 defeat of Scotland in 1943) and the 'Victory' international *v.* Scotland in 1946. Back in League football after the war Compton made a further thirty-two appearances and scored ten goals. Gained a cup-winner's medal in 1950, on which note of triumph he retired from the football scene.

Compton had, of course, in the meantime, carved a remarkable career for himself on the cricket field, where he was a carefree and brilliant England and Middlesex batsman. Scored 1,004 runs in his first season (1936), sixty-five runs in his first Test (*v.* New Zealand 1937) and 102 in his first Test against Australia (1938). Had a great season in 1947 when he smashed Hayward's forty-one-year-old record aggregate of 3,518 runs and Hobbs' sixteen centuries in a season which stood for twenty-two years. Compton's figures were 3,816 (average 90.85) runs and eighteen centuries. His highest innings was 252 not out.

Unfortunately, Compton's cavalier style was hampered in later years by a knee injury sustained in his football career.

Compton, L. (1932–52). *Centre-half.* A one-club man and a grand servant at Highbury for over twenty years. Joined Arsenal in February 1932 from the Athenian League club, Hampstead Town, and within three months played in Arsenal's senior team at Villa Park. Operating at left-back, Compton could not, however, command a regular place before the war, because of the brilliance of Male and Hapgood, but such was his excellent form that the England selectors chose him to appear in trial games in 1937 and 1938.

Compton took part in sixty-seven League games during those eight seasons and won, in 221 appearances, five London Combination championship medals. War-time soccer saw Compton playing in every position except on the wings; being particularly successful at centre-forward, where he once scored ten goals *v.* Leyton Orient, played in the 1941 Cup final *v*. Preston (heading the equalizing goal to earn a replay) and represented England.

After the war, at centre-half, he became the key-stone of Arsenal's defence; 'Big Leslie' commanded the middle, blocking the through-pass and heading away menacing centres from the wings—a real tower of strength. His first full cap (he played in four war-time internationals) in 1950 *v*. Wales and again *v*. Yugoslavia was a long overdue honour and was, incidentally, at the age of thirty-eight the oldest début in an English international. Won a League medal 1948 and a cup-winner's medal in 1950. Took part in 253 League games and retired to coaching staff at Highbury in 1952. Was a Middlesex county cricketer.

Cope, H. W. (1926–33). *Left-back*. A full-back from Notts County with whom he had both First and Second Division experience. Earned a Division II championship medal with them in 1922–3 when he made twenty-eight League appearances. Had made 126 outings in League matches for the Meadow Lane club when he moved to Highbury in December 1926. During the remainder of that season he made eleven League appearances for Arsenal and also played in an England trial game.

Sustained a knee injury in the Easter games of 1927 which did not mend in time to play in the Cup final against Cardiff City that April. So the unlucky Cope had to give way to the player he had displaced, Alf Kennedy.

Cope made twenty-four and twenty-three League appearances during the following seasons, 1928 and 1929; but, thereafter, the brilliance of the young Eddie Hapgood limited his first-team games to one during each of the next three seasons. His four outings in 1932–3 brought his total to sixty-five League games for the Gunners. This fine club-man, who was content to return to the reserve team when displaced by a much younger man, later became the trainer of Blackburn Rovers, and was, incidentally, serving in that capacity when Hapgood was appointed manager of the Rovers after the war.

Copping, W. (1934–9). *Left-half*. Worked in the pits and played for Dearne Valley Old Boys and Middlecliff Rovers. After an unsuccessful trial with Barnsley (his home town), he joined Leeds in 1930 and became a member of the famous Edwards, Hart,

Copping half-back line of that club. Had already won six England caps when he moved to Highbury in June 1934 for a fee of £8,000.

The harder the game the better he liked it. Known as the 'Iron Man', he was in his element in the famous rough-and-tumble international against Italy in 1935 when his courage set a fine example to his side. Copping, who was never cautioned or sent off the field, always said: 'The first man in a tackle never gets hurt.'

While with Arsenal he gained fourteen further caps, against twelve different countries, and, in addition, won two championship medals 1935-8 and a cup-winner's medal in 1936. His League appearances were: 1934-5 (31), 1935-6 (33), 1936-7 (38), 1937-8 (38) and 1938-9 (26). A total of 166. He returned to Leeds in 1939 and in 1946 became trainer to Southend United. Afterwards he joined his old Highbury colleague Pat Beasley at Bristol, and then moved to Coventry City as trainer.

Cox, F. (1949-53). *Right-winger*. Joined the ground staff at White Hart Lane from St. George's Lads' Club (Reading) and graduated through the nursery team Northfleet to sign professional forms in 1938. Played in all five forward positions for the Spurs. Was in Transport Command during the war and operated in the Far East. Arsenal paid a five-figure fee for his services in September 1949.

Had a wonderful match v. Sunderland in the following December, when his speed and trickery continually had the opposition reeling and his passes made goals for Forbes, Goring and Logie in a 5—0 victory. The semi-finals in 1950 and 1952 v. Chelsea, however, are remembered as 'Cox's matches'. In the first he scored direct from a corner on the stroke of half-time, to put Arsenal back in the game after being two down, and in the replay he scored the only goal of the game after a superb piece of individualism. Two years later Chelsea met Cox again in the semi-final round, and again this bundle of energy scored the goal to earn a replay and netted twice in the latter when Arsenal triumphed 3—0. Had therefore scored five goals in four semi-final games v. Chelsea but was not generally a prolific scorer, since in seventy-nine League appearances for the Gunners he totalled only nine goals.

In August 1953 was transferred to West Bromwich Albion, the club against which he first played in Arsenal's colours, and later became coach. Was appointed manager of Bournemouth in April 1956 and later became manager of Portsmouth. Won a cup-winner's medal in 1950 and a cup-finalist's medal in 1952.

Crayston, W. J. (1934–9). *Right-half.* Born at Grange-over-Sands and was a League player with Barrow at the age of sixteen. After eighty consecutive appearances for them was transferred to Bradford in 1930. Was unlucky to break a wrist and a leg in 1933, but Arsenal signed him during the close season 1934. Made his League début for the Gunners at Highbury *v.* Liverpool 1st September 1934 and went on to play in thirty-seven games that season to earn a championship medal.

The following season (1935–6) was a particularly successful one for him, because, in addition to gaining a cup-winner's medal when Arsenal beat Sheffield United at Wembley, he represented the Football League *v.* the Irish League, and played for England against Scotland, Wales, Austria, Belgium and Germany. In 1938 he won a second championship medal, appeared in an England trial and gained further caps *v.* Wales, Ireland and Czechoslovakia.

Never appeared in fewer than thirty League games in a season for Arsenal and had a final total of 168. Crayston gave up active football during the war after a leg operation. After service as a flying officer he returned to Highbury and became assistant manager. Was appointed manager in November 1956 after the death of Mr. Tom Whittaker but resigned at the end of the following season. Was afterwards manager of Doncaster Rovers.

Curtis, G. (1938–47). *Inside-forward.* A clever footballer who signed for Arsenal at seventeen from West Thurrock, Essex. As a schoolboy once had a badly bruised right foot but continued to play—plimsoll on right foot, boot on the left—and so Curtis became a natural player with either foot. In fact, it was said that he was one of the best 'two-footed' players in the game just after the war.

Had made two appearances in Arsenal's League team when he joined the Army at the outbreak of the war. Eventually he went to India and was a star in Denis Compton's touring team out there. On returning to this country Curtis played in eleven League games during 1946–7. In addition, he had twenty-seven outings in the reserve side, was a member of the victorious Arsenal team in the

Football Combination Championship match (*v.* Portsmouth 3—0) and just missed a Football Combination cup-winner's medal, losing 2—1 *v.* Swansea at White Hart Lane in the final.

Curtis captained Arsenal's reserve side in the first public trial of 1947 and half an hour after the game was signed by Southampton for £8,000. Was a regular first-teamer at the Dell for five seasons, 1948–52. Afterwards played in France and in August 1956 was appointed manager-coach of the England Youth side.

Daniel, R. (1946–53). *Centre-half.* Was an amateur full-back in Swansea Town's senior team when only fifteen and came to Highbury in September 1946. Due to Army service made only eight appearances in the reserves during the following two years but returned, after a further nine Combination matches, to make his début in the League team in the last match of season 1948–9—a home game *v.* Charlton which was won by two goals to nil.

Played regularly in the reserve team during 1949–50, in addition to six appearances in League games, with such splendid form that it was obvious the Club possessed a completely adequate reserve to take over when Compton was unavailable or injured. Came under the notice of the Welsh selectors in 1951, and whilst still a reserve was honoured *v.* England, Ireland and Portugal. In the same season Daniel also gained a Combination championship medal with twenty-five appearances.

Stepped into the senior team on Compton's retirement in 1952 to win a cup-loser's medal at the end of the season and a League championship medal in the following campaign, missing only one match. Broke his forearm against Blackpool a month before the Cup final, but played at Wembley with a plastic covering on it. After eighty-seven League games for Arsenal requested a transfer and moved to Sunderland, summer 1953, for nearly £30,000. Gained twelve Welsh caps while with Arsenal. Later moved to Cardiff and then back to Swansea.

Dickson, W. (1953–6). *Half-back.* Born in Lurgan and was transferred from Glenavon to Notts County in November 1945. Two years later, when Lawton joined the County, Dickson moved in the reverse direction as part of the transfer deal. At Chelsea he gained a regular place in the League side in 1950 which was quickly followed by one in the Irish team. After 101 League games and eighteen cup-ties for Chelsea, differences arose between player and club. Refusing to re-sign for the start of 1953–4, he stayed in Ireland, and nearly agreed to join Preston, but eventually signed for Arsenal in October 1953.

Made twenty-four League appearances during the remainder of the season, but afterwards became the game's unluckiest footballer with a long string of injuries. He dislocated his shoulder in the second game of 1954–5—out of football until the end of September. Two more games—knee trouble; and whilst having treatment for that came an appendix operation. Recovered and played several Combination games, when just before Christmas back trouble put him in a plaster spinal jacket. Came back v. Spurs on Good Friday 1955, tore ligaments in his knee—out for the rest of the season.

Spent the whole of the summer getting fit once more, but, sad to say, his shoulder was again dislocated in the very first game of the season (1955–6) and subsequently played in no further senior games for Arsenal. Was surely Arsenal's unluckiest footballer. Placed on the open-to-transfer list at the end of 1955–6 season, Dickson returned to Ireland, but Mansfield signed him early in the following campaign.

Docherty, T. (1958–61). *Left-half.* Born in Glasgow and joined Celtic after being demobilized from the Army in July 1948. Was kept in the reserves due to the splendid form of Bobby Evans, the Scottish international, and was transferred to Preston in 1949. Made his first-team début with the North End as an emergency outside-left on Christmas Day 1949 and quickly became their regular wing-half. Apart from season 1953–4, when a broken ankle-bone put him out of action for a considerable period, Docherty missed only eleven League games in seven seasons at Deepdale.

Won a Division II championship medal in 1950–1 and a cup-finalist's medal in 1953–4. League appearances for Preston: 1950–1 (42); 1951–2 (42); 1952–3 (41); 1953–4 (26); 1954–5 (40); 1955–6 (41); 1956–7 (37); 1957–8 (40). Was a member of the Rest of Great Britain XI v. Wales at Cardiff in the Welsh F.A.'s 75th Anniversary match in December 1951, and while at Preston was capped nineteen times by Scotland.

Joined Arsenal in August 1958, and his energetic and inspiring play has done much to revitalize the young team at Highbury. Was unfortunate enough to break a leg against his old club in October 1959. Arsenal were placed fourth in the League table at the time, but when Docherty came back again, for the cup-ties against Rotherham, Arsenal had slumped to sixteenth position. Made thirty-eight League appearances for Arsenal in 1958–9 and won three more Scottish caps. Total League appearances at the end of 1959–60 stood at 371. Appointed coach at Chelsea in 1961.

Dodgin, W. (1952–61). *Centre-half.* Comes from Wardley in County Durham and is the son of the former Brentford manager. Was a Fulham player with thirty-five League appearances when his father was team manager at Craven Cottage, but was unsettled there by some barracking from a section of the crowd. His directors refused to transfer him but agreed to play him in the reserves. Six weeks later, however, in December 1952, Arsenal signed him in exchange for Healey, a reserve full-back, plus a moderate fee.

Dodgin showed very good form in the Combination side at Highbury during the remainder of the season and looked a very capable centre-half on his League début on a Wednesday evening in April 1953, when Daniel was on duty for Wales at Belfast. The international winger Langton, converted to centre-forward, had few chances against Dodgin in this game, when Arsenal beat Bolton 4—1. The victory put the Gunners on the top of the table for the first time in the season and there they remained to the end.

On Daniel's departure to Sunderland, Dodgin stepped into the League side and settled down to make the position his own, even surviving the sweeping team changes which were made in the worst start of any season. Was chosen to captain Young England *v.* Young Italy at Bologna in January 1954 and missed only three League games during the season. The next, 1954–5, was not a lucky one for he was back as a regular reserve. Sharing the senior-team place with Fotheringham in 1955–6, Dodgin played himself back as the first-choice centre-half with the following appearances: 1956–7 (41); 1957–8 (23); 1958–9 (39) and 1959–60 (30). Had made 191 League appearances at the end of 1959–60. Moved back to Fulham in 1961.

Drake, E. J. (1934–9). *Centre-forward.* A happy and plucky player who, despite an unfortunate crop of injuries, was Arsenal's best centre-forward of modern times. Scored many goals for Southampton Schoolboys and had experience with Winchester City (Hampshire League) before Southampton signed him in 1931. Got a hat-trick for them in his first game and had totalled forty-eight goals in seventy-two games when he joined Arsenal in March 1934. Quickly made his mark at Highbury and, in the following season, set up a new Club record with forty-two goals—the best total in the League that year! In December 1935, at Villa Park, he equalled the Division I individual goal-scoring record by netting all seven in Arsenal's 7—1 victory over Aston Villa. Was badly injured in the England *v.* Wales international of February 1936, but turned out in the Cup final of that season with his knee swathed in bandages to score the only goal of the game.

Honours include: England caps *v.* Ireland and Italy 1935; *v.* Wales 1936; *v.* Hungary 1937 and France 1938. Championship medals 1935–8; cup-winner's medal 1936 and Charity Shield medals 1935–8. Appearances and goals: 1933–4 (10—7); 1934–5 (41—42); 1935–6 (26—23); 1936–7 (26—20); 1937–8 (27—17); 1938–9 (38—14). Total: 168 apps. 123 goals. An unfortunate spinal injury in a war-time match at Reading in 1945 terminated his playing career, but has since made a name for himself as manager of Reading and, more recently, of Chelsea.

Drury, G. B. (1938–47). *Inside-forward.* Born at Hucknall in Nottinghamshire and was on the books of Sheffield Wednesday when Arsenal signed him as an outside-left. Made his League début for the Gunners in 1937–8 and had eleven outings at inside-forward during that campaign. Was chosen, along with team-mates Compton, L., Compton, D. and Lewis, to represent the London Combination against the Central League in 1938. His craft and ball control earned him twenty-three appearances and three goals in 1938–9, and then came war service with the R.A.F.

On the resumption of League football in 1947, Drury made four appearances in Arsenal's first team and then joined West Bromwich Albion to be near his aging parents. He played in five League games for them, scoring one goal, during the remainder of the season and gained a regular place in the next, scoring seven goals in twenty-three appearances. Hapgood signed him for Watford in July 1948, but after a change of managership there he returned to the Midlands to play for Darlaston in the Birmingham Combination.

Moving to Linby Colliery, he joined another ex-Arsenal player, Ernie Coleman, who was the player-manager of this Central Alliance side. These two inside-forwards did much to put Linby on the 'football map' in 1950–1 when they helped the Colliery reach the first round proper of the F.A. Cup for the first time. Drury finally assisted another Central Alliance club, South Normanton.

Eastham, G. (1960–). *Inside-forward.* Signed by Newcastle United from Ards for a fee of £8,000 and made eighteen League appearances in season 1956–7 and scored two goals. Twenty-nine appearances and three goals in 1957–8, thirty-five appearances and six goals in 1958–9 and forty-two appearances with eighteen goals in 1959–60 made up a total of 124 League appearances and twenty-nine goals for the United. Represented the Football League *v.* Irish League 1960 and played for England (Under-23) *v.* France, Scotland, Holland, East Germany, Poland and Israel 1960.

Refused to re-sign for Newcastle in the summer of 1960, and after prolonged negotiations joined Arsenal in November. Made his début in Arsenal's colours in a Combination game at Highbury against Leicester City Reserves on 19th November. The reserve gate swelled to nearly 10,000 to see this £47,500 buy in his first game as a Gunner. Three weeks later Eastham wore the number-ten shirt in the League team against his father's old club Bolton Wanderers and netted two goals in a highly satisfactory début.

Eastham's father was a well-known player of the 1930's who possessed uncanny skill as a ball player. He developed with Cambridge Road and South Shore Wednesday (Blackpool juniors) and signed for Bolton in 1932. Played for England *v.* Holland 1935. Saw service with Brentford and Blackpool before joining Swansea Town in August 1947.

Evans, D. (1951–). *Left-back.* Made steady but regular progress since joining Arsenal from Ellesmere Port F.C. in January 1951. Had several games in the London Mid-week League side during the remainder of that season and became a regular right-back in the Eastern Counties team in the following campaign

(1951–2) with twenty appearances. Also made four appearances in the Combination side in the same season, before establishing a regular place at left-back in the reserves during 1952–3 with thirty-four appearances.

Continuing his progress, Evans made his League début in the first home game of 1953–4, when Huddersfield drew 0—0 at Highbury, and totalled ten outings during the season. Played in exactly half of the League matches in 1954–5 and was the only ever-present player in 1955–6, when he took part in fifty-two senior games. At the end of season 1959–60 he had made 189 League appearances, every one of which was at left-back.

Season 1959–60 was an extremely unlucky one, for Evans fractured an ankle at Wolverhampton in the third match, recovered to appear in the team again on Boxing Day, but, only three games later, had the dire misfortune to break the other ankle at White Hart Lane. Turned out in the Metropolitan League and Football Combination sides during the last month of the season but did not reappear in the senior side.

Is a very dependable penalty-kicker and his successes include four in each of the seasons 1956–7 and 1958–9.

Forbes, A. (1948–56). *Wing-half.* Gave up soccer for a spell after leaving school to concentrate on playing ice-hockey, at which he represented Scotland against the Canadian Army. Returned to football with Dundee North End, a Scottish junior club, as a centre-forward and was transferred to Sheffield United in 1944. On settling down at wing-half, he quickly won Scottish honours and, like Macaulay, played for Scotland *v.* England 1947 and for Great Britain *v.* Rest of Europe a month later. Also gained further caps *v.* Wales and Ireland 1948.

Was on the transfer list and recovering from an appendicitis operation in February 1948 when Macaulay visited him in hospital and persuaded him to move south to Arsenal. Forbes made a record recovery and played his first League game for the Gunners on 6th March, scoring a goal in a 5—2 victory over the Wolves. It was an ironical fact that he was preferred to Macaulay for the 1950 Cup final, but his hard direct tackling blotted out Liverpool's dangerous winger Liddell, which did much to enable Arsenal to dictate the run of play in this vital game.

Forbes, always willing to take the ball through, scored twenty goals for Arsenal, won a League championship medal in 1952–3 and collected Scottish caps *v.* England, Portugal and France 1950; *v.* Wales, Ireland and Austria 1951 and *v.* Wales, Denmark and Sweden, 1952. Cartilage trouble kept him out of the League team for much of 1955–6 and at the end of the season Forbes was transferred to the newly promoted Division II club, Leyton Orient. Totalled 217 League games made up as follows: 1947–8 (11); 1948–9 (25); 1949–50 (23); 1950–1 (32); 1951–2 (38); 1952–3 (33); 1953–4 (30); 1954–5 (20); 1955–6 (5).

Fotheringham, J. (1951–9). *Centre-half.* Born in Hamilton, Lanarkshire, but at an early age moved with his parents to Corby in Northamptonshire. Played for his adopted county against Gloucestershire in a schoolboys' representative game and, at the age of fifteen, had a trial for Arsenal *v.* Leyton Orient in a London Mid-week League match in October 1949. Signed professional forms on reaching his seventeenth birthday in March 1951. This 6 ft. 4 in. centre-half made his début in the Combination team at Watford in the following October and continued to develop rapidly in the reserves, with twenty-seven appearances in 1951–2, eight in 1952–3 and thirty-eight in 1953–4.

After Forbes (8 games), Dickson (3) and Dodgin (3) had held in turn the centre-half position, at the start of season 1954–5, Fotheringham was drafted into the League side at Bolton on 6th November. The game ended in a 2—2 draw and, although up against the England centre-forward Nat Lofthouse, he played a splendidly cool and efficient game. Not only was he retained for the following match—a friendly against Spartak—but he kept his place for the rest of the season, making twenty-seven appearances.

Was still first choice during the first half of 1955–6 but in January, after twenty-five League outings, lost some of his commanding form and gave way to Dodgin again. Made twenty further appearances, totalling seventy-two, before being transferred to Heart of Midlothian at the end of season 1958–9.

Goring, H. (1948–60). *Centre-forward or wing-half.* Born at Bishop's Cleeve and was discovered by Jimmy Brain, the former Arsenal forward and manager of Cheltenham Town, playing for the village team. Son of the local postman, Goring, who on leaving school was first a butcher's assistant and then a market gardener, was a member of Cheltenham's Southern League side at eighteen.

Signed for Arsenal in January 1948 and took part in the Club's tour of Brazil in May 1949 with promising results. Made his League début at Chelsea in the following August, scoring the winning goal, and quickly became one of the discoveries of 1949–50. He not only topped the Club's scorers in his first season with twenty-one goals but his intelligent play, particularly in the Cup final of that campaign, earned many bouquets.

With a shortage of wing-halves on the staff, Arsenal tried Goring at right-half in the reserves during 1953–4 with such success that, after his first League game in the position against Portsmouth in April 1954, he was a regular for two seasons and was also honoured by the F.A. on their tour of the West Indies in 1955 at right-half.

Was captain of Arsenal in 1956 and made 220 appearances (ninety-four at right-half) and scored fifty-one goals. Honours: League championship medal 1953; cup-winner's medal 1950. League apps.: 1949–50 (29); 1950–1 (34); 1951–2 (16); 1952–3 (29); 1953–4 (9); 1954–5 (41); 1955–6 (37); 1956–7 (13); 1957–8 (10); 1958–9 (2).

Groves, V. (1955–). *Inside-forward or winger.* After experience with Leytonstone and Walthamstow Avenue, turned professional with Leyton Orient. Made thirty League appearances and scored fifteen goals in 1954–5 and a further twelve games (nine goals) in the following season before joining Arsenal in November 1955. Made his début for the Gunners 12th November in a home game v. Sheffield United and scored one of the goals in a 2—1 victory. His ribs were severely injured in the next game at Preston and he missed two matches before he was back in the side v. West Bromwich Albion to make a further twelve appearances. Groves scored five goals in his first five games and also netted an equalizer five minutes before time in the third-round Cup replay at Bedford.

Bad luck with injuries dogged his career towards the end of the season. Had a cartilage operation during the summer of 1956 and was not really fit when he returned to the side at Hillsborough on 22nd September. Recalled for the Villa game 3rd November, he scored two goals but sustained concussion and an injured right knee.

Was out of the game for three months. Unsettled and discouraged by his series of injuries, he requested a transfer but, instead, eventually returned to first-team duty and recaptured the form which had interested the England selectors twelve months earlier.

Played in thirty League games in 1957–8 (ten goals) and thirty-three for another ten goals in 1958–9, during which season he was appointed captain of the side. Was converted to a wing-half in 1959–60 with considerable success. Up to the end of that season Groves had made 113 League appearances and had scored thirty-one goals.

Represented England 'B' v. Yugoslavia 'B' 1956, England Under-23 v. France Under-23 1957, London v. Frankfurt 1956.

Hapgood, E. A. (1928–39). *Left-back*. Known as the 'Ambassador of Football'. One of the most polished full-backs the game has ever known, whose unruffled calm, uncanny positional play and sure kicking set a wonderful example to footballers everywhere. Captained Arsenal and England many times and was truly one of football's gentlemen. Born in Bristol, Hapgood was an amateur with the Rovers at the age of eighteen, but Arsenal signed him in October 1927 from the Southern League club Kettering. Gained a regular place in the side in 1929 and in the following ten years never played in fewer than thirty-two games each season. Totalled 393 League games for Arsenal.

His numerous honours include five championship medals (1931–3–4–5–8), two cup-winner's medals (1930–6) and a loser's medal (1932). Including twelve war-time internationals, he made forty-three appearances for England and was captain in thirty-four of them. Won his first cap in May 1933 v. Italy and subsequently played against fifteen different countries. Hapgood lost his place in 1937 and 1938 to Catlin (Sheffield Wednesday) and Barkas (Manchester City) but won it back v. Scotland 1938. In addition, he represented the Football League four times and took part in five England trial games.

After spells as manager of Blackburn Rovers and Watford, Hapgood became manager of the Southern League club, Bath City.

Harper, W. (1925–32). *Goalkeeper.* Along with David Jack, was one of Herbert Chapman's first captures. Harper was already well established as a Scottish international goalkeeper when he came south from Hibernian, for he had played in all three 'home' internationals in each of the seasons 1923–4–5. He won a tenth cap *v.* England while an Arsenal player in 1926.

Formerly a heavyweight boxing champion in the Scots Guards, Harper used his physique to full advantage with tremendously long goal-kicks. He was a daring goalkeeper and a favourite of the football public. After losing his place in the first team to Lewis, he decided, at the end of 1926–7 season, to try his luck in the United States. His hopes were not fulfilled there, however, and he returned to this country somewhat disillusioned three years later.

He signed once more for Arsenal and vied with Preedy and Keyser for a place in the League side in 1931 season. He made nineteen appearances and so qualified for a championship medal. The arrival of Moss from Oldham, and his speedy promotion, led to Harper moving to Plymouth Argyle in 1932, by which time he had taken part in sixty-three League games for Arsenal. When Harper retired from the playing field, he became the Argyle's trainer.

Haverty, J. (1954–). *Outside-left.* A diminutive bundle of tricks who is quite a favourite with the Highbury crowds. A native of Dublin, he represented Eire in a youth international and helped his club, St. Patrick's F.C., reach the final of the Eire Cup before joining Arsenal in July 1954.

A month later Haverty was introduced to First Division football in an evening game at Goodison Park where, partnered by Tapscott, he formed one of the smallest left-wings in football. Played in six League matches during 1954–5 and eight in 1955–6 when, apart from the very last match, he took part in Arsenal's strong finish in gaining fifteen points out of the last possible eighteen. At the end of the season he won a full 'cap', being selected to play for his country against Holland.

During 1956–7 Haverty gained a regular place on the Arsenal left-wing, scoring eight goals in twenty-eight appearances. His ability to dance round his opponents with impish regularity inspired the seven-goal rampage against Manchester City in October, while

175

his wonder display, crowned by a vital second goal, for Eire against Germany in November made him the hero of Dublin. Played for Eire in the World Cup qualifying competition against Denmark (October 1956) and England (twice in May 1957) and gained further caps in 1958, 1959 and 1960. Had made 112 League appearances (twenty-one goals) at the end of 1959–60.

Henderson, J. G. (1958–). *Outside-left.* Glasgow-born. Joined Portsmouth in 1951–2 from a Glasgow youth club. Had seven seasons at Fratton Park, during which time he appeared in 214 League games and scored seventy goals. Was first capped at outside-right for Scotland *v.* Sweden in 1952–3. In the following campaign he appeared at centre-forward *v.* England and Norway, and at outside-left *v.* Ireland when he scored in the 3—1 win at Windsor Park, Belfast. Appearances and goals for Portsmouth: 1951–2 (27 apps. 8 goals); 1952–3 (20—11); 1953–4 (34—8); 1954–5 (41—13); 1955–6 (35—16); 1956–7 (33—11); 1957–8 (24—3).

Moved to Wolverhampton towards the close of 1957–8, making nine appearances with three goals for the Midland side. Was transferred to Highbury in September 1958. Scored two goals in his first game in Arsenal's colours *v.* West Bromwich Albion and struck such good form that he regained a place in Scotland's team, which he had last occupied in 1955–6.

Honours: Scotland *v.* Sweden 1953; *v.* England, Ireland and Norway 1954; *v.* Wales 1956; *v.* Wales and Ireland 1959. Scotland 'B' *v.* England 'B' 1953 and 1954. Has been troubled by injuries while at Highbury but has made over fifty League appearances and scored nineteen goals for Arsenal in two seasons. Henderson, a versatile forward, has played in all five positions in the Gunners' attack.

Herd, D. (1954–). *Inside-forward.* Son of Alex Herd, the Scottish international who gained a cup-winner's medal with Manchester City in 1934. Joined his father as a player for Stockport County in April 1951 and, before the season was over, father and son appeared together in the County's League team. They filled the inside-forward positions in a match against Hartlepools United—David scoring one of the winning goals.

National Service interrupted his career with Stockport but, all the same, several 'big' clubs were interested in this tall, well-built forward when, on demobilization in August 1954, he celebrated by scoring three goals in the County's pre-season trial game.

Amid very keen competition from Liverpool, Arsenal eventually signed him for £10,000. Scored two goals in his first game in the Londoners' colours—a 2—2 draw *v.* Brentford Reserves in the Combination Cup—and netted the winning goal, three minutes from time, in the London F.A. Cup final *v.* West Ham in March 1955. Made his League début for Arsenal in February 1955 *v.* Leicester City at Highbury and had two further outings at the end of the season for one goal. Came to the front with a bang in 1956–7 as a centre-forward and was in the following campaign Arsenal's leading scorer with twenty-four goals in thirty-nine appearances.

Deservedly won Scottish caps in 1959 *v.* Wales, Ireland and England. By the end of 1959–60 Herd had had 126 League outings for Arsenal and had scored sixty-eight goals in those games.

Hill, F. (1932–6). *Wing-half.* Transferred from Forfar Athletic to Aberdeen in 1928 and gained his first Scottish cap *v.* France 1930. Two more *v.* Wales and Ireland followed in 1931, when he also played for the Scottish League against the Football League. Joined Arsenal in May 1932 and made his League début for the London club at Blackburn in the following October. Despite competition from wing-halves Jones, John, Crayston and Copping, Hill earned a championship medal in each of his first three seasons at Highbury. Sometimes played at wing-forward or, on occasion, at centre-forward. Although only a lightweight, his tenacious tackling earned him the title of 'Tiger' Hill.

Moved to Blackpool in June 1936 after seventy-six League outings with Arsenal and helped them regain Division I status in 1937. At that time he was permanently on the left-wing and he scored eight goals. Reverted to wing-half with Southampton in 1939. Since the war he has made his mark in the management side of football with Crewe Alexandra, Burnley, Preston North End and Notts County. League appearances with Arsenal were: 1932–3 (26), 1933–4 (25), 1934–5 (15) and 1935–6 (10).

Hoar, S. (1924–9). *Outside-left.* Joined Luton Town in 1914–15 and stayed to make 209 Third Division appearances and score thirty-six goals for them before donning an Arsenal shirt in 1924. In his first season at Highbury Hoar had eighteen outings in the first team and, in addition, took part in an England trial. Made twenty-one appearances (three goals) in the following campaign and sixteen, for another three goals, in the next when he also played in Arsenal's first Cup final. After sustaining an injury in the Easter games of that year, there was some doubt whether he would pass a fitness test for the final. He came through the test all right but had a lean time in the match against Cardiff's Scottish international right-back Nelson, who was on top form. Incidentally, six years later the same Jimmy Nelson, then a Newcastle player, once again helped beat Arsenal in a Cup final.

Hoar's best season was in 1927–8 when he missed only four matches and scored ten goals. A further six appearances and one goal in 1928–9 gave him an aggregate of ninety-nine games and eighteen goals for Arsenal. He then moved on to Clapton Orient for whom he played in twenty-six matches.

Holton, C. (1947–58). *Centre-forward and wing-half.* Centre-half at school in Oxford, left-winger with Marston Minors and full-back with Oxford City. Came to Arsenal in October 1947 as a right full-back. Played for the Army when on National Service and after playing five games at full-back turned centre-forward in a Combination game at Fulham, April 1950. Had netted five goals in six matches by the end of the season. In 1950–1 Holton's success as a goal-scoring leader was continued with twenty-seven goals in thirty Combination appearances, together with a further five in ten League games. Had made his début in the latter on Boxing Day at Stoke.

Was a regular centre-forward during the three seasons 1951–2 (28 apps. 17 goals,), 1952–3 (21–19), 1953–4 (32–17), but made only eight appearances in 1954–5. In the following campaign he came back into the side at left-half in October, *v.* Everton, and was such an instant success in his new position that he was appointed captain for eleven games. Holton's versatility is illustrated by the fact that during this season he played seventeen times at left-half, ten at centre-forward, three at right-half and one at centre-half.

Has represented London F.A. and holds a cup-finalist's medal (1952) and a League championship medal (1953). After 198 League appearances and eighty-three goals for Arsenal was signed by Watford in October 1958 for £9,000.

Had a wonderful season when Watford gained promotion to the Third Division in 1959–60; was captain of the side and broke the club's scoring record with forty-five goals, this being ten more than the previous best credited to McPherson (1928–9) and Lane (1934–5). At the end of 1959–60 Holton had made seventy-five League appearances for Watford with a tally of fifty-one goals.

Hulme, J. H. A. (1926–38). *Outside-right.* In his day was the fastest man in football and his lightning dashes down the wing repeatedly caused havoc among defences. Although born in Stafford, he developed his soccer talents with York City. Blackburn Rovers paid £250 for his services in February 1924, but he cost Arsenal £3,500 a year later. His first honour came in 1926 when he was chosen for a Football League XI *v.* the Army. Capped for England *v.* S. 1927–8–33; *v.* W. 1928–9; *v.* I. 1928–9; *v.* Bel. 1927; *v.* France 1927. Represented Football League *v.* S.L. 1928–9–33; *v.* I. L. 1928–32. Won championship medals 1931 (32 apps.) 1933 (40 apps.) and 1935 (16 apps.), cup-winner's medals 1930–6, cup-loser's medals 1927–32. Scored 108 goals in 333 League appearances for Arsenal.

Was transferred to Huddersfield in January 1938 and was a member of their Cup-final side of that year, making his fifth appearance in a Wembley Cup final (a record). He retired from the playing field on that day when Preston won by a penalty. Incidentally, Huddersfield had another ex-Arsenal player on the left-wing in Pat Beasley.

Hulme was also a notable and hard-hitting cricketer for Middlesex during the 1930's and shared the record sixth-wicket stand of 212 runs with G. O. Allen in 1934. Was the manager of Tottenham Hotspur for some years after the war, and is now a well-known journalist.

Hutchins, A. V. (1920–3). *Full-back.* From Croydon Common, a club which used to operate in the Southern League together with such well-known Football League teams of today as Swindon, Southampton, Queen's Park Rangers and Northampton and the First Division club West Ham United.

During his last season with Croydon Common, Hutchins created a remarkable goal-scoring record. Although playing in the full-back position, he ended the season as the top individual goal-scorer for his club, having scored seven times—all from penalty kicks! In contrast, Hutchins scored one goal during his spell at Highbury.

He made a total of 104 League appearances for Arsenal in the four seasons immediately following the First World War and missed only three matches in season 1920–1 and only five during 1921–2. From Arsenal, Hutchins joined another London club, Charlton Athletic, who were at that time, it will be remembered, an average Third Division side. He played in twenty-one League games for the Athletic.

Jack, D. B. N. (1929–34). *Inside-right.* A tall graceful player who was in every way a worthy successor to Buchan. Had already made a name for himself with Bolton Wanderers whom he joined from Plymouth in 1921 for £3,000. Had the distinction of scoring the first goal at Wembley in that never-to-be-forgotten final of 1923, when Bolton beat West Ham 2—0 before the biggest crowd ever to assemble there. Three years later he scored the winning goal for the Wanderers against Manchester City in the 1926 Cup final. In addition, he gained England honours in 1924 *v.* S. and W. and in 1928 *v.* France and Belgium. He also played for the Football League *v.* I.L. 1923–9 and *v.* S.L. 1928.

Jack was transferred to Highbury in 1929 and further honours came his way including England caps *v.* S., Germany and Austria in 1930 and *v.* W. and Austria in 1933. Also took part in Football League games *v.* S.L. 1930 and *v.* I.L. 1931. Won a third Cup-final medal in 1930 and just missed creating a record of Wembley victories when he appeared in Arsenal's losing side of 1932. He finally completed his collection of football trophies with championship medals in 1931–3. He made 181 League appearances for Arsenal as follows: 1928–9 (31), 1929–30 (33), 1930–1 (35), 1931–2 (34), 1932–3 (34), 1933–4 (14). His League goals were ten for Plymouth, 143 for Bolton and 112 for Arsenal. Later became manager of Southend United and then of Middlesbrough. Also had a similar appointment in Ireland until he passed away in September 1958.

James, A. (1929–37). *Inside-left.* Undoubtedly the greatest footballer between the two wars. Originally a goal-scoring inside-forward, but is usually remembered for his uncanny gift of making openings for his colleagues. Transferred from Raith Rovers to Preston in 1926 where he scored fifty-three goals in four seasons. Earned four caps while at Deepdale (*v*. W. 1926; *v*. E. 1928–9; *v*. I. 1929) and was a star member of the 'Blue Devils' Scottish side which won 5—1 at Wembley in 1928. Moved south to Highbury in 1929 for £9,000 and took a little time to settle down, but never looked back after a dazzling display in a cup-tie at Birmingham in 1930.

Became the arch-schemer of the Arsenal team although, when the occasion demanded, he could still score goals (he netted the first goal in the 1930 Cup final and once scored a hat-trick *v*. Sheffield Wednesday). Won championship medals 1931–3–4–5, cup-winner's medals 1930–6 and Charity Shield medals 1931–3. Played in all three home internationals of 1930 and was capped again in 1933 *v*. W. Missed the 1932 Cup final through injury. Made 231 League appearances for Arsenal (26 goals) and was captain for five years. Retired in 1937 but returned to Arsenal after the war to coach the 'A' side at Hendon. His untimely death in June 1953 was an irreplaceable loss to the game.

John, R. F. (1922–37). *Left-half*. Sterling displays for Barry Town and Caerphilly in the Welsh and Southern Leagues made John a much-sought-after player, but Arsenal beat their keenest rivals Cardiff City for his signature in January 1922. Made his League début in the following October *v*. Newcastle at Highbury. Was capped for Wales while still a reserve and gained his fifteenth cap in 1937 fifteen years later. His many honours include championship medals 1931–3–4, cup-winner's medal 1930, cup-loser's medals 1927 and 1932, three Charity Shield medals, and caps *v*. England 1926–7–8–30–2–7, *v*. Scotland 1923–30–6, *v*. Ireland 1923–5–8–33–5, *v*. France 1933.

John made more League appearances for Arsenal than any other player—421. He was noted for his fine distribution of the ball and Hapgood rated him as the best wing-half he had played behind. He also played many games at full-back and was Arsenal's outside-left in the 1932 Cup final, when he scored his side's only goal. On retiring, he became trainer to Torquay, Crystal Palace and Cardiff City.

Jones, B. (1938–49). *Inside-left.* A brilliant little ball-player whose three-star performances for the Wolves continually earned headline notices in the Press. Born in Merthyr, was spotted by Wolverhampton in October 1933 while playing for Aberaman. Played in twenty-seven First Division games and scored ten goals during the remainder of the season. Gained his first Welsh cap *v.* Ireland in 1935 and from then until the war was chosen for all the Welsh internationals. Made 163 League appearances for the Wolves in the space of five seasons and was then transferred to Arsenal, who paid a record fee of £14,000 for his services.

Unfortunately, the limelight and focus of the price-tag was a heavy burden for Bryn on the football field and it affected his play. In addition, he altered his style to fit in with the team which was used to the James type of scheming. Won a Charity Shield medal and made thirty appearances for the Gunners before the war. Served in the Army and returned to play in another forty-one games. Found international form and was capped *v.* S. and I. 1947; *v.* E. 1948 and *v.* S. 1949. Also won another Charity Shield medal 1948. Moved to Norwich in 1949 and later returned to the Highbury area to open a business.

Jones, C. (1929–34). *Outside-left and right-half.* A Welsh international outside-left from Notts Forest who caught the eye of the footballing public with a dazzling display for his country against England at Selhurst Park in 1926. Wales won 3—1 on that day and it was Jones who caused most of the trouble to the England defence. He went on to win three further caps (1927 *v.* Scotland and Ireland, 1928 *v.* England) before moving to Highbury.

Although he was small and rather light, manager Chapman decided to solve his team troubles by moving him to right-half. He was an instant success. His terrier-like tackles and tenacious play— he never knew when he was beaten—were an inspiration to his team-mates and, no matter how heavy the odds were against the team, Jones was always there doing his utmost to stem the tide.

Further honours came his way in the shape of three caps (1930 *v.* England and Scotland, 1932 *v.* England), a cup-loser's medal in 1932 and two championship medals in 1931 and 1934. He made 176 League appearances for Arsenal in the six seasons 1929–34.

Was a studious type of player who was happiest thinking up new tactics to use on the field. Left Arsenal to become manager of Notts County for a spell. Had experience with Cardiff, Stockport and Oldham before joining the Forest in 1925.

Jones, L. J. (1937–9). *Inside-right.* A clever inside-forward who started with Aberdare while assisting in his father's butcher's shop. Quickly attracted the attention of Cardiff City and Swansea Town and it was the former who signed him in 1929. Cardiff were, at that time, in the process of their unfortunate slide from Division I (1929) to the foot of Division III (1934) and Jones' 129 appearances (thirty-four goals) for them embraced both Second and Third Division fare.

He joined another Division III club, Coventry City, in January 1934. During his five-year stay at Highfield Road he earned five Welsh caps (1935 *v.* I.; 1936 *v.* S.; 1937 *v.* E., S. and I.) and a Division III championship medal in 1936. In helping the City to promotion he was the club's second leading scorer to Bourton, with twenty goals in thirty-two appearances. When he moved to Highbury in 1937, in exchange for Davidson, Jones had taken part in 139 League games for Coventry, during the course of which he had notched sixty-nine goals.

In his first season with Arsenal he won a First Division championship medal and continued to be first choice for Wales (1938 *v.* E., S. and I.; 1939 *v.* E. and S.). In addition, he gained a Charity Shield medal in 1938. Made twenty-eight appearances (three goals) in 1938 and eighteen (no goals) in 1939—total forty-six appearances for Arsenal. During the war he played in five more internationals and was the manager of Scunthorpe and Lindsey United on their election to the League in 1951.

Joy, B. (1936–47). *Centre-half.* A 6ft. 1in. centre-half who made a name for himself in amateur circles before joining the Arsenal ranks (still as an amateur incidentally). Played for the two famous amateur clubs Corinthians and Casuals and represented England in the three amateur internationals against Ireland, Scotland and Wales in each of the three seasons 1934–5–6. One of the few amateurs of modern times to win a full England cap—*v.* Belgium 1936—and, in addition, had the unique experience during the same season of taking part in the Olympic Games in Berlin. Was also a member of the amateur Australasian tour of 1937.

Joy made two League appearances for Arsenal in 1936 and a further six during the following campaign. In 1937–8 the injury to Roberts gave Joy his chance of a regular place in the side and his twenty-six appearances that season earned him a championship medal. With Compton established at centre-half after the war, Joy played a few games at full-back, but he retired from League football in December 1946 after making eighty-six appearances for Arsenal. He returned for a time to his old loves Corinthian-Casuals who had by this time amalgamated. Is now a well-known sports writer and author of *Forward Arsenal*.

Kelsey, J. (1949–   ). *Goalkeeper.* Came to Highbury after experience with Winch Wen, the Swansea League club, in September 1949. In the following month made his first appearance in Arsenal's Combination team on his native soil at Cardiff and made thirteen appearances in this side during the rest of the season.

Kelsey made his League début 24th February 1951 and was unlucky enough to run up against a top-form Hans Jeppson, Charlton's Swedish centre-forward, who notched a hat-trick. The Athletic won this game at Highbury 5—2 and Jeppson's hat-trick was the first against Arsenal since Balmer's (Liverpool) three in 1946–7. Kelsey's next two League games also ended in defeat, but his final one of 1950–1 resulted in a 2—1 home win over the Wolves.

Thirty-seven games in the reserves during the following campaign gave him the confidence and experience needed for first-team duty and he was back in the League side in 1952–3 for more than half of the season, thus winning a championship medal.

Becoming first-choice 'keeper in 1953–4, in which he missed only three League games, Kelsey was honoured by the Welsh selectors with caps against Ireland and Austria. Since then his magnificent play has made him a regular choice for the position in the Welsh team.

At the end of 1959–60 he had won thirty international caps and had made 255 League appearances for Arsenal. But for a broken arm, sustained in the cup-tie replay at Sheffield in February 1959, his total would have been more. Kelsey is the senior of the present Arsenal players as far as experience goes and is unreservedly recognized as the best 'keeper in Great Britain. Represented Great Britain *v.* Rest of Europe in the F.I.F.A. Anniversary match at Belfast in August 1955.

Kennedy, A. L. (1923–8). *Left-back.* A product of Ireland who came to Highbury on the recommendation of the old Distillery and Derby County player J. (Toby) Mercer. The latter will be remembered as a right-wing partner of that Derby favourite Steve Bloomer. Mercer, who gained eleven Irish caps, was a particularly good friend of Arsenal's about this time, for he also introduced left-winger Joe Toner, right-back Alex Mackie and inside-forward Jimmy Hopkins, all of whom gained regular places in the Gunners' League team. So sure was he of the prospects of Kennedy and Toner that he paid their fare to London to give them a trial with the Club.

Kennedy made his first League appearance for Arsenal in the 1922–3 season and during that first campaign was honoured by Ireland against Wales. In 1925 he gained another cap and, that time, played against England. Made 122 League appearances in all— his best season being 1924–5 when he missed only two games. In 1927 took part in Arsenal's first Cup final at Wembley.

Kirchen, A. (1935–9). *Outside-right.* A fast, sharp-shooting and very dangerous winger—possibly the most dangerous Arsenal have ever had. A terrific shot. After appearing at outside-right in the King's Lynn Schoolboys side, he gained Norfolk county honours at centre-half. Former Arsenal full-back Tom Parker, then manager of Norwich City, signed him at the end of 1933–4 season. He played fourteen games (seven goals) for them and joined Arsenal in March 1935 for £6,000. Made a happy League début for the Gunners at Tottenham when he scored two goals in a 6—0 victory, but did not command a regular place until 1937.

Was capped on the Scandinavian tour at the end of that season *v.* Finland, Norway and Sweden as a right- and left-winger. Played in England trials of 1937–8. Won a championship medal and a Charity Shield medal 1938. League appearances: 1934–5 (7), 1935–6 (6), 1936–7 (33), 1937–8 (19), 1938–9 (27). Total ninety-two in which he scored thirty-eight goals. In all games for Arsenal he scored eighty-eight goals in 162 matches.

Had to retire at the early age of twenty-eight, when a severe leg injury in the 1942 war-time game against West Ham ended his playing career. Is now a farmer in Norfolk and is also a director of his former club Norwich City.

Lambert, J. (1926–34). *Centre-forward.* Born at Greasborough, near Rotherham, and played for the local side in the Sheffield Minor League. After unsuccessful trials with Rotherham and Leeds, Lambert joined Doncaster Rovers in 1924 for two seasons, during which he scored fourteen goals in forty-four League outings. Moved to Highbury in 1926 and, at inside-right, paired up well with Hulme on his début at Bolton. Settled down at centre-forward and gained a regular place in 1930. In the following season, he broke Brain's record with thirty-eight goals in thirty-four games. Honours include the following medals: cup-winner's 1930; cup-loser's 1932; League championship 1931 and Charity Shield 1930–1.

Scored ninety-eight goals in 143 League matches and played, in all, 326 games (249 goals) for Arsenal. His first-team figures were divided thus: 1926–7 (16 apps., 1 goal); 1927–8 (16—3); 1928–9 (6—1); 1929–30 (20—18); 1930–1 (34—38); 1931–2 (36—22); 1932–3 (12—14); 1933–4 (3—1). In 1934 Lambert joined Fulham, for whom he made thirty-five League appearances. A former miner, his pluck and courage made him a centre-forward to be feared but, at the same time, he was a fine club-man and a gentleman—on and off the field. He returned to the Arsenal staff in 1938 to coach the 'A' team, but was tragically killed in a road accident early in the war.

Lawton, T. (1953–5). *Centre-forward.* One of England's greatest centre-forwards who graduated to soccer fame via the Burnley ground staff. Netted a hat-trick in his first professional appearance, when Burnley beat Spurs 3—1, and soon afterwards Everton paid the record fee for a seventeen-year-old of £6,500 for his services. In 1938–9 he won a League championship medal, played in eight English internationals and was top scorer in the League with thirty-five goals. Captained England in war-time.

Joined Chelsea in November 1945 for £14,000, but after two seasons at Stamford Bridge Lawton requested a transfer. After much speculation he moved to Notts County for a record fee of £20,000 in December 1948 when the County were struggling in seventeenth place in Division III. By the end of the campaign they were in sixth position and in the following season, although no higher than eleventh, no other League club matched the County's tally of 102 goals. By leading his side to promotion in 1949–50, Lawton added a Third Division (S.) medal to his collection.

Moved on to Brentford March 1952, where he was player-manager for a time, and then to Highbury in September 1953. Lawton gained twenty-three full international caps between 1939 and 1949 and his tally of League goals is as follows: Burnley (16), Everton (66), Chelsea (30), Notts County (90) and Arsenal (13), making an aggregate of 215. Left Arsenal to become player-manager of Kettering and was appointed manager of Notts County during the summer of 1957.

Lewis, D. (1924–30). *Goalkeeper.* Came to Highbury from Clapton Orient, making his League début for Arsenal and sixteen appearances in 1924–25. Took over from Robson, who had the distinction of being the only Arsenal goalkeeper to be ever-present during any season between the two wars. Robson moved to Bournemouth during the following season, but by then the Scottish international Harper had arrived from Hibernian, and Lewis still remained second-choice 'keeper.

He displaced the Scotsman, however, towards the close of 1926–7 season and kept his place for the Cup-final team of that year. His unfortunate experience of allowing a simple shot to slip through his arms into the net to give Cardiff the only goal of the match is well-known history. Gained his first Welsh cap against England in 1927, while another followed in 1930. Also played against Ireland in 1928.

Lewis made more than thirty League appearances in each of the three seasons between 1928 and 1930, and his final total was 142. When Arsenal reached the Cup final in 1930 he hoped that he would have the chance to atone for his costly error of the previous final, but injury prevented him playing. Instead, the young goalkeeper Preedy from Wigan stepped into his place to earn a winner's medal.

Lewis, R. (1937–52). *Inside-forward.* Born Ross-on-Wye. Was an amateur with Nunhead before signing pro for Arsenal 15th March 1937. Created a club record by scoring forty-three goals for the Combination side 1938–9 and came right to the front in war-time football, when he played many fine games and bagged goals galore for the B.A.O.R. team on the Continent. While on leave, in 1943, played for Arsenal in the Cup final against Charlton at Wembley, where his splendid opportunism in scoring four goals helped his side win by the record Wembley Cup Final score of 7—1.

Lewis, a brilliant ball-player who possessed the happy knack of positioning himself in the right spot to finish off attacks, started his first post-war season with a bang: scored six goals in the first Arsenal trial; played for England v. Scotland in the Bolton Disaster Fund match; scored nine out of Arsenal's ten goals in the first six games. Although limited to twenty-eight appearances, due to injuries, netted twenty-nine goals during the season.

Was the hero of the 1950 Cup final, when, at inside-left, he twice positioned himself intelligently to take passes from Logie and Cox, strode clear of the defence and coolly drew the Liverpool goalkeeper Sidlow before stroking the ball home. Played for England 'B' v. Italy and Luxemburg; in the latter game he scored both goals in 2—1 win and just missed a hat-trick. Gained championship medal (1947–8) and cup-winner's medal (1950) and totalled 103 League goals in 154 appearances.

Lishman, D. (1948–56). *Inside-left.* Took over the inside-left position from Lewis, and, like his predecessor, was a fine opportunist and most dangerous in front of goal. Was Walsall's regular inside-left when signed by Arsenal in May 1948 and made his First Division début in the following September at Sheffield against the United. Had twenty-two further outings for twelve goals during the season, but at the beginning of 1949–50 a series of boils affected his form and he made only fourteen League appearances.

Was established as Arsenal's first-choice inside-left in 1950–1 until he was unfortunate enough to break a leg in the Christmas game against Stoke. Came back, however, v. Bolton in the last home match of the season, scoring in a 1—1 draw. Fully recovered for the opening of 1951–2, Lishman quickly struck his top form. He was selected as a reserve for England v. France in October; netted a hat-trick in successive home games v. Fulham, West Bromwich Albion and Bolton and won a cup-finalist's medal at the end of the season.

In the next campaign he gained a championship medal and also played for England 'B' *v.* Scotland 'B'. Lishman, who was Arsenal's leading scorer in the League for five seasons, claimed hat-tricks on eight occasions and had an aggregate of 125 goals in 226 League appearances. Was transferred to Notts Forest in March 1956.

Logie, J. (1939–55). *Inside-right.* A native of Edinburgh and came south in June 1939 from Lochore Welfare F.C. Within five weeks, however, Logie was in the Navy, sailing in trawlers, which was to be his occupation for the duration of the war. After hostilities, he immediately commanded a place in the League side, being inside-left to Bastin in the opening match of 1946–7 season when Arsenal lost 6—1 at Wolverhampton. He played two further games at inside-left and four at left-half before settling down to make the inside-right berth his own and to score his first League goal—at Blackpool.

Logie, a very clever ball-player, became the schemer-in-chief of the Arsenal attack for nine seasons. His form was so consistently brilliant that he was unlucky not to win many more than just the solitary Scottish cap gained in October 1952. In each of those nine seasons Logie never appeared in fewer than thirty-two games and only eight Arsenal players have made more League appearances than his total of 296. He could also score goals as well as 'make' them, as his aggregate of sixty-eight shows, and none was more important than the one to put Arsenal 3—1 up against Burnley in the last match of 1952–3, to give the Gunners the championship title for the seventh time.

Logie, who captained the Arsenal side on several occasions, played in twenty-nine cup-ties for the Club, scoring eight goals, and gained two League championship medals (1948 and 1953), a cup-winner's medal (1950) and a cup-finalist's medal (1952). Besides his Scottish cap, he was also honoured by the London F.A. and the Football Combination. Moved to Gravesend and Northfleet in February 1955.

Macaulay, A. (1947–50). *Right-half.* This Falkirk-born player was signed by Glasgow Rangers from the Camelon Juniors club. As an inside-right at Ibrox he gained Scottish League and Cup medals and his stylish display in one of the Arsenal *v.* Rangers matches at Highbury led him to join West Ham in 1937 for a £6,000 transfer fee.

Played in the first war-time Cup final at Wembley in 1940 when West Ham defeated Blackburn Rovers 1—0, and appeared in seven Scottish internationals during the war. Brentford, who were then struggling against relegation, paid £7,500 for his services in 1946. Was selected for the Scotland *v.* England game in 1947 and, with Forbes on the other flank, gave one of the finest wing-half displays ever seen at Wembley. These two were then chosen to represent Great Britain a month later against the Rest of Europe.

Brentford were relegated at the end of the season and insisted on full-time players only, so Macaulay, a sports coach at a London college, asked for a transfer. Amid strong competition Arsenal were successful in signing him for £10,000. Gained a League championship medal in his first season (1948-9) at Highbury with forty appearances. Had thirty-nine outings in 1948-9 and twenty-four in 1949-50 for a total of 103 for Arsenal. Was unlucky not to gain the only honour to elude him (a cup-winner's medal) because, after playing in the semi-final replay, Forbes was preferred for the 1950 winning final. Moved to Fulham in the close season of 1950 and made forty-nine League appearances for them before joining Guildford City as player-manager in 1953. Now manager of Norwich City.

Mackie, J. A. (1923-6). *Right-back*. Belfast-born right-back who joined Arsenal from Forth River in 1922. Made twenty-three League appearances and gained an Irish international cap *v.* Wales in his first season at Highbury. Had thirty-one League outings in 1923-4, nineteen in 1924-5 and thirty-five in 1925-6, after which he lost his place to Tom Parker. Was then transferred to Portsmouth in 1928, having played in 108 League games for Arsenal.

Mackie made a remarkable recovery from a severe leg injury which threatened to terminate his playing career and appeared twice at Wembley in Cup finals for Portsmouth 1929 (beaten by Bolton Wanderers 2—0) and 1934 (beaten 2—1 by Manchester City). Although in the veteran stage, was again honoured in 1935 by Ireland in internationals *v.* Scotland and Wales.

In a spell for Portsmouth which spanned eight years, Mackie made over 280 appearances. Was ultimately secured by Northampton in March 1936. Was at one time a deep-sea fisherman.

McPherson, I. (1946–51). *Winger.* Distinguished war service in the R.A.F. as a Mosquito pilot in a Pathfinder squadron earned a double D.F.C. Was originally an inside-forward with Glasgow Rangers but signed for Notts County during the war and after 'guesting' for Arsenal several times moved to Highbury in 1946 in exchange for Welsh international Cumner.

In his first season at Arsenal, McPherson's clever ball control and speed was put to good use on the right-wing in thirty-four games. Was switched to the left flank in the following campaign, when Denis Compton was out of action with a knee injury, and was an outstanding success in this position in Arsenal's sixth championship season. Thereafter, his first-team appearances were evenly divided between outside-right and -left.

McPherson, who possessed a terrific shot, wonderful ball control, speed and strength, was something of an enigma at Highbury. At times he looked in the international class, at others exasperatingly mediocre. Returned to Notts County in August 1951, where he was captain for a time, and then, two years later, moved with Broome to Brentford where Lawton was player-manager.

Won a championship medal in 1947–8 and made 152 League appearances, scoring nineteen goals, for Arsenal. His seasonal totals were as follows: 1946–7 (37 apps. 6 goals); 1947–8 (29—5); 1948–9 (33—5); 1949–50 (27—3); 1950–1 (26—0).

Male, G. C. (1930–48). *Right-back.* Although West Ham born, Male slipped through the 'Hammers' scouting network and was an amateur centre-half with Clapham when Arsenal signed him in May 1930. League début following December *v.* Blackpool when Arsenal won 7—1. His last (and 285th), seventeen years later, ended on a similar note—Arsenal 8 *v.* Grimsby 0. Played his first cup-tie in the final of 1932 at left-half but later became one of the greatest right-backs the game has known. His display in the 1936 Cup final is remembered as a rare example of full-back technique.

Besides his nineteen caps, Male collected four championship medals (1933–4–5–8), a cup-winner's medal (1936) and a cup-loser's medal (1932). Also played for the Football League twice. Furthermore, he holds the distinction of being the only Football League player to figure in six championship seasons.

Partnered his club-mate Hapgood in the England side on

thirteen occasions and captained his country on the Scandinavian tour of 1937. Now spends his time imparting his soccer knowledge and skill to the Highbury youngsters.

Marden, R. (1950–5). *Outside-left.* Developed with Chelmsford City under the watchful eyes of Arthur Rowe, who was at the time manager of the club, and Frank Soo, the former Stoke City wing-half. Had a two months' trial at Highbury before signing as a professional in January 1950.

After splendid progress in the 'stiffs', the sturdy Londoner graduated to the League side on 3rd March 1951 against Manchester United. It was quite a testing début for him, because he was opposed by that versatile and experienced Irishman Carey. Marden, though unlucky to have four 'goals' disallowed in his first few games, scored his initial League goal at Portsmouth on Easter Monday and then got another at Sunderland on the following Saturday—his sixth and seventh games. Took part in each of the eleven remaining matches of the season.

Scored Arsenal's first League goal of season 1951–2 against Huddersfield but made only seven appearances in 1951–2 and eight in 1952–3, scoring two and four goals respectively. Had nine outings in 1953–4 and scored all of his three goals in the 5—1 victory at Charlton. When Marden joined Watford in the summer of 1955 he had totalled forty-two League games and scored eleven goals for Arsenal. Stayed two years at Vicarage Road, during which he netted eleven goals in forty-one Third Division games and had the distinction of scoring all five goals for Watford Reserves in their victory over Swindon Reserves.

Mercer, J. (1946–55). *Left-half.* A classical half-back and the inspiring captain behind Arsenal's post-war successes. Born in Ellesmere Port, was in the Cheshire Schoolboys' team which included Cullis (Wolves) and Soo (Stoke), graduated to the local side and then in 1931, at the age of sixteen, joined Everton. Was first capped in 1938 and made twenty-two appearances for England in war-time (seven times as captain). Also gained a championship medal in 1938–9 while with Everton.

Lost his place in the first team at Goodison Park early in 1946–7 season when a troublesome knee injury threatened to end his career.

Arsenal, seeking an experienced player, signed him in November 1946 and the gamble paid handsome dividends—Mercer made a complete recovery and for nearly ten years his amazing stamina and keen strategy helped Arsenal back to the heights again.

In this period the Gunners won the League championship twice (1947–8 and 1952–3), the F.A. Cup (1950) and were losing finalists in 1952. Mercer was chosen as the 'Footballer of the Year' in 1950 for his outstanding personality and his bearing on and off the field. Announced his retirement at the end of championship season 1953, but his love for the game was too great and he was back at the opening of the next; unfortunately, towards the end of the season he broke a leg in colliding with his team-mate Wade and thereafter had to accept the fact that his playing days were over.

Made 247 League appearances for Arsenal and was appointed manager of Sheffield United in August 1955. Now manager of Aston Villa.

Milne, J. V. (1935–8). *Outside-right.* Another winger who was secured by Arsenal from Blackburn Rovers. A Scot this time. Was born at Stirling and was a centre-forward in schoolboy football. Gave up the game for two years while he worked in Glasgow as a barman, but was persuaded to turn out at centre-half for a junior team. Ashfield then signed him and converted him into a winger.

Missed a junior-international cap by joining Blackburn on the day before the match. Came to Highbury in the summer of 1935 and made fourteen League appearances in the following season. Played in the Charity Shield games of 1935 and 1936 when Arsenal lost 1—0 to Sheffield Wednesday at Highbury and 2—1 to Sunderland at Roker Park. His nineteen appearances in 1936–7 and sixteen in 1937–8 brought his total to forty-nine League games and nineteen goals for the Gunners before his transfer to Middlesbrough.

Gained more opportunities at Ayresome Park and his consistent displays were rewarded with Scottish caps against England in 1938 and 1939; the latter match being the memorable one in which England beat the 'Hampden roar' for the first time for twelve years.

Milne, W. (1922–7). *Right-half.* Born in Buckie. Won the D.C.M. during the 1914–18 War for gallantry in the field. First appeared in Arsenal's League team in the 1921-2 season and chalked up 114 appearances before a broken leg caused him to give up the game, his last match being against West Bromwich Albion at Highbury 16th April 1927.

Was appointed assistant trainer to Tom Whittaker when George Hardy left for Tottenham in the same year, and continued in this capacity until 1939. His valuable work behind the scenes did much to help Arsenal's reserve team win the championship of the London Combination nine times in twelve seasons. Brentford wrested the title from the Gunners in 1932 and again in 1933, while Portsmouth were the champions in 1936.

Billy Milne, a popular personality at Highbury for so many years, stepped up to the post of first-team trainer after the war when Tom Whittaker was appointed manager of the Club. Has also acted as trainer to the England team on several occasions. Retired at the end of 1959-60 season.

Milton, A. (1945-55). *Outside-right.* Signed amateur forms for Arsenal straight from school in April 1945 and turned professional fifteen months later. Made first appearance in the Combination side at Plymouth 2nd October 1946, just before his call-up for Army service in the same month. Returned after two years and gained a regular place in the reserve eleven, making twenty-six appearances and netting ten goals during 1949-50. Helped Combination team carry off the championship in the following campaign and also made his début in the senior team against Aston Villa in March 1951.

Became first-choice right-winger in the League side during September 1951 and after only twelve such appearances was chosen to represent England v. Austria at Wembley in November 1951. Totalled twenty League appearances, scoring five goals, during the season and followed it up with a further twenty-five appearances and seven goals in 1952-3 to earn a League championship medal. Twenty-one outings in 1953-4 and eight in 1954-5, with three goals in each, gave Milton a total of seventy-five League appearances and eighteen goals for Arsenal.

One of his best games was against Huddersfield (h) 3—5, 13th November 1954, when he twice equalized with brilliant goals and never put a foot wrong. Moved to Bristol City in February 1955 where, with the former Arsenal winger Beasley as manager, he helped the team clinch the Division III (S.) championship.

That achieved, Milton retired from soccer to concentrate on cricket. Is a right-hand batsman and excellent fieldsman for Gloucestershire and has been chosen to play for England.

Moss, F. (1931–6). *Goalkeeper.* Born in Lancashire and a product of the works side Leyland Motors where he was employed. Had a spell with Preston but was the reserve to international Jack Hacking at Oldham when Chapman spotted his promising talent. Moss, who, by means of his excellent anticipation, made goal-keeping look easy, was a fearless player and he quickly gained prominence after his transfer to Arsenal in 1931.

In his first season with the Gunners he played in the Cup final against Newcastle, and in the following campaign he was chosen to represent the Football League *v.* Irish League. In 1934 Moss played for England *v.* Scotland, Czechoslovakia and Hungary, and again in the infamous match against Italy at Highbury in 1935 when seven Arsenal players were included in the England team. In addition, he won championship medals in 1933–4–5 when he made forty-one, thirty-seven and thirty-three League appearances respectively.

Apart from Hibbs of Birmingham, Moss was considered to be the most competent 'keeper of the 'thirties and, coupled with Swindin, one of the best ever to wear an Arsenal jersey. Unfortunately, he suffered a recurring dislocation of the shoulder and an injury in a match at Everton in 1935 led to the finish of his career. In this game he insisted on returning to the field at outside-left and, although injured again, capped a gallant display by scoring a splendid goal. A year later, after another accident at Blackburn, Moss had to retire from active football. He had made 143 League appearances for Arsenal. Became manager of Hearts.

Parker, T. R. (1926–33). *Right-back.* Came from Southampton and had already earned an England cap (*v.* France 1925) when he arrived at Highbury. Parker established his place in the Arsenal side towards the end of the 1925–6 season and missed only two League games during the following five seasons, during which time he played in 155 consecutive matches. Appeared in Arsenal's first three Cup finals and was captain in two of them. Gained one winner's medal and also earned a championship medal in 1930–1. Played altogether in 258 League games for the Gunners, 246 of which were in six consecutive seasons.

Parker was unlucky to be a contemporary of the famous England full-backs Goodall (Huddersfield Town) and Cooper (Derby County), for, otherwise, his consistent form and grand positional play would surely have earned him further honours. On leaving Highbury he became manager of Norwich City and, later still, of his old club, Southampton.

While in Southampton's colours Parker assisted them to win the Division III (South) championship in 1921–2 and appeared in three F.A. trial games. Was also chosen for The Rest *v.* England game in 1927.

Platt, E. (1938–53). *Goalkeeper.* Born at Wolstanton in Staffordshire but moved to Gloucester at an early age. Was originally an outside-right when at school but was spotted as goalkeeper with local village side Charfield by Bath City scouts. After a brief spell with the City, Platt joined Colchester United 1936–7.

Arsenal became interested in this young goalkeeper and in December 1938, when still under eighteen years of age, he was signed by the Highbury club. Was a Royal Fusilier during the war and saw service in North Africa and Egypt. Back in football at the end of hostilities, Platt spent seven seasons as an efficient deputy to Swindin and usually could get a First Division game only when the first choice was injured. Totalled fifty-three League games for Arsenal as follows: 1946–7 (4); 1948–9 (10); 1949–50 (19); 1950–1 (17); 1952–3 (3).

In September 1953 Portsmouth's Irish international and ex-Arsenal goalkeeper Uprichard seriously injured a hand and Platt was recruited to fill the gap. So, after fourteen years as a reserve at Highbury, Platt stepped into First Division football as a regular first-team man at Fratton Park. In the following season, however, Uprichard made a brilliant come-back and Ted was once more in the reserves. Having made thirty League appearances for Portsmouth, Platt joined Aldershot (1955) for a short spell, where he strengthened the defence in a bright start to the 1955–6 season. Differences with the club led to him joining the Southern League club Worcester City after sixteen League games.

Roberts, H. (1926–38). *Centre-half.* Played little football at school but made rapid strides with Oswestry Town (his birthplace). Had four seasons with them when he joined Arsenal in December 1926. This shy unassuming footballer was a natural for Chapman's 'third-back game' and, on taking over from Butler, became the most talked of centre-half of his era. Unfortunately, his style of play did not fit in with the defensive system of the England team and he won only one cap—against Scotland 1931—although his consistent form richly deserved more.

Roberts gained four championship medals (1931–3–4–5) and played in the Cup finals of 1932 and 1936. His worst moments were when he put through his own goal twice in as many minutes *v.* Derby County 8th October 1932. Arsenal were leading 3—1 at the time. An injury in his 297th game for the Gunners when Middlesbrough visited Highbury in 1937 ended his playing career. Was then appointed trainer of Margate, the Southern League 'nursery' club, and his excellent work there promised further successes in the administration side of football. Sad to say, he died suddenly in June 1944 from erysipelas, while serving as a captain in the Royal Fusiliers.

Rooke, R. (1946–9). *Centre-forward.* Attended Stoke School in Guildford and, after playing for an amateur side in the area, joined Crystal Palace in 1933 where he spent most of his time in the reserve side scoring 150 goals. On being transferred to Fulham in 1936 he was their leading goal-scorer for many seasons and once netted six goals in a cup-tie *v.* Bury (1938). After service abroad with the R.A.F. during the war, Rooke came back to play in a war-time international for England *v.* Wales and in 1945 led Arsenal's forward line as a guest player *v.* Moscow Dynamos.

In the opening half of the first post-war season Arsenal were languishing in a desperate position near the foot of Division I. A centre-forward of the Drake type was needed to bolster the attack and get goals. Although Rooke was then thought to be approaching the end of his playing career, it was felt at Arsenal that this energetic whole-hearted player would fill the bill. How right they were!

Rooke scored the winning goal in his first game for Arsenal (*v.* Charlton 14th December) and in his first ten matches notched twelve goals. By the end of the season he had totalled twenty-one goals in twenty-four appearances (including four against Middlesbrough) and had helped Arsenal climb to the thirteenth place.

In the following season (1947–8) Rooke, ever-present, banged in thirty-three goals to become the top scorer in Division I and help the Gunners win the championship. With fourteen goals in twenty-two appearances in 1948–9, he scored sixty-eight times in eighty-eight games for Arsenal. Later player-manager with Crystal Palace and Bedford Town.

Roper, D. (1947–57). *Winger.* Born Botley, Hampshire, and played for Bitterne Nomads in the Hampshire League. Spotted in 1940 by Southampton scouts, signed for the club at seventeen and for a time was in and out of the side at centre-forward. Settled down on the right-wing after 1943 and partnering Bates formed a dangerous combination.

Joined Arsenal August 1947 and delighted the Highbury crowds with his thrilling raids from the wing for nine seasons. Totalled 297 League matches and scored eighty-eight goals, having played in all five forward positions for the Club. For the first two seasons was a regular outside-right, but thereafter was most often on the left flank. Returned to Southampton in 1956.

Made a first-class full-back in emergencies, and is remembered for this in October 1949 against Blackpool when Compton, L., was injured. Smith, L., moved to centre-half and Roper dropped to left-back, where he successfully blotted out Matthews. Furthermore, he took the corner from which Lewis nodded in the only goal of the match. In the Cup final of 1952 Roper again showed splendid form at right-back when Barnes was injured.

His greatest performance was in the floodlit match in October 1952 *v.* Hibernian when, in irresistible form, Roper scored five goals. Goalkeeper Younger, flown over from Germany on special Army leave, could do nothing against his unstoppable shooting. Played for England 'B' *v.* Scotland 'B', March 1953, won two championship medals 1948 and 1953 and a cup-finalist's medal 1952.

Rutherford, J. (1914–26). *Outside-right.* A famous right-winger who did yeoman service with Newcastle United before becoming an Arsenal player. Born in the Tyneside area at Percy Main and, after experience with Wilton Athletic, joined Newcastle in 1902. Made a grand League début v. West Bromwich Albion, scoring two goals. Was an inside-forward for the first two years, but then settled down at outside-right. Gained every honour open to him while at St. James' Park: championship medals 1905-7-9; cup-winner's medal 1910; cup-loser's medals 1905-6-8-11. Capped for England v. Scotland 1904; v. Scotland, Ireland and Wales 1907-8; v. Austria (twice), Hungary and Bohemia 1908. Played for Football League v. Scottish League 1904.

His blond hair was thinning a little when he came to Arsenal in 1914, but, nevertheless, this quiet fellow rarely had an 'off-day' and was a model of consistency. Made twenty-one League appearances in his first season at Highbury and twenty-six in 1914-15. After the war his appearances were as follows: 1919-20 (36), 1920-1 (32), 1921-2 (36), 1922-3 (26), 1923-4 (22), 1924-5 (21), 1925-6 (3). Total: 223 League games and twenty-five goals.

Went to Stoke City as manager in 1924 but returned to Arsenal after a short interval. Was finally transferred to Clapton Orient in 1926.

Scott, L. (1937-51). *Right-back.* Sheffield-born and discovered by former Fulham manager the late Jack Peart. Signed amateur forms for Bradford City when fourteen and became a professional three years later. Played thirty-nine League games for the City before following Swindin to Highbury in February 1937. Won two Combination medals and made eighty-one appearances in the reserve side prior to the war.

Developed into one of the fastest backs in the country, and was chosen to play for England in twelve war-time internationals. Making his League début for Arsenal at Wolverhampton in the first match of the 1946-7 season, Scott was the automatic choice at right-back in the England team in seventeen successive full internationals.

Ill luck then dogged his career, for after an appendicitis operation in Norway, where he was coaching in the summer of 1948, he suffered a severe knee injury when playing against Wales at Villa Park in November 1948. Made a temporary come-back at the end of the season but broke down again v. Liverpool in September 1949. Returned to the side in December v. Manchester United and in company with three other international full-backs, Barnes (Wales), Carey (Eire) and Aston (England), looked the best back on the field.

Still as fast as before, he fought his way back into the England side as well.

Gained a League championship medal (1947–8) and a cup-winner's medal (1950), and after 115 League games for Arsenal was transferred to Crystal Palace in October 1951 as player-manager. Honours included England caps 1947 *v.* Ireland, Eire, Wales, Holland, Scotland, France, Switzerland, Portugal; 1948 *v.* Belgium, Wales, Ireland, Sweden, Scotland, Italy; 1949 *v.* Denmark, Ireland, Wales. Football League 1947 *v.* Scottish and Irish Leagues; 1948 *v.* League of Ireland; 1949 *v.* Scottish League; 1950 *v.* League of Ireland. League appearances were made up as follows: 1946–7 (28); 1947–8 (39); 1948–9 (12); 1949–50 (15); 1950–1 (17); 1951–2 (4).

Shaw, A. (1948–55). *Wing-half.* Had experience in amateur circles with Hounslow Town, Hayes, Southall and Queen's Park Rangers before turning professional with Brentford. Was a regular first-team player with the 'Bees' when Arsenal signed him in April 1948. His League début for the Highbury club came early in 1949–50 when he turned out against Chelsea on 31st August. During the same season he was chosen by the F.A. to play against the Army.

After Daniel had fractured his arm at Blackpool, on the Good Friday of 1952, Shaw came into the first team as stand-in centre-half but he, too, was unlucky enough to suffer a similar fate to his predecessor—against Manchester United in the very last match of the season.

Shaw was a very valuable reserve because he could be depended upon to give a good display in almost any position. His best season was 1952–3 during which he appeared in the wing half-back positions as well as inside-left. With twenty-five League outings he qualified for a championship medal: a fitting reward for his versatility.

Totalled forty-one League games for Arsenal, which were made up as follows: 1949–50 (5); 1951–2 (8); 1952–3 (25); 1953–4 (2); 1954–5 (1). Moved to Watford during the close season of 1955 and made three first-team appearances at Vicarage Road in 1955–6.

Shaw, J. (1908–22). *Right-half.* A famous Arsenal personality, known the world over, who has been associated with the Club since the 1907–8 season. Was born in Bury and came to Arsenal from Accrington Stanley who, at that time, were competing in the Lancashire League. Made one League appearance in season 1907–8 and from then until 1921 was a regular choice in the side.

Had the distinction of being the only ever-present during the worst-ever season in the club's history (1912–13, when only three matches were won!) and again played in all the games in 1914–15 when in the Second Division. Totalled 308 League appearances for Arsenal and by his splendid example proved to be a great captain.

After retiring from the football field he became team manager of the reserve elevens and on the death of Herbert Chapman in 1934 he very ably filled the post of acting manager until the appointment of George Allison. Since then, Mr. Shaw has continued to give yeoman service to the Club behind the scenes at Highbury, and a good deal of the Arsenal's success can be attributed to this quiet and modest philosopher.

Joined the staff of Chelsea during the war, because Arsenal were without a reserve team to look after, but returned to Highbury as head coach and chief representative until he retired at the end of season 1955–6 at the age of seventy-three. Was within a few months of completing fifty years' service.

Sidey, N. W. (1929–38). *Centre-half.* A former inside-forward with Nunhead (Isthmian League) who was an amateur with Arsenal in 1929. Signed professional forms two years later. Converted to centre-half and learned his 'policeman' tactics from Roberts. Never gained a regular first-team place due to the brilliance of Roberts and Joy, but, nevertheless, could always be relied upon to give a first-class performance when called upon. Gained many honours in the London Football Combination with the highly successful reserve side during the 'thirties. Represented the London Combination against the Central League in 1936 and again in 1937.

Sidey appeared in the Arsenal side in the Charity Shield matches of 1933 and 1934; each of which ended in decisive wins for the Gunners. In 1933 they beat the cup-winners Everton 3—0 at Goodison Park, and a year later the cup-winners Manchester City fared even worse at Highbury, losing by four goals to nil. Sidey's best seasons for League appearances were 1933–4 and 1935–6 when he made twelve and eleven outings respectively. His final figure was forty, which was spread over the six seasons 1933 to 1938.

Combination appearances totalled 228, which earned him four championship medals.

Sloan, J. A. (1946–8). *Inside-forward and wing-half.* Known as 'Paddy', he came to Highbury in the summer of 1946 from Tranmere Rovers where he was a recognized centre-forward. Nevertheless, it was at inside-right that Sloan made his mark in the 'Victory' internationals of 1945–6. He played for Ireland *v.* England in September 1945 and *v.* Wales in May 1946. In the latter he partnered Arsenal's Dr. O'Flanagan and scored the only goal of the game. At the end of the season he toured Spain and Portugal with the F.A. of Ireland team and against Spain, once again, scored the only goal of the match.

After three appearances in Arsenal's forward line at the beginning of 1946–7 Sloan was tried as a right-half in the Football Combination side and he displayed such good form against Reading (won 5—1), Tottenham (won 3—1) and in Paris *v.* Racing Club that he was back in the first team after these three games. He retained his place for the remainder of the season, making twenty-seven League and three cup-tie appearances and, in addition, was capped in his new position by Ireland against Wales.

With the signing of Macaulay and Forbes, Sloan felt there was little future for him at Highbury and joined Sheffield United in February 1948. Later played for Norwich and also in Italy.

Smith, L. (1939–54). *Left-back.* Born in Mexborough and worked in local butcher's shop after leaving school. During this time played football for Yorkshire Tar Distillers. Came south to Highbury in May 1939 as an amateur and turned professional three months later. Was a regular captain of the reserve side immediately after the war, making fifty-four appearances in the first two seasons.

Made his League début in the last game of 1947–8 season at centre-half when Compton was on cricket duty for Middlesex and Fields was injured. Arsenal beat Grimsby in this match by eight goals to nil. Smith was retained for the summer-tour matches in Belgium and Portugal and then in the following season gained a regular place in the League side at left-back—Barnes moving to the right flank. Very soon he became one of the best backs in the country, for he was good in the air, able to recover quickly and could ply his winger with splendid passes along the touchline with an uncannily accurate left foot.

Was first honoured by the Football Combination *v.* Diables Rouges in 1948 and graduated to the England team *v.* Wales in 1951. Played at Wembley in the losing Cup final *v.* Newcastle and for England *v.* Wales and Ireland in 1952. Won a League championship medal 1953 and gained further caps *v.* Wales, Belgium and Scotland.

Totalled 162 League games for Arsenal, made up as follows: 1947–8 (1); 1948–9 (32); 1949–50 (31); 1950–1 (32); 1951–2 (28); 1952–3 (31); 1953–4 (7). Transferred to Watford 1954.

Standen, J. T. (1953–60). *Goalkeeper.* Played for Rickmansworth Town before turning professional with Arsenal in April 1953. Was the third-team 'keeper until Sullivan sustained a back injury and then made rapid strides with the reserves. Made one League appearance in 1957–8 when, in December, Kelsey went down with influenza on the trip up to play Burnley. Another débutant in this game was the South African outside-right, Le Roux.

Standen returned to the senior side in October 1958 when Docherty, Herd and Henderson (for Scotland) and Kelsey and Bowen (for Wales) appeared in the Scotland *v.* Wales international and Arsenal, with five 'stand-ins', held Wolverhampton to a 1—1 draw at Highbury.

Made his mark after Kelsey broke his arm in the Sheffield United cup-tie of the same season and showed brilliant form. This was particularly so at West Bromwich, when he helped his side to a 1—1 draw, while Henderson was a crippled passenger for eighty minutes, Groves limped with a pulled muscle for nearly as long and Wills was dazed by a kick on the head for the last twenty minutes. After at least a dozen daring saves was himself injured, and a swollen knee kept him out of the following game *v.* Leeds. Played in the remaining games of the season except the last, totalling thirteen appearances. Was first-choice 'keeper at the beginning of 1959–60 until Kelsey won his place back again. At the end of season 1959–60 had made thirty-four League appearances. Was transferred to Luton Town in October 1960.

Swindin, G. (1936–54). *Goalkeeper.* Born in Doncaster and gained experience with Bradford City, for whom he played twenty-six League games. Joined Arsenal in April 1936 and made his first-team début at Brentford in the same year. Gained a championship medal 1937–8 with seventeen appearances when sharing the position with Boulton and Wilson.

Stepped into the League side immediately after the war and became automatic choice after several brilliant performances when the side was struggling to settle down in the keen competition of soccer in 1946. Swindin's cool efficiency helped spread confidence among his fellow team-mates.

Two of his outstanding games, though one can rarely remember him playing a bad one, were against the Wolves in December 1946 and a cup-tie replay *v.* Chelsea in the following month. That each game ended in a 1—1 draw was largely due to the goalkeeper's faultless play. Roy Peskett, of the *Daily Mail*, described him as 'the goalkeeper perfect'. It was sheer bad luck that he was a contemporary of Manchester City's Swift—otherwise he would have won an England cap which he so richly deserved.

Gained a second championship medal 1947–8, a cup-winner's medal 1950 and a finalist's 1952. After 272 League games for Arsenal, Swindin succeeded Fairbrother at Peterborough United as player-manager in February 1954 and piloted them to the Midland League championship. Returned to Highbury as manager August 1958.

Tapscott, D. (1953–8). *Inside-right.* This speedy and enthusiastic inside-right enjoyed a rapid rise to fame after his transfer to Arsenal in October 1953. Born in Barry, South Wales, he assisted his local town team while on National Service. Then two days after moving to Highbury made his London Combination début and proceeded to net thirteen goals in the next fifteen reserve games—form which was good enough to warrant a run in the senior side before the end of the season.

Tapscott grabbed his opportunities in the League team in fine style, scoring two goals in his first match (a 3—0 victory over Liverpool, which is also remembered for Mercer's unfortunate farewell to the Highbury playing scene). Three days later was chosen to play for Wales *v.* Austria in Vienna in May. Meanwhile, Tapscott scored three further goals in the four remaining games of the season.

In the following season, 1954–5, was an automatic choice for club and country, making thirty-seven League appearances with thirteen goals and representing Wales against England, Scotland, Ireland and Yugoslavia. Was Arsenal's leading goal-scorer in the League during the following two seasons with seventeen in thirty-one appearances (1955–6) and twenty-five in thirty-eight appearances (1956–7). Injuries caused a loss of form in 1957–8 when he had only eight League outings. Scored all four goals in Arsenal's 4—3 victory over the Racing Club de Paris 1956. Moved to Cardiff City in September 1958.

Thompson, L. (1928–33). *Inside-forward.* A Sheffield schoolboy international who had amateur experience with Barnsley before signing pro for Birmingham in 1918. Four years later he moved to Swansea and was a member of their promotion team of 1924–5, when he netted sixteen goals in thirty-four appearances. Scored the winning goal which knocked Arsenal out of the Cup in the sixth round of the 1926 competition. Had totalled 187 League games and eighty-four goals for the Vetch Field club when he came to Highbury in 1928.

Was dogged by injuries while at Arsenal and had few chances in the League team. Was, nevertheless, a great influence in the Combination side, for which he scored eighty-five goals in 160 games. His League appearances were limited to twenty-six over a span of five seasons. Transferred to Crystal Palace in 1933. Was later reinstated as an amateur and assisted Islington Corinthians. Later still, one found him in charge of the Spurs' second team. Now has a business in North London and is also an Arsenal scout.

Toner, J. (1920–6). *Left-winger.* Discovered in Ireland by the former Derby County winger Toby Mercer, who was a contemporary of Steve Bloomer. Recommended to Arsenal and quickly won a place in the League side during the Club's early struggles on its return to Division I after the war. Was not a prolific goal-scoring winger—he notched only six goals in eighty-seven League games for Arsenal—but was speedy and accurate with his centres.

His League appearances and goals while at Highbury were as follows: 1919–20 (15 apps., 1 goal); 1920–1 (11—3); 1921–2 (24—1); 1922–3 (6—0); 1923–4 (3—0); 1924–5 (26—1); 1925–6 (2—0). Won

Irish caps 1922 *v*. Wales; 1923 *v*. Wales; 1924 *v*. England and Wales; 1925 *v*. England and Scotland.

Moved on to Burnley, where he played thirty-seven games, and then to St. Johnstone. Gained further international recognition while at Muirton Park, Perth, in 1927, with games against England and Scotland. Returned to Ireland on retiring from the game and lived at Castlewellan, County Down, until his death, November 1954, at the age of fifty-seven.

Wade, J. (1944–56). *Right-back*. A very useful full-back who captained the Combination side over a period of ten years (making 274 appearances) and who very adequately filled the breach in the first team when called upon.

A Londoner by birth, Wade signed amateur forms for Arsenal in May 1944 and became a professional in August 1945. Won a Combination championship medal 1946–7, a second one in 1950–1 when he was ever-present with forty-seven appearances, and was honoured by the London Combination F.A. *v*. Diables Rouges 1950.

Made his first-team début in the annual match *v*. Racing Club de Paris on Armistice Day 1946; had two League outings in the same season and a further three in the championship season 1947–8. A single appearance in 1949–50 and eight in 1951–2 were the limits of his League experience until, with Barnes put out of the game by the 1952 cup-final injury, Wade grabbed his chance in 1952–3 with forty appearances, thereby earning himself a League championship medal. The Football League also recognized his excellent form by choosing him to represent them against the League of Ireland in March 1953.

A knee injury in a floodlit friendly *v*. Queen's Park Rangers reduced his appearances to eighteen in 1953–4, and a further fourteen in the following campaign brought his total League games to eighty-six. Wade, a qualified F.A. coach, left Arsenal in the spring of 1956 to become player-manager of Hereford United, the Southern League club.

Ward, G. (1952–). *Wing-half*. A Londoner, born in October 1936, who played for Leytonstone, London and Essex boys and was an England schoolboy international. Was in those days a left-winger. Joined Arsenal's ground staff when he left school in August 1952 and gained a place in the reserve side during his first season. Had the satisfaction of scoring the only goal in the final of the Combination Cup of that season against Southampton.

Came into the League team for the second match of season 1953–4 when Marden was injured, and at sixteen was the youngest player to wear an Arsenal shirt in senior football. This was on 22nd August 1953 at Highbury against Huddersfield—a match which nded without any goals, although Ward did get the ball into the net but was adjudged off-side. Held his place in the side on the following Monday at Bramall Lane where Sheffield United won 1—0 and again at Villa Park a few days later.

Very soon after these three League games Ward won an England amateur cap v. Ireland, but he had to wait for three seasons before returning to the first team. By then he had developed into a very fine wing-half. League appearances: 1953–4 (3 apps.); 1957–8 (10 apps.); 1958–9 (31 apps., 4 goals); 1959–60 (15 apps.).

Wills, L. (1949–   ). *Wing-half or full-back.* A Londoner who joined the playing staff at Highbury from Eton Manor Boys' Club. First Combination match v. Reading at Highbury on 12th November 1949 and became a regular wing-half in the reserve side, making the following appearances: 1949–50 (26); 1950–1 (44); 1951–2 (37); 1952–3 (36).

In the following season Wills had made twelve appearances in the reserve team when he was drafted in as a substitute right-back during a friendly floodlit match against Queen's Park Rangers (October 1953)—Wade having to go off with a badly damaged knee. Played so well that he not only kept his place in the side for his League début against Tottenham on the following Saturday but also retained it for the rest of the season, making thirty appearances.

Wills shared the right-back position with Barnes during the next campaign (1954–5), taking part in twenty-four League games and twelve reserve fixtures. Barnes kept him out of the side in 1955–6 until the Welsh international retired after the eighth match of the season. Wills again grasped the opportunity of a regular place for another fifteen matches and was then displaced by Charlton in December. Has since, however, made further League appearances both at wing-half and at full-back. Up to the end of 1959–60 had totalled 171 League appearances.

Wilson, A. (1933–9). *Goalkeeper.* Joined Arsenal in May 1933 from Greenock Morton where he had spent five seasons. Had earlier experience with Overton Athletic and was a lathe operator in a steel works. Due to the brilliance of Moss, Wilson made only five and nine appearances in 1934 and 1935 respectively, but his chance came in 1936 after Moss was injured, and he became a thoroughly efficient member of the team's remarkable defence. He enjoyed thirty-seven League outings and also collected a cup-winner's medal in that campaign.

In the following season, however, Boulton (21 appearances) and Swindin (19 apps.) kept Wilson's total of League games down to two. Wilson's share in 1938 was ten compared to Swindin's seventeen and Boulton's fifteen, while in the season immediately prior to the war Wilson (19) and Swindin (21) played in forty League encounters, Boulton having left Highbury for Derby County; the remaining two games gave Marks his only League appearances with Arsenal.

During the six seasons 1934 to 1939, Wilson played in eighty-two League games for Arsenal. He later qualified as a masseur.